Black Youth Aspirations

Black Youth Aspirations: Imagined Futures and Transitions into Adulthood

BY

BOTSHABELO MAJA

Independent Scholar, Republic of South Africa

United Kingdom – North America – Japan – India – Malaysia – China

Emerald Publishing Limited
Howard House, Wagon Lane, Bingley BD16 1WA, UK

First edition 2022

Reprints and permissions service
Contact: permissions@emeraldinsight.com

British Library Cataloguing in Publication Data
A catalogue record for this book is available from the British Library

ISBN: 978-1-80262-026-9 (Print)
ISBN: 978-1-80262-025-2 (Online)
ISBN: 978-1-80262-027-6 (Epub)

Printed and bound by CPI Group (UK) Ltd, Croydon, CR0 4YY

ISOQAR certified
Management System,
awarded to Emerald
for adherence to
Environmental
standard
ISO 14001:2004.

Certificate Number 1985
ISO 14001

INVESTOR IN PEOPLE

To all youth whose fathers are ABSENT, even when they are present, I see you! I dedicate this book to my father, Moloto Harrison Maja, for being present. My mother, Thokozile Mathilda Maja, for always being there. My grandmother, Gogo Agnes Mncube, for raising me.

Table of Contents

List of Figures

Acknowledgements

There are a number of people I would like to acknowledge for their contribution to this publication.

Let me start with my family: Matselane Maja (my wife) and Diphenyo Moloto Maja (my son) – who triggered the genesis of this research and served as an unwitting guinea pig in my experimentation of various ideas and concepts in this publication.

A publication like this one depends to a great extent on the 'shoulders of giants' that we can stand on. These giants include Professor Mokubung Nkomo; Professor Jonathan Jansen, Professor Derrick Swartz, Professor Matseleng Allais, Professor Yael Shalem and Dr Presha Ramsarup – all of whom played key roles in critiquing and advising on various aspects and stages of this study. Thank you very much for your support and the time you took to read and engage with me.

I also would like to acknowledge the teenagers who informed this research, all nine of them, from both Soweto and Pretoria East. Their insights and willingness to share with me proved invaluable and will hopefully benefit many other youth coming up the ranks of youth life.

I would also like to extend my appreciation to Ms. Kamogelo Gaesite for proofreading and editing this publication.

Lastly, I would like to acknowledge and thank Professor Brahm Fleisch for guiding, informing, and critiquing this publication.

Of cause as the saying goes, I take and remain solely responsible for the contents of this publication

Chapter 1

Introduction

South Africa as a young democracy has come of age. The born-frees qualified to vote for the first time in the national and provincial elections in 2014. They were then considered adult enough to contribute to the direction the country is taking by voting for their own political party, president, and provincial premiers. They voted for the first time in the year 2016 at municipal and local government level. Like South Africa, they also turned 25 years old in 2019.

South Africa's population stands among the youngest in the world at an average age of 24.9 years. According to Statistics South Africa (2019), South African citizens under the age of 35 years constitute 77.6% of the total population, with

> ...youth aged 15–24 years the most vulnerable in the South African labour market as the unemployment rate among this age group was 55.2% in the 1st quarter of 2019.

Similarly, according to Unicef's 'Generation 2030 Africa' report, out of South Africa's projected population of 53 million people, 18 million of those would be under the age of 18 by 2015 (2014). Globally, 'already, nearly half the world's population is under twenty-five years old. That represents about three billion people' (Elmore, 2010). The numbers and consequent importance of this young generation cannot be ignored, and today's youth are key to the future of the world.

Knowing and understanding this generation are therefore critical to understanding society today, and the future it holds. At the core of this research is therefore an attempt to answer the key question – how are young South Africans, particularly young black urban South Africans, imagining themselves into the future? This will be done by looking at one group of South African youth – black urban youth, and one variable of this black urban South African youth – their capacity to aspire.

Understanding the Capacity to Aspire

The theoretical framework shaping this theory is informed by Arjun Appadurai's notion of the 'capacity to aspire' (2004). It is a notion that talks to more than just the concept of aspiration as commonly utilized in our everyday conversations,

Black Youth Aspirations, 1–20
Copyright © 2022 Botshabelo Maja
Published under exclusive licence by Emerald Publishing Limited
doi:10.1108/978-1-80262-025-220211001

i.e. the what and how of aspiration, but more to the enablers and constrainers of aspiration.

The capacity to aspire is defined by Appadurai as a 'future-oriented cultural capacity', and not – as is commonly understood – an individual motivational trait (2004). It is about aspirations, however, not looked at narrowly from an individual perspective, but understood in its broader socio-economic context – the political economy of aspiration. Thus, according to Appadurai, an individual's capacity to aspire is shaped more by the socio-economic context within which they find themselves, rather than an individual's inborn trait. It has two dimensions built into it.

Firstly, it is future oriented and thus constitutes 'a map of a journey into the future' (2004). All youth have the map 'into the future' equally distributed amongst them. For young people to grow into productive citizens of the world, they need maps early in life to give them a glimpse of possibilities for the future. These maps consequently inform pictures they gradually form of themselves as adults of the future. Therefore, all youth have maps of the future with them.

However, two key points arise with regards to these maps, which separate the working class from the middle class. First, they do not all look the same; some maps are less helpful and others are more helpful for the future. Secondly, some come with navigational information and others do not. Thus 'the availability of navigational information, is not equally distributed' (Bok, 2010). A map with no navigational information is equivalent to no map and this tends to be the reality for the less affluent and members of society (Fataar, 2010; Ramphele, 2002).

The concept has been used explicitly and implicitly by two South African authors. The youth studied by both Fataar and Ramphele came from less affluent backgrounds, and either had unhelpful maps or had maps with no navigational information. Navigational information in a map provides the traveller with key information on the journey to be undertaken, enabling better estimation of travel time and overall requirements of the journey. The typology that Appadurai utilizes, of maps and navigational information, is critical. Whilst in modern times such maps and navigational information come through one mobile device loaded with all these geographic positioning systems, this has not been traditionally the case. Before the advent of today's modern technologies one needed a map, a compass and a sextant – particularly when sailing from one point to another. The compass and the sextant were key to navigating from one point to another, whilst the map only showed you the departure and arrival points without any assistance in between. This is the key difference pointed out by Appadurai with regards to maps with navigational tools, and maps without navigational tools – let alone the complete absence of maps in some cases.

Therefore, those with no navigational information are less able to know what the journey will require from them and thus might not be able to arrive at the intended destination. Consequently, their capacity to aspire becomes limited, the choices they have of their futures become limited, the risks they should take in building their futures become limited, and ultimately their life-prospects are limited. Navigational information on the map of a journey into the future provides options of routes to take, it points to risks along the route, it points to resources and time required to arrive into the future per route chosen. It even points to safety nets available alongside the routes chosen – for emergencies and available refreshments. However, the more affluent (who are provided with the required navigational information for the good map into the future) must still be able to read the map and adhere to the navigational instructions provided. This brings us to the second aspect of the capacity to aspire.

The capacity to aspire is a 'cultural capacity' and not an 'individual motivational trait', and it is consequently shaped by knowledge and experience (Appadurai, 2004). Youth gain knowledge and experience from their immediate environment which mainly constitutes the family, the school and the community. The family, the school and the community in turn are shaped within the context of politics, class, economy, race and gender amongst others. Thus, for young people to develop their capacity to aspire, their families, other people within their local communities and those they encounter in their daily lives must have the experience of navigating particular fields and pathways (Bok, 2010). In less affluent communities, such people tend to be missing; leading to what Ramphele refers to as the absence of 'valuable regenerative resources'. These are resources the more affluent are able to tap into for knowledge and experience – educated parents, cousins and sisters studying further at a higher education institution, uncles and aunts owning and managing successful businesses as well as friends whose members of families occupy leadership positions in the country. Equally important in South Africa's case, parents who are present and employed.

Key amongst the youth studied by Ramphele was the absence of positive male role models, which raised the question: 'how this affects young men growing up without positive male role models' (2002). These are all what Ramphele calls 'valuable regenerative resources' that are available to affluent youth but are absent for marginalized youth. Thus, people who live in poverty have available to them a much smaller number of aspirational nodes and thinner pathways by which to enact their desires for mobility (Fataar, 2010). According to Appadurai, equally providing the map into the future to all, equally distributing the navigational information for the map and expanding the scope of knowledge and experience for marginalized youth may 'allow the poor to contest and alter the conditions of their poverty' (2004).

The segment of youth focused on are young people roughly at the end of schooling, 16–18 years of age. Given that aspiration is understood as 'future oriented', youth younger than 16 years old is regarded as largely in its infancy in terms of aspiration. Fifteen-year-olds and below are generally still grappling with the challenges of the immediate, navigating through the schooling system, and only entering the high school phase of their education. Youth older than 18 on the other hand are completing or have completed schooling and have begun entering into spaces of realism that tend to constrain aspirational capacity. Ordinarily, by the time youth leave the schooling system they should be on their way to realizing their aspirations, and not still be developing their capacities to aspire. Even though the 16–18 age group is targeted, it is acknowledged that the literature on youth in South Africa tends to generally deal with persons between the ages of 14 and 35 years as per South Africa's national definition of youth.

Beyond the age categorization of what constitutes youth which lends itself easily to statistical manipulation, youth in this case is further understood as a 'transient social cohort' which is permanently flexible, dynamic and on the move (Van Zyl Slabbert, Malan, Marais, Olivier, & Riordan, 1994). Youth are not simply passive victims of society's crises; and cannot be understood simply in terms of the impact politics and education has on them. They respond to the environment in which they find themselves, for better or worse.

There is a need to understand South African black township youth aspirations and the implications it carries for South Africa as a nation. This is so because black people constitute the majority of the South African population, currently at 80.9% of the total population, with youth constituting 77.6% of the total population (Stats, 2018). The South African population is also more urban inclined than rural, with 64.3% of the population based in urban environments (Stats, 2011). Whilst Ramphele's work in this area was conducted in the formative years of South Africa's impending birth as a democracy (1992–1993), Aslam Fataar represents a very small group of South African scholars who have done work recently in this area.

Internationally, Appadurai points out that the capacity to aspire, understood as a cultural capacity, is a weak feature of most approaches to cultural processes and frequently remains obscure (2004). This is because culture tends to be understood mainly as being about the past and to some extent about the present – never about the future. The futuristic aspect of understanding culture is Appadurai's main contribution to the field. Fataar takes this futuristic outlook on culture and utilizes it within the 'school (*as*) the crucial site for understanding the composition of these newer youth subjectivities' (2010). I believe understanding the youth's capacity to aspire as futuristic and more holistically shall require a focus both in and out of school.

The main body of academic work on the youth challenge facing South Africa has correctly confined the casual nature of unemployment and poverty to the issue of culture, as highlighted in the literature review section below. However, such literature has tended to understand culture in its narrow traditional sense as mainly being about the past and the present – and nothing about the future. This has explained the absence of literature that understands culture utilizing Appadurai's lens – as futuristic (also being about the future) and core to development, i.e. closing the poverty gap and creating jobs. This is the new dimension that Appadurai brings into the literature, which has thus far been missing – that of understanding the 'capacity to aspire' as a cultural conception, and consequently related to the future.

In conceptualizing the capacity to aspire as one key dimension of the understanding and conceptualization of culture, Appadurai allows the space to grapple with the central worry and ultimately its significance – understanding and dealing with unemployment and poverty as it affects the primary members of society – mainly the black youth. He does so because such a conceptualization makes 'real progress on the relationship between culture, poverty and development' (Appadurai, 2004). Thus, the capacity to aspire, understood as cultural and futuristic, does not become an end in itself. It is central to the envisioning of a future with minimal poverty and marginalization of specific sectors of the community, as is the case with South Africa's black urban youth.

Appadurai's conceptualization of culture as futuristic and aspirational is fairly new and thus rarely featured in most academic work on culture and youth culture in particular. Pre-2004, scholarly work on culture never had the advantage of Appadurai's conceptualization of culture. Literature pre-2004 on culture and youth culture in particular, simply defined culture in relation to its link to the past and the present. Similarly, South African studies on culture tended, and largely continued to refer to culture in relation to only the past and the present. This is the first gap that this research fills – that of adding a reference to culture as inclusive of the future as much as it is about the past and present.

At the core of this body of work are two key concepts – youth and culture. These concepts are linked to the central conceptual framework informing this research, that of Appadurai's 'capacity to aspire'.

South Africa's definition of youth includes all people between the ages of 16 and 35 and thus official statistics categorize them as such (Stats, 2012). The focus here is only on the component of youth between the ages of 16 and 18, i.e. at the crossroads of completing schooling and entering into the world of employment and/or higher or further education.

The extended focus is on culture (norms, beliefs, values etc.) – but understood broadly as not only being about the past and present, but more importantly about the future. It will therefore only focus on one dimension of this futuristic conceptualization of culture, only that which relates to the capacity to aspire. The literature on this broader conceptualization of culture, and specifically on the aspect of the capacity to aspire, is however limited. Most literature on culture however, and specifically youth culture, can be categorized into two categories as detailed in part two of the literature review, i.e. youth culture pre-democracy and youth culture post-democracy, under the section youth culture past and present.

The conceptualization of culture as inclusive of capacity to aspire and thus futuristic has opened new doors to research on youth. Internationally, there is an increasing number of scholars using this conceptualization to study youth, communities and societies. Appadurai himself has used this conceptualization to study slum communities in India (Mumbai) and how, by enabling their capacities to aspire through providing them with maps and rich navigational tools, they could reclaim their citizenship and extricate themselves from poverty and deprivation (Appadurai, 2004). In Australia, this conceptualization is being used to study learners from low socio-economic status with the aim of enriching their aspirational maps to participate and succeed in higher education, which has subsequently been adopted into government policy (Bok, 2010; Commonwealth of Australia, 2009; Prodonovich, Perry, & Taggart, 2014).

South African literature has been slow to connect with this conceptualization, except for three authors who have grappled with this notion.

The first academic who grappled with the notion of capacity to aspire, even before Appadurai's formal conceptualization of it, is Mamphele Ramphele – back in 1991 (Ramphele, 2002). In her attempt to 'understand how post-apartheid South Africa was being experienced at the grassroots level by those growing up in poverty', she selected a group of black urban youth in New Crossroads (a township in the Western Cape province of South Africa) with the aim of understanding 'their potential to succeed if given the opportunity to identify their talents and play their strengths'. She provided these youths with maps and navigational tools through constant workshops, tasks and weekend trails with a team of professional guides and leadership development experts, and also opened a world that was not ordinarily open to black township youth. In Appadurai's terms, Ramphele sought to provide these youths with maps and navigational tools so as to 'increase the ability of poor people to navigate the cultural map in which aspirations are located' (Appadurai, 2004). What comes out strongly however in Ramphele's work is the aspect of risk, which affects the poor most and their 'confidence to explore unmapped possibilities' (Bok, 2004). Of the 15 youths who formed part of the more in-depth intervention to provide maps and navigational tools, only two were a success. The narratives of other members of the group showed a mixture of success and failure as they too were steered by the stars into an uncertain future. Their personal resources were found wanting in many respects and they could not handle the pressures of their inadequate and unpredictable society (Ramphele, 2002). These 13 youths had maps, but lacked the navigational tools and the ability required to use them. They also did not have the required safety nets that would enable them to explore, experiment and take risks.

Lesley Powell is also among the few South African scholars who have begun engaging with the notion of capacity to aspire. She applies it to the field of vocational education and training (Powell, 2012). Importantly, in her research focusing on students in the vocational education and training field, she finds that not only does this new lens of studying vocational education and training students suggest a 'paradigmatic shift which results in different questions being asked', but equally that 'strengthening the capability to aspire is central to the role that education and training is to play in poverty alleviation' (Powell, 2012).

The most insightful academic work on the 'capacity to aspire' relevant to here is the work done by Aslaam Fataar – both in relation to its South African grounding and location in the schooling sector. It is a book attempting to 'open a window onto the lives of young persons' educational navigations in a democratic South Africa' (Fataar, 2010). Fataar's narrative analysis of (Fataar Aslam), a young boy's encounter with his schooling across the rural and urban landscape, relates that his 'life circumstances were incommensurate with his desire to become educated'. Fataar Aslam had to overcome difficult material circumstances and forced mobility to realize his capacity to aspire for better education (2010).

Both Ramphele and Fataar deal with the issue of the capacity to aspire, even though not pronounced as such by Ramphele. Whilst they both deal with 'how human beings engage their futures' (Appadurai, 2004), they however do so from two divergent angles.

Ramphele, through her intervention, attempts to create the maps for the youth and provide the navigational tools required. She seems to embrace Appadurai's notion that 'aspirations are never simply individual' and that they are 'formed in interaction and in the thick of social life' (Appadurai, 2004). This must have informed the workshops and group trails that she facilitated in an attempt to create the different 'social life' that would provide the good maps and navigational tools.

Fataar on the other hand, seems to put more reliance on the realization of the capacity to aspire on the individual's 'active self-formation and disciplining' (Fataar, 2010). Fataar refers to Fuzile's case as that of being about 'desire to become educated'. Thus he uses desire, just like Aristotle (1949), and not aspire – as used by Appadurai.

Thus for Fataar, the individual comes first before the social. This means that whatever the social imposes on the individual, the individual remains capable to 'subvert(s) and invent(s) space, *and* how he moves to extend beyond its physical limits' (Fataar, 2010). Thus the role of agency, for Fataar, seems to be more pronounced than that which is seen by Appadurai as being about 'interaction in the thick of social life' (2004). The suggestion is rather the balancing of both the individual and the social that remains unresolved.

Inherent in Appadurai's conceptualization of the capacity to aspire are two key concepts – capacity and aspire. In further elaborating on this conceptualization Appadurai provides some deeper analysis of one concept and very little on the other.

The concept that Appadurai defines a bit further is that of capacity. Appadurai uses what he refers to as a 'navigational metaphor' to further elucidate the concept of capacity. He sees the concept of capacity as entailing what he calls maps and navigational tools. According to Appadurai, the presence of maps and navigational tools – which are not equally distributed – is a form of capacity that is central to shaping aspirations. Appadurai's navigational metaphor helps in dealing with the notion of capacity at its basic level. We will know where to go and how to get there – as per the navigational metaphor Appadurai utilizes. For the youth under study here they will know what subjects to choose, for what career options, and what pass and entrance requirements are linked to their future trajectory.

If we continue with Appadurai's navigational metaphor, however, maps and navigational tools don't help us with higher order information. This includes information such as why we need the careers we have chosen (why we need to go there) and what likely impact they will have on our lives and those of others (what will happen once we get there). Appadurai only deals with tools as part of his navigational metaphor.

Appadurai further refers to the notion of 'hope to achieve' (Appadurai, 2015). What many people 'hope to achieve' is also not equally dispersed. In the economic field, it initially grappled with various economic systems such as Marxism and capitalism and their socio-political dimensions, inclusive of slavery and later colonialism. It has shaped academic debates from Max Weber on modernity and all its subsequent critiques – all about how to build a modern and equal society for all of humanity. Human existence is and will forever be intertwined with the quest to achieve sustainable livelihoods – no matter how elusive this quest has been thus far. This journey about 'hope to achieve' has traversed various scholarly debates. From liberal theory through Marxism and its attempt to understand how social class is reproduced to Bourdieu on how inequality is produced and later to

Nussbaum and Sen on what it means for freedom and well-being, and recently to Appadurai on 'changing the terms of recognition'.

Bourdieu, in his 1986 seminal writing on the forms of capital, argued that capital can present itself in three fundamental guises: as economic capital, which is immediately and directly convertible into money and may be institutionalized in the form of property rights; as cultural capital, which is convertible, on certain conditions, into economic capital and may be institutionalized in the form of educational qualifications; and as social capital, made up of social obligations ('connections'), which is convertible, in certain conditions, into economic capital and may be institutionalized in the form of a title of nobility (Bourdieu, 1986). Such inter-disciplinary approaches have over time helped us grapple with our quest towards sustainable livelihoods by using the past (mainly data generated which tended to be quantitative), to help us understand the present in order to plan for the future. These approaches have further helped us understand how social class is reproduced, and how social advantage is created. 'How human beings engage their futures' is the question Appadurai has grappled with in the last decade, and it is a question herein grappled with (Appadurai, 2004). Appadurai, in grappling with how human beings engage their futures, builds on work previously done by Amartya Sen and Martha Nussbaum, based on their capabilities project (Nussbaum, 1997). Sen's capabilities approach, in an almost similar manner to Appadurai's, was born from a need to relate economics to development, and ultimately to freedom.

Thus, Appadurai's capacity to aspire, as is the case with Sen and Nussbaum, is central to our understanding of development and ultimately liberation and/or freedom. It connects with the sociological traditions of Bourdieu's cultural and social capital. Appadurai recognizes Bourdieu's social capital in defining what he calls 'social spaces' and the impact they consequently have in shaping one's capacity to aspire. These social spaces, as Appadurai puts it in recognizing Bourdieu's argument on the forms of capital, are not equally distributed and favour the middle class more than the working class. Appadurai further connects with Bourdieu in recognizing the importance of cultural capital, albeit 'as futuristic', and not just an inheritance from the past and present that talks only to practices and traditions. Appadurai asserts that this change requires us to place *futurity*, rather than *pastness*, at the heart of our thinking about culture (2013).

Appadurai, in his quest to 'change the terms of recognition' through inculcating capacity to aspire, not only connects to Sen on freedom and well-being, but also to Fraser on the aspect of justice. For freedom is about justice, and an adequate understanding of justice must (also) encompass at least two sets of concerns: those cast in the Fordist era as struggles over distribution and those often cast today as struggles for recognition (with a bias towards Nancy Fraser's 'perspectival dualist' analysis) (Fraser & Honneth, 2003). The bias towards Fraser is important in the South African context. The political settlement of 1994 in South Africa was about recognition. To varying degrees, as argued by Honneth, it gave previously dispossessed South Africans – mainly black people – the 'normative monism' of recognition. These include the recognition of rights, cultural appreciation etc., all of which are now enshrined in the Constitution of the Republic of South Africa of 1996 (Fraser & Honneth, 2003).

Today, some in South Africa would however argue that our democratic dispensation nonetheless failed to realize the redistributive goals it promised – a better life for all. More importantly, it failed to cultivate the necessary capacity to aspire among black South African youth. In the South African context under which the black youth are studied, this becomes a central proposition. Thus, without realizing these youth's capacities to aspire, we cannot claim to have attained freedom, liberation and justice in South Africa. Dreze and Sen make the point that capability is essentially about freedom (Dreze, Sen, & Hussain, 1995). Thus the expansion of human capability is about the freedoms people actually enjoy to choose the lives that they have reason to value (Sen, 1992). Thus, capabilities are opportunities or freedoms to achieve what an individual reflectively considers valuable (Walker, 2007).

In her earlier work, in an attempt to deal with what Appadurai calls 'changing the terms of recognition', Nussbaum went further in her capabilities project by further offering a list of what she refers to as 'the most central human capabilities' (Nussbaum, 1997). In this list of 10 central human capabilities, Nussbaum takes us back to Aristotle in listing among her 10 capabilities 'senses, imagination, and thought. Being able to use the senses, being able to imagine, to think, and to reason' (Nussbaum, 1997). Of the 10 capabilities listed by Nussbaum, three are associated here; namely senses, imagination and thought capability.

Senses, imagination and thought feed aspirations. They are as concerned about Appadurai's 'ethics of possibility' as they are about the 'politics of hope' – the capacity to aspire. Next, what Nussbaum further does is to list what she calls 'three different types of capabilities' which are basic capabilities, internal capabilities and combined capabilities (Nussbaum, 1997). The combined capability is internal capabilities combined with suitable external conditions for the exercise of function (Nussbaum, 1997; Sen, 1980). The key elements of combined capability that Nussbaum refers to are further extended by Appadurai in his later work (Appadurai, 2015). Thus the internal capabilities needed in the combined capability of Nussbaum, is referred to differently by Appadurai as materiality (which I define further later). Appadurai further defines the 'external conditions' that also shape Nussbaum's combined capability simply as social spaces. All these sociological constructs and traditions go back to what Aristotle grappled with earlier when he argued that 'desire necessarily leads to action... the efficient cause of praxis (deliberate action) is *prohairesis* (a certain kind of desire)' (Aristotle, 1959). Thus focusing on the capacity to aspire, is an important ingredient towards action.

Here is an attempt to understand, in an unequal socio-economic context, 'how human beings engage their own futures' (Appadurai, 2004). Rather than being neither about understanding the past nor grappling with the present, this is about using the present to engage better with the future. Similar to Appadurai's concerns, this work is concerned with the socio-political mechanism by which class, race and gender inequality is reproduced. It posits the idea of futuristic thinking, as aspiration is by nature futuristic, such that new socio-political mechanisms – alternatives – are made available in order to 'change the terms of recognition'.

By its nature, this body of work has emerged from a multi-disciplinary understanding of how human beings and societies are able to build sustainable livelihoods, even though it has borrowed heavily from the economics field. Amartya Sen began grappling with this aspect of how human beings engage their own futures in as early as the 1970s, in what he termed 'well-being and advantage' (Sen, 1980). Sen's theoretical construct later developed into what he referred to as the capabilities approach, which is an attempt to deal with an internalized process of inequality. The essence of this approach is captured in Sen's explanation of capabilities as: 'a person's ability to do valuable acts or reach valuable states of being represents the alternative combinations of things a person is able to do or be' (Sen, 1993). According to Sen, the quest to understand how human beings engage their own futures is shaped by how human beings 'do valuable acts' and 'reach valuable states of being'. Thus the freedom to lead different types of life is reflected in the person's capability set. The capability of a person depends on a variety of factors, including personal characteristics and social arrangements (Sen, 1993). These 'social arrangements' are what Appadurai refers to as social spaces. Steve Biko, as early as 1973, engaged with similar issues of how human beings engage their own futures through the black consciousness movement. Amongst the core tenets of Biko's black consciousness was how human beings (in this case black people) are able 'to explore his (their) surroundings and test his (their) possibilities' (Biko, 1973, pp. 87–98).

Appadurai brings into this debate two dimensions. First is the notion of capacity, and secondly that of aspiration – which is a strong feature of cultural capacity, as a step in creating a more robust dialogue between 'capacity' and 'capability' (Appadurai, 2004). Appadurai refers to this aspect, as 'the capacity to aspire'. How do people, in an attempt to engage with their own futures, realize their own 'capability set', or as put by Appadurai, 'aspirational capacities'?

The black youth in sampled here are at the prime of engaging with their own futures – at the crossroads of finishing schooling and entering the world of work and/or further education – in an attempt to realize their own capability sets. There are key theoretical constructs that Appadurai gives us in our quest to understand how these youths engage with their own futures in a manner that ultimately realizes their 'capability set', as put by Sen.

The engagement with 'capability' and 'capacity' is however not an entirely new engagement. It is an engagement which Aristotle dealt with earlier on the issue of body and soul. Aristotle's account of the relation between body and soul, according to one of Aristotle's earlier definitions, is that 'the soul is the form, or first actuality, of a natural body with organs' (Sorabji, 1974). Sorabji further puts it that Aristotle

> ...for the rest of the work considers in turn the capacity for nutrition, the capacity of sense-perception, the related capacity of imagination, the capacity for thought, and the capacity for voluntary movement.
>
> (Sorabji, 1974)

It is the capacities of imagination and thought that scholars such as Appadurai and Nussbaum borrow heavily from.

Appadurai further adds an important dimension to his theoretical construct, that of *aspire* (aspiration). Again, this notion borrows heavily from Aristotle's notion of desire. As Aristotle puts it,

> ...a man with such a desire, we are told, will necessarily act accordingly... provided that (i) he has the ability, (ii) he is not prevented, (iii) he is fully aware of the relevant observational facts.
>
> (Aristotle & Webster, 1923)

Thus, aspiration (desire) has as much to do with capability/capacity (ability), which materializes under conditions of 'not prevented' – freedom. Desire, of course, is one of the key words of Deleuze's (Deleuze & Guattari, 1987) remarkable corpus and was his way to introduce multiplicity, vitality, energy and creativity (following Spinoza) as alternatives to the narrower mechanic idea of 'agency' (Appadurai, 2015). Thus, framing aspiration with a related adjective of capacity is in itself a deeply rooted sociological construct by Appadurai. To aspire requires a related capacity (what Aristotle calls 'ability') which, according to Aristotle, 'is not prevented'. Thus, the field of 'not prevented' that Aristotle talks to is the same 'social space' that Appadurai refers to as unequal. This is the same space that Weber, Marx and Bourdieu refer to as reproducing social class.

The capacity to aspire is thus similarly about capability/capacity (Appadurai, 2013; Nussbaum, 1997; Sen, 1980) as it is about desire/aspire (Aristotle & Webster, 1923; Deleuze & Parnet, 1987; Appadurai, 2013). Whilst Appadurai simply refers to the capability/capacity nexus as being 'two sides of the same coin', I would argue they denote more than that. Sen and Nussbaum's utilization of the concept of capability, instead of capacity, denotes a more action oriented competency than capacity does. Its close alliance to ability pushes one to the kinds of definitions Nussbaum gives us in her attempt to give more action to the concept of capability – hence the list of 10 central human capabilities of Nussbaum referred to earlier. Nussbaum's central concern with action in itself is borne out of the push that using the concept of capability tends to nudge one towards. Capacity on the other hand, whilst slightly removed from the immediate action requirements that come with the concept of capability, is a higher order competency that can serve as a precondition to capability. It is even more of a higher order competency as conceptualized by Appadurai, who refers to it as a 'sort of meta-capacity' (Appadurai, 2013). This is

> ...because the better off, by definition, have a more complex experience of the relation between a wide range of ends and means, because they have a bigger stock of available experiences of the relationship of aspirations and outcomes, because they are in a better position to explore and harvest diverse experiences of exploration and trial, because of their many opportunities to link

> material goods and immediate opportunities to more general and
> generic possibilities and options.
>
> (Appadurai, 2013)

The meta-capacity that Appadurai refers to here also applies to the aspiration dimension of his construct.

There are a number of basic elements that however inform the 'aspire' aspect of Appadurai's construct. To aspire, one must be able to see – as it is a meta-phorical way of seeing the future. Having eyes to look (the materiality that Appadurai talks about as further shown below) is however not enough, as the capacity aspect of this construct requires of one to metaphorically see. Thus to see, one must look. It is the seeing, and its inherently unequal nature – according to Appadurai, that defines the capacity to aspire as a meta-capacity. The seeing that shapes the capacity to aspire, according to Appadurai, requires maps and navigational tools. This combines both the personal characteristics and social arrangements that Sen referred to earlier (Sen, 1993). Whilst seeing and looking are personal characteristics, maps and navigational tools on the other hand arise out of social arrangements and are shaped by same. These social arrangements are the same as the social spaces Appadurai refers to, and they are no different from the conditions of 'not prevented' that Aristotle referred to. Thus, in talking about the capacity to aspire as a meta-capacity, Appadurai argues that it is socially constructed in that the rich possess richer maps and navigational tools whilst the poor tend to possess poor maps and navigational tools (2013). Appadurai later refers to this as mediants, material-ity, and normativity (2015). The eye (and its sensory-neural infrastructure) is the materiality through which seeing – as a practise of mediation – takes effect (Appadurai, 2015). In order to 'bring normativity back into the new material-isms', we will need to

> ...recognise the dynamic materiality of mediants, seen as dividuals
> that interact to produce various materialities; ideas such as class,
> interest group, multitude, mass, and public will all need to be
> rethought.
>
> (Appadurai, 2015)

The youth here and those who serve as their role models and map/navigational tool providers in shaping their capacities to aspire are what Appadurai would refer to as 'actants'. Appadurai borrows this term from Latour, who defines actants as

> ...something that acts or to which activity is granted by others. It
> implies no special motivation of human individual actors, nor of
> humans in general. An actant can literally be anything provided it
> is granted to be the source of an action.
>
> (Latour, 1996)

Both the working class youth and the male middle class youth have an obsession with Hip-Hop and celebrities whom they idolize – which Appadurai defines as mediants. These mediants 'produce various materialities' of what I referred to earlier as a better life, or put another way, the good life – that feeds and shapes aspirations and similarly talk to issues of class and identity. It is what the Hip-Hop stars and other celebrities (as mediants) represent to these youths in terms of materiality – bling, girls, parties and the like. This is the stuff the capacity to aspire is built around.

Understanding South African Youth Culture in a Global Context

In dealing with the rise of job insecurity globally, Standing (2011) suggests the emergence of a new class that he refers to as the 'precariat'. Standing defines this new class as having 'insecure labour, flitting in and out of jobs, often with incomplete contracts or forced into indirect labour relationships via agencies or brokers' and thus subject to 'precariatization', which is the 'habituation to expecting a life of unstable labour and unstable living' (Standing, 2011). Understanding youth globally and the challenges they face cannot be done in isolation from class specifically, and the economy broadly. Appadurai's conceptualization of the capacity to aspire is itself about class and the economy. Thus, the emergence of this new class, the precariat, which standing refers to is relevant in attempting to understand how and where youth see themselves in their future. It however, does not negate locating the current space this youth occupy in the traditional working class/middle class dichotomy which is utilized.

Across the class divide however, whether middle class or working class, youth globally face a number of challenges today than was previously the case. Michelle Fine and Jessica Ruglis (2009) document in the USA what they refer to as 'circuits and consequences of dispossession'. These detail

> …how educational policies laminate credentials of merit onto most White and Asian elite youth, while tattooing the material and psychic scars of "lack" onto most Black, Latino, immigrant, and/or poor students.
>
> (Fine & Ruglis, 2009)

Their work illustrates how systems and institutions meant to serve nations can themselves become instruments of dispossession and subjugation, blunting the youth's capacity to aspire. Not only do these systems and institutions blunt the youth's capacity to aspire, they also tend to naturalize (tattooing) black youth failure whilst similarly naturalizing (laminating) white youth success. Thus the maps and navigational tools that Appadurai talks about tend to be different for white youth as against those for the black youth in the USA areas of their work. Class tends to be central in the determinations. The challenges black youth face can trigger identity issues such as those Fine and Sirin (2007) refers to as the 'hyphenated self'.

The hyphenated selves frame develops out of standpoint theory (see Collins, 2006), assuming that youth who live at the dangerous intersection of political and cultural contestation feel deeply the static electricity of politics and surveillance in their bones. On the other hand, the frame also recognizes that individual lives – particularly youth – are affected by structures, policies, ideologies, practices that may be quite remote and concealed, even as they penetrate intimately. Although youth may experience these force vectors, in the language of Lewin, they may not be able to name them or even recognize their impact.

(Fine & Sirin, 2007)

John Ogbu's cultural-ecological theory confirms a similar pattern among minority groups and migrant youth (mainly black) in the USA. Ogbu argues that,

...the historical, economic, social, cultural and language or dialect situations of minority groups in the larger society in which they exist tends to be a critical determinant to their educational success.

(Ogbu, 2003)

Ogbu, in his cultural-ecological theory makes two related points. First that the school and community collude to shape academic outcomes for youth. Secondly, and most importantly, that both the school and community are influenced by societal structures that privilege some groups at the expense of others (2003). Appadurai refers to this as an unequal distribution of maps and navigational tools.

Joan DeJaeghere (2018) focused his work in this field on young girls in Tanzania, and how they activate agency in taking steps towards the realization of their aspirations. The strong element of agency that DeJaeghere brings into this field is similar to that of Fataar (2010) and his case study of Fuzile Ali – and how he transitions from the Eastern Cape Province of South Africa to the Western Cape Province in pursuance of his aspirations. DeJaeghere however takes us even closer to Appadurai's conceptualization with two key arguments he makes. First that aspirations and agency are dialectically related. Secondly, that as Appadurai points out, both aspirations and agency are socially situated – in the thick of social life.

Lew Zipin, Sellar, Brennan, and Gale (2015) help us understand the global challenges facing youth by engaging further with Appadurai's notion of aspiration when proposing three logics for aspiring. These include the doxic logic – which is founded in populist ideological mediations, the habituated logic – which is founded in biographic and historical legacies, and the emergent logic – which focuses on senses of future potential grounded in lived cultures and hold possibilities for imagining and pursuing alternative futures. It is this emergent logic that I engage further with. Not only does it help focus the research, but I use it to reconnect with Appadurai in redefining the future itself in terms of what Appadurai calls 'mediants' and 'actants'. Appadurai also redefines what 'lived cultures' are, what 'imagining' entails and what these 'alternative future' could embody in expanding on what he calls 'the terms of recognition'.

Gale and Parker (2015), in their work looking at low socio-economic students in Australia, propose

> ...four overlapping concept-clusters with potential to explain aspiration: social imaginary (Taylor & Taylor, 2004); taste/distinction (Bourdieu, 1984); desire/possibility (Butler, 1987; Bourdieu, 1984); and navigational capacity/archives of experience (Appadurai, 2004; de Certeau & Randall, 1984).

I utilize the fourth cluster of maps and navigational tools more closely.

South Africa's youth culture and its gradual political activism can be traced back to 1908 through the Scouts movement – which were generally segregated and provided skills training – to the formation of youth clubs in 1937 onwards, and culminating in the 1976 student uprisings and the later formation of various youth leagues and the United Democratic Front (UDF) in the 1980s. 'From the early 1980s, politics and activism in particular became the arena of the youth' (Van Zyl Slabbert et al., 1994). As a consequence, as pointed out by Pelser, 'key institutions of informal authority – families and schools – were critically wounded by the 1976/80s' (Pelser, 2008).

The South African context of segregation, oppression and brutality by the state towards its own people had created a youth anomaly for the country. Such an anomaly meant that whilst ordinarily, as is the case globally, youth between the ages of 16 and 18 are supposed to be in school or transitioning into further and/or higher education; in South Africa, youth had begun carrying into their own shoulders the future of the country. Thus, education had to be the first victim.

By the advent of democracy in 1994, youth, politics and schooling had become interlinked in South Africa, with the resultant inevitable 'breakdown in the culture of learning and teaching' (Maja, 1994). Studies undertaken by various scholars during this period, including Carrim and Shalem (1999), Morrow (1988, 1989, 1992, 1994), Ntshingila-Khosa (1994), Motala (1993), Cross (1991), Narsing (1989), Mundell (1992), Ritchken (1990) and Rule (1990) all sought to understand the culture of learning and teaching in disadvantaged schools and its impact on education quality and effectiveness.

Thus, the advent of democracy in 1994 inherited a breakdown of the culture of learning and teaching in a number of schools. With Nelson Mandela released and the country ushering in a new period of peace and democracy, many of the youth had to find new purpose and goals. It is this search for new purpose and goals that the post 1994 period sought to engage with, and in many respects this search continues through studies such as these on the capacity to aspire.

The family and the broader out of school society plays a critical role in the creation and harnessing of any particular culture and for purposes of this study – youth culture. Children are born into families, and continue to grow within specific neighbourhoods and society. Thus, in as much as youth are a transient social cohort, the socio-political context within which they find themselves plays a major role in shaping their own flexibilities and dynamisms. The government, the community, the church and various other social clubs all matter in the formation of youth culture. Thus, according to Pelser (2008), the wounding of the family and societal structure in the 1970s and 1980s cannot be overlooked in the analyses of youth culture in South Africa today.

The nature of the family structure, whether nuclear, extended, compound, single parent or as has become common in recent years, child headed household does contribute to the kind of youth culture that emerges. 'Latchkey children', that is, children who are left to their own devices usually outside school hours (Van Zyl Slabbert et al., 1994) are likely to form their own system of values, knowledge, beliefs and actions through which they will make sense of their lives and establish their own identity. Such values, knowledge and beliefs, according to Appadurai, will constitute their maps and navigational tools into the future.

Thus by 1994, talk of the 'lost generation' had become a common definition describing South African youth. This concept, refined and contested in various ways, sought to capture a generation of youth that had no future, and was consequently lost.

1994 was a pivotal moment in the history of South Africa. The struggle for liberation had been won and years of struggle against apartheid were over. Suddenly, there was nothing to fight for, nothing to take over, nothing to mobilize for, nothing to blame – even though the effects of apartheid where bound to be felt for many years to come. South Africa's youth, understood as flexible, dynamic, on the move, sought to define their new and changing roles within society in a multiplicity of ways. These new and changing roles of South African youth have thus far not been adequately studied and explored by the literature, particularly in the last 10 years.

Thus, despite the youth bias of the South African population as illustrated earlier, there remains a silence about youth culture in and out of school in South Africa. This is particularly the case when one focuses on youth between 16 and 18 years, i.e. about to complete general education and on the periphery of work, further education, and/or higher education. This is the critical stage of the crossroads into adulthood. The mainstream of youth studies in South Africa has generally focussed on issues of health (Delius & Glaser, 2002; Harrison, Xaba, & Kunene, 2001) – particularly on sexual activities and related HIV and AIDS studies, and to a lesser degree, on other health matters such as obesity, substance/ alcohol abuse as well as crime (Chabedi, 2005; Glaser, 2009; Harber, 2001; Pelser, 2008; Seekings, 2010); bullying/violence, rape etc. The only studies focussed on youth culture and schooling broadly are those done in the 1990s by Maja (1994, 1995), Dolby (1999), Cross (1993), Van Zyl Slabbert et al. (1994), Christie (1998), with the latest being that of Dass-Brailsford (2005) which was more in the field of psychology. In the last 10 years there has been no substantive work done to understand youth culture in and out of school in South Africa.

Whilst the diversion of focus from youth culture in and out of school is regrettable, it is at the same time understandable. The advent of South Africa's democracy coincided with a new world both negatively and positively. In the positive sense, the period 1994 onwards saw the emergence of information and communication technologies as the new drivers of tomorrow's societies. The centrality of youth in this ICT age could thus not be ignored. As Manuel Castells argued, societies that were not party to the ICT world were bound to be left behind in all respects (economic, political and social). The computer, the laptop, the mobile phone and the tablet were all gradually entering the human world. The implications of this shift, which some have argued further contributed to the demise of apartheid, made the world more connected than ever before. Countries could no longer survive and prosper as an island. Thus, South Africa's youth, who had suffered deliberate isolation in a world that was itself not that connected, were now being exposed to an entirely new world that had become one. Thus, the effect of what can be loosely termed 'double-exposure' set in. By 2006, '72% of 15–24 year olds were reported to have a cell phone' (Kreutzer, 2009). Thus, increasing work has been undertaken to measure the effects and/or lack thereof of 'technology usage ... on societal issues like civic engagement and social capital' (Castells, 2011; Putnam, 2001). Work on 'how mobile phones seem to have brought about societal change by enabling collective action in various countries and contexts' has also been undertaken (Rheingold et al., 2003 in Kreutzer, 2009). The intention here is to take advantage of this reality through data collection methods explained in the research design. In the negative sense, the advent of HIV and AIDS took place during the same period. Youth culture was thus studied in relation to issues of health and sexuality and the implications thereof, inclusive of the increasing number of child-headed households.

In this new world that South Africa's youth inherited in 1994, they had to define and create their own world as a transient social cohort. Selikow et al. identify five key areas in which South Africa's youth sought to define and create their own youth culture post democracy (Selikow, Zulu, & Cedra, 2002). The first is what is referred to as the depoliticization of youth. Secondly, they point to a culture of consumerism – 'material belongings, dress code and luxury cars'. This culture could be linked to the perception that 'black youth tend to live for the present, as they do not see a future or the future looks bleak' (Mokwena, 1992 in Selikow, Zulu, & Cedra, 2002). Third is the culture of crime and violence. Ramphele links the culture of crime and violence to

> ...more and more blacks with requisite resources are fleeing from these townships and settling in previously exclusive white areas. They are the professional and skilled people who have hitherto provided positive role models for young people in these townships. Their flight deprives the townships of valuable regenerative resources and leads to a concentration of deviant and crime-ridden sub-culture, which then takes over whole communities.
>
> (Everatt & Jennings, 1996)

Fourth is gendered socio-economic marginalization – which is caused by the lack of education and jobs – and thus manifests itself in men resorting to criminal action for survival and women using sex as a commodity. Fifth, and lastly, a culture of patriarchy – 'men's dominance, promiscuity and sexually assertive behaviour … many men defining their power by their ability to affect their will, especially over women' also contributes to youth culture today (Selikow, Zulu, & Cedra, 2002). All the elements of this 'transient social cohort' that Selikow points to relate in key ways to issues of desire and agency that Fataar points to, on those of the capacity to aspire as identified by Appadurai. Whilst Selikow looks at these five areas of youth definitions of self in relation to culture as being about the present and past, they equally remain key in our understanding of culture as futuristic. Depoliticization, consumerism, crime and violence, marginalization, and patriarchy all form part of 'subvert(s) and invent(s) space' and shape how youth 'move(s) to extend beyond (its) physical limits' (Fataar, 2010).

The South African youth has historically been an important component of the country's history. Whilst the role and centrality of the youth and their engagement in politics might have been a recent phenomenon in a number of Middle East countries in the last 10 years, in South Africa this has been the case since the 1970s. The 1976 June Soweto student uprising is a case in point. Thus, up to 1994, the role and centrality of South African youth in the socio-political economy of the country was critical and well documented (Nkomo, 1984). By the dawn of democracy in South Africa (by 1994), there had been an element of transition for the youth into other life activities other than politics, some as a consequence of decades of political activism against the apartheid system. Some among the youth were categorized as 'the lost generation' or 'latchkey children' (Marks, 2001; Van Zyl Slabbert et al., 1994). Others took on new identities. Instead of 'comrades', some became the 'ingagara', or 'regte' or 'cherry' as Selikow puts it in the title of his book (2002). In some ways these new identities were also imposed by the realities of the present, and not only as a consequence of past political activism – with the advent of HIV and AIDS and the third industrial revolution. Thus, a lot of youth studies between 1994 and 2010 focussed on youth lifestyles and the impact they were having on their health, consumerism, crime and violence as summarized by Selikow in 2011 in the five key areas defining youth as shown earlier.

It is only since 2010 that a more futuristic analyses of youth culture begun to emerge through the work of Fataar (2010) and Powell (2012), utilizing the capacity to aspire as a possible lens through which to look at youth.

The gap in scholarly work that I sought to fill is that which occupies the space between childhood and adulthood and the resultant transition demanded by this space. It seeks to capture and analyse black urban youth narratives of this space, and how it impacts on their capacity to aspire. It further seeks to dig deeper than the statistics can provide, in answering the question – who is the South African youth? What defines them? What preoccupies them mentally, physically, and emotionally; and what drives them? It argues that understanding the youth will be tantamount to understanding the country, and thus the only way of building a future not only for the youth, but equally for the country.

There is a general dearth of such studies in South Africa, as illustrated by the common areas of focus on youth as indicated earlier. The work of Aslam Fataar, who has done work on 'youth self-formation and the capacity to aspire' – using case study methodology – looks at 'how young people now go about navigating their educational aspirations in light of their contingent life circumstances'.

Utilizing Kennelly and Dillabough (2008) and Appadurai's notion of 'capacity to aspire' (2004), Fataar explores 'the complex webs of interactions by which people in impoverished terrains construct viable lives'. The argument presented, as amplified by Ramphele, is that 'people who live in poverty have available to them a much smaller number of aspirational nodes and thinner pathways by which to enact their desires for mobility' (2002), as similarly argued by Appadurai (2004). However, absent as the 'valuable regenerative resources' might be, and limited as the number of aspirational nodes might be, Giddens' (1984) structural theory reminds us of both structure and agency, and the tension it presents. Therefore whilst individuals might not be completely free agents, they however do act with some freedom of choice. Thus, the social structures within which we are located both enable and constrain choice and action – but agency is always there. In the case of Fuzile Ali, Fataar sees agency as critical in that it is about 'active self-formation and disciplining' (Fataar, 2010).

Across the body of literature reviewed in this chapter, two main trends seem to emerge. The first trend is that which I would like to refer to as the traditional body of literature, which looks at youth in relation to its past and present. The second body of literature, whilst not necessarily divorced from the past and present, dips into the past and present to try and focus on the future and explain it better. Most of the work on youth in South Africa mainly falls into the traditional school of thought. Internationally however, an increasing amount of scholarly work on youth has taken a more a futuristic lens utilizing agency, capability and capacity as some of its main instruments.

Second, there are a number of strands that have begun to emerge in our attempt to understand and redefine what we mean by youth culture as futuristic. These strands and their interrelatedness shall continue to be the subject of debate and critique in this field moving forward. Whilst I privilege some of these strands over others, I hope to add to the body of conceptual clarity-seeking on how we understand youth moving forward. The role of the individual – agency – vis-à-vis the role of society is one of the debates opened up in the literature. Is the capacity to aspire 'not an individual motivational trait' as Appadurai (2004), DeJaeghere (2018), Michelle Fine and Jessica Ruglis (2009), Ogbu (2003) put it or is agency equally important as Fataar (2010), Zipin Sellar, Brennan, and Gale (2015) and others propose.

Third and most importantly, however, most of the literature does not move us beyond describing and understanding the problem. Much as the literature is rich in helping us define and understand the problem, very little exists on possible solutions. It is this solutions oriented focus that is mainly lacking, and this is where the bias towards Appadurai emerges. Appadurai is among the few scholars that attempted to provide us with a solution, albeit in a less detailed manner. He proposed a solution without delving sufficiently deeper into its dynamics, possibilities and nuances. Appadurai proposes two instruments which he believes will help solve the problem of triggering the capacity to aspire – maps and navigational tools. A map is a different instrument from a navigational tool. He proposes these instruments because his primary concern in defining the capacity to aspire was not just about helping us understand the challenge of poverty, but more about the altering of the terms of recognition, or the politics of hope, or the ethics of possibility (2004). It is these three concerns that lead Appadurai to utilize the capacity to aspire as a terms changing concept, and thus the need for instruments that will trigger its realization.

Chapter 2

Narratives of Black Youth

Narratives of Black Female Youth

Introduction

This is an exploration of young, black urban South Africans' capacity to aspire. The purpose was to discover what maps of the future do the youths have and how their immediate environments in and out of school served as instruments that help them interpret the maps. The theoretical basis of this study was informed by Arjun Appadurai's (2004) conceptualization of the capacity to aspire. In conceptualizing the capacity to aspire, however, Appadurai does not give us much to go with beyond the surface level. He argues that the capacity to aspire is about looking at culture beyond past and present and more futuristically. It is also not an individual motivational trait, but rather shaped by society. It is informed by both the politics of hope and the ethics of possibility. Appadurai then proposes two important tools that could help realize the capacity to aspire; these are maps and navigational tools. We therefore do not have much more than this to go with in order to run with the concept. What makes it even more complex is that the context within which Appadurai conceptualized the capacity to aspire and mine differ. Appadurai conceptualized the concept in the context of adult slum dwellers in India and various other parts of the world as an instrument that could assist them 'alter their terms of recognition' (2004). It was meant for those in poverty and how they could take charge of their lives and extricate themselves from their position of poverty and degradation.

I use Appadurai's conceptualization to better understand, define and hopefully empower young school goers in their last two years of formal schooling to develop and embrace their capacity to aspire. I use Appadurai's conceptualization to test its applicability to these youths in the South African context – including how they define their maps of the future, how they construct the maps and navigational tools, how they navigate cultural spaces as well as what informed the development of their maps and navigational tools. I use three different descriptors of space to tell the story of these youths in relation to how it shapes their capacity to aspire. The first two elements of space – the personal and external space – are an attempt to grapple with Appadurai's notion of the capacity to aspire as 'not being an individual motivational trait'. This view is shared by Michele Fine and Sirin (2007), John Ogbu (2013) and various other scholars. Equally Joan DeJaeghere (2018), based on his work with young girls in Tanzania, stresses the importance of

Black Youth Aspirations, 21–86
Copyright © 2022 Botshabelo Maja
Published under exclusive licence by Emerald Publishing Limited
doi:10.1108/978-1-80262-025-220211002

activating agency in taking steps towards the realization of aspirations. This view seems to be shared by Fataar (2010) in his case study of Fuzile Ali. Thus, the descriptive cases in this section use the notion of personal and external space to narrate the stories of the youths in both Soweto and Pretoria East. The last element of space utilized in the descriptive case is the virtual space. This space, which comes through the various online spaces that the youths were using, straddles both the personal and external space. Social media has increasingly shown how it can blur the space between the personal and external in ways unimagined before.

This first part of my descriptive cases focusses on female urban youth, both middle and working class. As will be the case in the second part which focuses on their male counterparts, I report here on three areas affecting each informant which includes – their personal family space, their external space and lastly their virtual space. Each of the spaces of the youth covered here is therefore captured in a different context. The personal family space reflects their individual spaces within their family inclusive of siblings and parents and home environment. The external space reflects all their related spaces outside the home such as friendships, and related institutions such as the school, church and the broader community. The virtual space reflects their presence online mainly through three social media platforms inclusive of Facebook, Instagram and Twitter. These were observed through online lurking utilizing accounts established specifically for this purpose. Four female black urban youth are covered in this chapter.

The Case of Karah

Personal Family Space

Karah is a 16-year-old girl born in Lubumbashi in the Democratic Republic of Congo. She regards herself as 'exciting and creative'. She moved to South Africa in 2004 when she was five years old. She comes from a family of seven children, two boys and five girls, of which she is the youngest child.

Karah's father is however mainly still based in the DRC and travels frequently between South Africa and the DRC, whilst her mother is based in South Africa with all seven children. Whilst the father remains part of the family and sustains it financially, he is largely physically absent.

Karah started her education at this school in Grade Three. She resides in the most exclusive security estate in Pretoria East which is in the same estate as the school she attends, which is itself an exclusive private school in the area. She plays a lot of sports such as tennis and netball at school and had been elected into the school leadership as the house captain for Fish Eagle house. She volunteered, and was subsequently elected into the leadership, so that she:

> ...could stop complaining about what other people are doing wrong and start correcting the wrong things they were doing myself.

She believes that participation in leadership spaces at school 'teaches you how to become a leader and makes you more informed on how to work with people'.

Karah's chosen subjects at school are Science, Mathematics, Biology, Geography, English, Afrikaans and Life Orientation. She believes that Science 'opens the doors for one' and she 'loved Biology from the beginning'. She chose Geography after dropping Accounting, which she had initially chosen. She had initially chosen Accounting because

> ...all members of my family have done accounting and are good at it, and I was also good at it, but later decided that I don't mind it but it was not for me.

Thus the family influence from such a large family seems to have made a strong imprint on Karah, and most of her decision-making processes are linked to those of other members of the family as will be shown further below. What makes this decision-making process so intricately linked to the family for Karah is that of the seven children, six are female. Equally, the consistent presence of her mother, compared to constant absence of her father and the impact it might have on her brother, seems to have positively impacted on her and the choices she makes about her future. Thus the initial choice of accounting as a subject for her was mainly driven by all her other sisters having done and succeeded in the subject. Karah however remains herself and is able to filter some of these influences to her own personal benefit. Hence whilst 'I was also good at it, I later decided that I don't mind it but it was not for me'.

Karah also likes to paint and considers herself an upcoming artist in that regard.

> I started drawing when I saw my sister doing it and I wanted to be like her. I started attending art and drawing and as I improved I loved it more and more.

Here again the sister influence comes up. She seems to not only be influenced by the choices her sisters make, but also by who they are and what they have become. Being the youngest in the family, she has an added advantage of seeing her sisters mature into who they ultimately become whilst she still has the time to make choices for herself.

Three of her art pieces have been framed; 'one for my mom in her room, the other for my sister which was a birthday gift and is in her room, and the other for myself'. What is very telling in Karah's maps and navigational tools is the absence of men, both in relation to her brother and her father. Consequently, none of the best pieces of art she has produced and framed have been shared and/or given to any of the male members of her family. She also feels that 'art isn't much of a career' to choose and follow upfront, which is why she decided not to follow art as a career.

Karah spends almost '90% of my money on clothes'. 'I love shoes – sneakers'. Karah has between 15 and 20 pairs of shoes. Thus in other ways she is a typical girl in Grade 11 who believes in personal beauty and invests in aspects that would assist her enhance her own beauty – clothes and shoes in particular.

The worst thing that has happened to her was when she lost her aunt to diabetes, mainly because 'she could not access a good hospital in time', she says. Despite being born in the Democratic Republic of Congo and living there for the first five years of her life, Karah does not know and has not personally experienced hardship.

Karah's father was a Science Professor before he was a businessman. Her mother is a specialist in Accounting and 'used to work with my dad in the DRC, but now works with my brother in mining' which is one of the reasons she had initially chosen to study Accounting herself. She regards her relationship with her parents as 'great'. She regards her mother as 'lenient' whilst her father does not stay with them. Her mother allows her to do all the things she wants to do because 'she trusts me and knows that I wouldn't do anything bad'. Karah feels that her parents are lenient with all the children including the eldest. What is striking in Karah's narrative however is the consistent absence of her father, either through anecdotes, examples, the choices she makes, or her broader outlook on life. She knows her father and is aware of what he does, where he is and the fact that he is part of the family, but there is a very telling absence of him in her day to day life and outlook of her future. Thus she is able to share that her mother is lenient but in the same breath only indicates that her father does not stay with them instead of her own personal experience of him. Most of her sentences about herself and her family are prefix with a 'she' and there is never a 'he'.

Karah's family and home form part of her believes and values. She associates herself with people who share her belief system and values which include being 'trustworthy, honest, and treating others as you would like them to treat you'. Karah's parents have had a difficult life and upbringing back in the DRC, stories which they share frequently with her and her siblings.

> They do tell me stories like how they had to walk long distances to school and how they had to fetch water far away from their households at the river and walk like twelve kilometres for that. My mom had to also sell stuff in the streets so as to support her siblings and things like that.

Much as Karah herself has never experienced poverty and suffering, she has however 'seen it'. This usually happens when they visit her home country 'and go to the markets and I can see people in distress trying to make a small living off the streets of the DRC'.

Karah wants to study industrial engineering because it will allow her 'to interact and work with people'. She was inspired to study this field by her sister who also studied the same field. Thus, much as there is agency on her part in initially choosing Accounting because 'everybody in the family was good at it' and later deciding to drop it because 'it was not for me', she never strays too far from where her sisters and mother are. For instance her love and choice of art as shown earlier. She plans to study post schooling at the University of Cape Town. She is not keen to move to another country to study.

Karah hopes to work for a company when she grows up because 'she does not have the determination or drive to run her own business'. This is despite her father being a businessman and seemingly succeeding at it. Her father at times asks her about her future prospects whilst her mom holds such conversations with her more frequently, except recently because she now has a clearer idea where she intends going and what she wants to do. She has also learnt a lot from her parents telling her about their days when they were growing up and what they used to do when they were young.

Karah plays netball and follows tennis and soccer. Soccer in particular seems to be the only thing she shares with her brother. In all the narratives about her brother, they only become positive when sharing the times they spend together watching soccer. This is despite them being the last two children in the family and attending the same school, with her brother two classes ahead of her.

Karah feels that she is getting enough opportunities to practice the future. Karah has attended open days at various universities as per the school's guidance to learn more about her career of choice, which is industrial engineering. Being keen to follow a similar career trajectory, Karah draws a lot of inspiration from her sister who is already practicing as an Industrial Engineer.

> Even in the last open day at Tukkies (University of Pretoria), it was my sister who told me about it and that we should go and learn about our chosen career fields.

'I have my sister, so if I ever need advice and knowledge she is there for me'. Karah has done work shadowing every year since Grade Nine as part of the school programme.

> Once I went with Wandi to see a Medical Doctor. This year we had to go for two days, and I went to see a Neurologist; and I also went to see my uncle who is a Mechanical Engineer in aeronautics.

Evidently, Karah does work shadow in other fields not necessarily related to her intended field of study, but has never felt the need to specifically work shadow her sister who works in her intended field of study. This is because her sister is a guarantee that she has daily and is always there to guide and support her. Thus work shadowing for Karah has become more of a general testing ground for her to explore other fields 'just in case'.

Karah has had conversations with her mother about her future and what she wants to become. One of these conversations led to her mother arranging a visit to the BMW plant in Rosslyn because at the time 'I wanted to do mechanical engineering'. She was able to talk to and work shadow an Industrial Engineer for the company. She finds such conversations extremely helpful, especially with her sister already practicing in the field.

Karah's view of gender and the impact it has on her is mainly that 'it does not affect me'.

> But I feel like gender does not affect anyone in this country unless they are very cultured. I think that is the only time it affects women in South Africa.

She however seems to be oblivious to the absence of male examples and anecdotes in her own life. The fact that she comes from a female dominated household, five females and two males – one of whom tends to be absent, entrenches this blind spot to males in her family. Her love of soccer, which is a male dominated sport, also seems to be occupying a space that seems to help mask the absence of male role models in her family. Thus there is a gender lens to Karah's outlook on life which she does not seem to be alive to.

When quizzed in more detail about this blind spot on males in her family, and in particular her brother, it becomes clearer that the picture that emerges is different. Her sense of her brother's and other black urban youth's progress in life, who attended the same school as she does and lives in the same house as she, is that 'they don't try hard enough whilst at the same time they have very big dreams with very minimal effort'.

> 'Some of them have the delusion of the school they go to and the subjects they choose. Like Science is now in fashion for them and they feel like if they do Science they can go anywhere. But you need to still pass the Science for you to get anywhere. They also feel that because they have studied in an elite private school, they will get preferences wherever they want to go afterwards'. 'They do not take advantage of the resources they have. Like when we have a project and we are given two weeks to do it, how do you then submit a hand written piece of paper when we have all these computers around us at home and at school and you had two weeks to type it up? It is not neat and you can't even read it. You would even find that the project required you to submit fifteen pages, but the boys just submit three pages'. 'They struggle with Science and yet they do not go to Science extra lessons whereas the teachers are here until after 4pm, things like that. If you are going to loiter around the school until 5pm then why don't you use that time productively and consult with your teachers and do homework instead of just sitting around the benches?' 'It is only us who bother the teachers and consult with them'. These male youth also 'waste their parent's money because they always get tutors to help them when all they need to do is work harder to progress in life. All you need is to pay attention in class and study'. 'But even if you don't understand the teacher, like me, I can't understand my Maths teacher, but I go home and redo the work and study more. But we also have so many teachers available and

if you don't understand the one teacher you just go to the next. I
have even gone to my Science teacher for a Maths problem and got
helped a lot. Even the Maths Literacy teacher can teach pure
Maths. There is no reason to say "I don't understand"'.

Karah has experienced the problem of black boys at her school much closer to
home with her own elder brother. According to her, her brother 'didn't try'. Out
of a family of five girls, 'he was the only one that struggled, and it didn't make
sense'. 'He just didn't put an effort, he didn't go to extra lessons, always chilled
with his friends. My mom also tried the whole tutor thing and it didn't work'.
Everyone in the family tried talking to her brother but it didn't help, 'even when
he dropped from Pure Maths to Maths Literacy he didn't listen to anyone'.

> Sometimes you found him at nine in the evening before an exam
> the following morning still highlighting his books and reading
> them for the first time the night before the exam.

Thus the gender issue for Karah was evident on two fronts. On the one hand
was a father who is absent, and on the other hand the brother who 'didn't try'.
The narrative of the father and his absence was either a no go area, or was easily
managed from a perspective of necessity. She seemed to be comfortable and had
made peace with her father's constant absence likely because it could be ratio-
nalized from an economic perspective. It would seem that the father is a
responsible father who is a successful businessman who has also studied to the
level of professorship. He is running his businesses so successfully that he can
afford to not only move his entire family of seven from the Democratic Republic
of Congo to South Africa, but equally ensure that they live in the most prestigious
security estate and attend elite private schools. This seemed sufficient to justify
and understand the absence from home that comes with it for Karah. She was
managing the father's absence by absorbing maps and navigational tools from her
mother and her sisters. Then there is the brother who prefers to 'chill'. Karah was
very vocal about this part and shares her disappointment unreservedly. She
however did not understand what informed it in the face of all opportunity and
resources. Her brother ultimately did not pass Grade 12 with good marks and has
consequently remained home not doing much.

External Space

Karah is close friends with Wandi and they tend to influence and shape each
other's outlook on life. 'We became friends by association'. They got to know
each other through other friends and ultimately grew into becoming friends. She
feels that their friendship is because 'she is very nice, has a good heart and is very
funny'. There are significant similarities between Karah and Wandi, which they
themselves acknowledge and at times feel 'are you copying me?' 'It just ended up
like that'. Their shared spaces seem to be the first thing that connected them, that
is, they attend the same school and live in the same security estate. Secondly, the

fact that their parents are not of South African descent might have contributed further in bringing them closer together – one from a French speaking country of the Democratic Republic of Congo and the other from an English speaking country of Nigeria. Further to these facts, they do genuinely seem to have shared values, outlook, demeanour and purpose in life.

Karah does not have a boyfriend and has never had one, though 'it's not a problem if you have one but it's about how you let them influence your life'.

> If it is going to mess up your school and make you do things that you shouldn't be doing then I don't think you should have one. Sometimes emotionally it is a lot to ask and people at times get into it too early; before they are ready.

She feels that 'some people only do it like it is a trend and when they break up they are like, who is next?' Thus school comes first for her. Every other thing she does gets assessed on the basis of whether it will contribute positively or negatively to her schooling.

Karah and Wandi influence each other a lot as friends and they feed off each other. They have serious conversations about their futures and options moving forward but 'it always turns into a joke'.

> We talk a lot about our aspirations but always turn them into jokes because it is just easier that way and less stressful because if you talk seriously about these things sometimes you just create problems that were never there and then you worry too much. We don't want to be so serious about it.

Thus despite all the seriousness with which she takes her life, she is still a typical 17-year old girl who prefers not to take things too seriously. Like any other 17-year olds, they tend to talk about shoes and clothes and the fact that they always have no money and their need for it.

Karah does not have much sense of a community, except for 'knowing the neighbours very well and them becoming our Godparents'. The school and the estate where she lives does not provide much of a community as everybody does what they are supposed to do and minds their own business. The closest Karah has come to a sense of community space, other than her neighbours, is through the church she attends – which is a Catholic Church. She attends church frequently with her family and she regards it as part of her community because 'it is very welcoming and you can go and talk to someone there about anything. Members are trustworthy and support each other and are nice and friendly'. They also organize a lot of church activities and occasions and projects that bring them together and creates a sense of togetherness and comradery. She attends catechism classes at church every Sunday so as to get confirmed.

When it comes to role models, unsurprisingly, Karah's first role model is her mother. This is because 'she came to South Africa and sacrificed everything she knew back home to bring seven children to South Africa for a better education and life'. Her second role model is her sister,

> ...because when she came to South Africa she could only speak French and not English. And the school she attended in South Africa threatened to expel her if she did not learn English fast. She worked hard and ended up not only being fluent in English but also succeeding and becoming an Industrial Engineer. Now she is successful and working in South Africa and travelling all over the world.

Her third role model is the soccer star Christiano Ronaldo. This is because

> ...he too does not come from much but has made so much of himself and is very hard working and dedicated to what he does. These are characteristics that I admire so much and can approve of them.

Her identification with Christiano Ronaldo is not only because he is a superstar and a soccer player that she admires for his skill, but also because

> ...he comes from a very poor and difficult background and had to work hard to get to where he is today. He had to overcome many obstacles to be where he is.

Similarly, Karah's sister is an important role model because she too had to

> ...study hard and did her utmost best and overcame many obstacles not only to survive expulsion, but also to learn, pass, go on to University, and become what she is today – an Industrial Engineer in a multinational company travelling the world.

Adversity, hardship, poverty and overcoming all these seem to be the key hallmarks of character and role modelling for Karah. Thus her definition of a role model is 'someone who can overcome any situation and are positive in how they handle themselves, work hard and have a good influence on me'. The absence of her father in the list of role models she mentions is however interesting, especially when assessed against her last statement: '*and have a good influence of me*'. Karah's father's influence on her was never mentioned, whether positive and/or negative. This was more interesting because her father in all likelihood fit the rest of the criteria of coming from a poor background, being hardworking and overcoming adversity. In fact, besides being absent, he could be more fitting as a role model than the mother. Thus the issue, it would seem, related more to 'influence on me'. She seemed to be attaching more value to the aspect of influence which, for a 17-year old, was unsurprising. Equally, it would seem that Karah's brother did not have the same safety net. For him, as a boy, he did not seem able to revert to the mother and seek inspiration from her. Thus the gap created by his father's absence seemed to have impacted more negatively on him than it had on Karah.

Barack and Michelle Obama are Karah's role models in the political field. This is because they 'are very charitable and they also do not come from very rich backgrounds and they are hardworking and determined'. It is also because Barrack Obama 'does a good job running his country and I like the fact that he can relax and make jokes and is not always under pressure'. When pushed about political role models in South Africa, Karah could only identify Nelson Mandela because 'he fought for us to gain our freedom and was very courageous about it. He freed the country and changed the world'. Seeing that pushing Karah to reflect on her political role models in South Africa was only giving me Nelson Mandela, who had passed on years earlier, I then had to ask her to reflect on political role models in South Africa – but only those still alive. Her immediate response was

> ...it does not really qualify as a role model but there was a politician who was appointed when Pravin Gordhan was fired, they had another Minister of Finance who suggested politicians must spend less money on themselves and that there must not be any blue light thing? (Nhlanhla Nene) I like that because he was honest and bold about it.

Karah's view of President Zuma is that

> ...he is corrupt and that influences all the other politicians because the fish rots from the head. Like, when you go and build your house with tax payers' money, other Ministers will also go and buy themselves five million Rand cars and that is why I don't agree with what he does and the way he leads. He doesn't set a very good example. And he is like the face of the country and for other countries to look at us and see what he does, it doesn't look good.

'I guess I am more DA', is Karah's response to her political outlook in South Africa. Even though she is 'more DA', it was interesting that she could not revert to the Democratic Alliance in search of her own South African political role models. Similarly, even though not pronounced in any way but more out of its silence, except for Christiano Ronaldo, all of Karah's role models are black. Secondly, again something coming out of the silences, none of them related to her parents' home country. She seemed to be more South African and seemed not to have any connection to the parents' native country. She felt that the South African

> ...economy is doing very badly and no one wants to invest here. And this is because people in power are not doing what they are supposed to do and all this corruption is making it worse. People are too stuck in their own ways and I think it is time for a new

leadership and government. I also do not think the EFF is a bad party, Julius Malema does make some very good points, but I just don't think he is able to always put them across in the right way. I am not like a hundred percent DA.

Karah does not see herself as a politician one day because she thinks it is too 'dangerous' to be a politician in South Africa.

It is a very stressful job and very demanding. You always have to be at work and there is always like a problem and you don't have like a private life.

She felt bad 'that racisms is still an issue in South Africa after so many years'. Both Karah and Wandi didn't understand why some people in South Africa still want to discriminate against each other. She had however not really experienced racism directly and her views were informed by what she picked up in the public discourse.

Virtual Space
Karah feels that she watches too much TV. 'I love Comedy Central, cartoons, Suits, Chicago PD, the Mentalist, Hawaii Five O etc'. She also does watch YouTube videos and a lot of Rap and R&B music. Her favourite artists include Beyoncé, Otis Redding, Tracy Chapman and Mariah Carey. She also watches soccer a lot on weekends with her brother. She spends most of her weekends catching up on all the TV shows she couldn't watch during the week.

Unlike Wandi, Karah has been allowed and has had a cellphone since she was 12. She has an Instagram and WhatsApp accounts. She uses Instagram just 'to look at people's photos and get ideas on what to paint' in terms of her art projects.

Of all the pupils sampled, Karah was one of the most difficult to locate and track online. The fact that she indicated that the only social media she has joined is Instagram did not help because it further signalled minimal online participation. A Twitter account in her name was however later located and verified as part of the research process as elaborated further below. However, one of the telling things about the account is that her last tweet was on the 22 February 2014, two years before the narratives captured above took place. Based on this, it would seem that much as she has an account and was once very active, she has stopped using Twitter since the abovementioned date or is on a different account.

The difficulty with the virtual aspect of this research is that it was planned from the onset to run on its own without the pupils' knowledge and/or consent as online data is public data. Thus even during the interviews I could not ask any of the pupils the specifics of their online profiles as it would have compromised the research and likely to have led to some withdrawal from their side.

Another difficulty was that because online profiles can be created anyhow by anyone using any name, it became more difficult to locate and allocate them to specific real life individuals. The fact that most youth create these profiles specifically to live a different virtual life separate from their real life persona further complicates the matter.

Searching though Facebook and Instagram for Karah's online profile and persona proved to be unsuccessful. Whilst this development was not surprising in relation to Facebook as she never said anything about being on Facebook, it was however surprising in relation to Instagram as she had explicitly indicated that she has an online Instagram profile and went further to describe how she uses it. It was only after months and months of daily search that I inadvertently bumped on a Twitter account under the name Karah, with a code name attached to it. Since she had not indicated any Twitter presence and I had failed to locate her even on the Instagram that she had mentioned, I needed to find a way of verifying whether this account actually belonged to her without asking her. This is especially because reading through this virtual presence was not talking to the same person whose narrative I had been capturing.

I was able to conclude that that was the same Karah by cross-checking a number of tweets against the information that she had provided me. Firstly, it was clear that the Twitter account belonged to someone who was residing in South Africa due to a number of South African topical issues that she tweeted about such as Rihanna coming to perform in South Africa and her wanting to go to the show in saying '*I wanna go to see @Rihanna so badly in October in South Africa… (if my black family pulls through for me)*'. What was also interesting about this tweet, is her conscious reference to being black, which I had earlier picked up in her identification of role models. Secondly, the account was only activated in 2012 with the first tweet on 7 February 2012, this coincides with the information Karah gave me during the narratives; that she received her first cellphone when she was 12; the account holder's 14th birthday also coincided with Karah's. Even though most of the tweets on this account did not identify with the person I had gotten to know through the narratives, some of the tweets where giveaways in linking to the Karah interviewed. From various tweets, it became clear that the owner of this account lives in Pretoria, specifically Pretoria East due to various references to Menlyn and Woodlands shopping centres in the east of Pretoria like '*AGGGG I wanted to go to Menlyn so I could hopefully bump into…*' The account holder often refers to her mother when it came to school matters such as: '*AHHHHHHHHHHH my mom said she'll talk to the heads at our school so I can move class tomorrow*'. This was after she had earlier tweeted that she has just been put in the worst class. On the other hand, the only time she referred to her father in her tweets was when '*that is the best part of the airport that's why I always go drop my dad there?!*' This was in response to *Mandy*, her friend, tweeting that '*don't you just love how the airport has attractive foreign guys?*' The account holder's tweets about friends tend to be the same as the friends she shared during the narratives such as '*today was the best day ever I lost so much weight from laughing…Mamazo you kill me'o*'. Mamazo is one of Karah's friends whom I had initially hoped to interview during the fieldwork. The account holder also, just like the Karah I had been interviewing, had great respect for Cristiano Ronaldo and holds him in high esteem, tweeting that '*when you have a name like Ronaldo people have high expectations on how you should look*'. She loves soccer too and at times tweets that '*I don't want to sleep because they are showing soccer and there are some hot players*', and of course '*there's nothing better than at the end of a soccer game when the players take off their shirts and swap it with another player*'. What was however very interesting about her love of soccer was that one gets two different pictures from the narratives versus the virtual world. In the narratives the conversation was about soccer as a sport and her love for the sport which she shares with her brother. It was about the hardworking Cristiano Ronaldo who is a role model and exemplifies hard work and overcoming adversity. Online however, a different picture emerged, which was about looks, body, and maybe even infatuation.

Even more important, the account holder is into art, and most importantly, one of the drawings she shared on Twitter bears a striking resemblance to one of the drawings Karah had given to me as part of her art collection. The most telling tweet however that links the Karah of the narratives to the Karah of the virtual world was this tweet where she complained, '*AHHHHHH there's no water in Woodhill today....I could die....and now I have to pee....and I'm thirsty...*' Woodhill Security Estate is the same estate Karah had informed me she resides at during the narratives.

Overall, except for being Christian, the online persona of Karah is totally different from the narrative related thus far. According to her online posts, Karah is '*the type of person to murder you than dance at your funeral...*' The virtual Karah sees men '*like bank accounts, if there is no money you lose interest*'. The loving sisterly Karah of the narratives is replaced by the virtual Karah who believes '*you don't have to love family you just have to put up with them*'. The good school going girl of the narratives becomes the virtual Karah who '*can't believe school starts tomorrow, if Monday had a face I'd punch it*', and believes that '*school literally murders you*'. The real Karah with helpful teachers at school suddenly becomes the virtual Karah who '*today I learned something at school. School isn't the problem, teachers are*'. Karah is one of the 'good' girls at her school, testimony attested to by one of the teachers, but online she hates it '*when your teacher asks u did u do ur homework...and u feel like saying do I look like the type of kid to do homework?*'

The Case of Wandi

Personal Family Space

Wandi is a 16-year old girl of Nigerian origin in Grade 11 at a middle class school in one of the wealthiest suburbs in Pretoria East. She started her schooling at the same school and has been there since. She stays in the most expensive security estate in Pretoria East, to which the school is attached. She comes from a family of four siblings comprising three girls and one boy, with both parents alive and present. She is the eldest sibling in the family. She studies Biology, Science, Geography, Mathematics, English, Afrikaans and Life Orientation.

She chose to study Geography amongst her subject choices because her 'grandfather was a Geography teacher in Nigeria'.

> Back then I didn't really know him (the grandfather) much, but
> people used to tell me he was a Geography teacher and I really
> didn't understand why he would choose Geography out of all these
> subjects. But then I thought let me take Geography and see. It
> turns out that it is one of my most favourite subjects. It is not
> necessarily him who influenced me directly, I was just curious.

Wandi's father is a family Physician and her mother is a Microbiologist, who is
currently a 'stay-at-home-mom'. The father owns a family practice in KwaMhlanga and also works in a hospital.

Wandi wants to become a Civil Engineer, but is worried that her 'Science mark
isn't high enough so if I can't, I will become an Architect'. She is 'good at art' and
wants to find 'the best way to do what I am good at'. She would like to work for a
company when she grows up 'just to learn the robes and understand more about
the field' and then consider going on her own.

Over and above studying, she would like to pursue art and continue doing
what she likes.

> I can't make a career out of art, but I could but my parents will not
> support me just going straight off into art. I also feel that I can't
> live off art. Some artists can become really successful at first, but
> some people go through some rough times and live a terrible life
> and I don't want to go through that. I wanted to do what I love,
> but also find a practical way of doing it.

As a consequence, 'civil engineering will pay the bills, but art will make me
happy'. It has been a very difficult balancing act between what Wandi loves and
what she has to do. Her parents have also been pushing her to focus on what will
pay the bills without discarding what she loves. In her conversations with her
parents, which began when 'she took art as a subject last year and Geography as
an extra'. Every time

> I was busy with an art project my parents would be like "you are
> taking too much time on the art projects and you must be
> focussing on all the other subjects".

'Then I was just like – I can do art later and I just dropped art and took
Geography as a main subject'.

These interventions from her parents have been critical in helping Wandi make
decisions about her future. They have helped her think through her options from
both a pragmatic and subjective point of view. This is both in terms of her subjective love for art on the one hand and her pragmatic choice of engineering on
the other hand.

> My dad supports what I do and he recognises that I am good at
> art, but he does not want me to do it at the expense of like having a

better future. He says I can't just throw away all my options and start off with art.

Wandi's father has framed two of her art pieces, one for his birthday and the other just to support her.

Wandi gets dropped off and picked up at school daily by her mother. She also participates in painting at school over and above attending classes.

The most difficult thing Wandi has experienced in her life is

> ...when I am arguing with my dad. It is because I am not allowed to do a lot of things. Like I can't sleep over at a friend's house and I am not allowed to go to parties, even day parties, I am not allowed to go to any of those. I am only allowed to visit a friend's house when my dad has met their parents, which is difficult because he is always working. I am not allowed a cellphone because my dad says ISIS will recruit me and I will become a terrorist, but now he has allowed me to get the cellphone, but every time I get an opportunity I spend my money on other things like art supplies and sometimes shoes.

Thus what initially comes through her father as do's and don'ts, ultimately ends up being internalized by Wandi herself in the choices she later makes. The fact that she was initially denied access to a cellphone by her father, but now she has been allowed to possess one and was even given money to purchase one, but rather chooses not to buy it, is a very interesting dynamic on the construction of maps and navigational tools. The best experience for her is buying shoes, 'I buy a lot of shoes and it is actually stupid because I have a lot of shoes but do not have clothes to wear them with'. She has between 20 and 30 pairs of shoes as 'I just know that my closet is covered with piles and piles of shoes'.

Much as Wandi is surrounded by the strong family space she has, she prefers not to discuss her educational options and future with her parents. She feels like 'it causes way too much stress for me'. This is because when her father 'makes up his mind he like makes up his mind, it's not like something you can go and argue. I would rather just leave it'. Thus her father is not only present in her life, but his presence is decisive. Wandi however understands what her parents are saying and why her father is so insistent about having these conversations and making the hard choices because

> ...back when they were younger in Nigeria and the country was experiencing a financial crisis it was hard for my parents and things where difficult for them. When he moved here, he didn't have anything. He just scraped enough money for a plane ticket. And South Africa would not even let him practise medicine even with his qualifications. He had to get piece jobs in some shops to survive. My dad has seen the rough side of life and doesn't want us to go through that.

It would seem that the conversations between Wandi and her parents are not only about her, but also about them and the journeys they as parents have traversed to get to where they are today. Thus it is not only about Wandi's maps and navigational tools, it is also about her parents' maps and navigational tools and how these helped them to be where they are. It is the infusion of past maps and navigational tools with future maps and navigational tools that seems to be shaping Wandi's traversing of her own journey to her own future.

Whilst Wandi feels that her father is very strict, she at the same time feels that he is more lenient with the last sibling in the family.

> It is like he wants me to be the role model to my younger siblings and expects me to set the standard. It is also not that he doesn't trust me, it is more that he doesn't trust other people.

In consequence, there are two additional elements shaping Wandi's future – being a role model and setting the standard. These are very high standards for a 17-year old girl in Grade 11. Her father has however set her up to believe and accept these elements as part of who she is. Wandi herself seems to be increasingly embracing these elements as part of her maps and navigational tools for her own future.

Community Space
Wandi and her family also belong to a church and prayer group whose members are very close to each other. Some of these families have become Godparents to Wandi and her siblings. Wandi derives most of her values and beliefs from church because 'we are actually very big on church' at home. The family attends Hatfield Christian Church which is also located in the east of Pretoria. 'We go to church every Sunday and belong to a prayer group which actually comes to our house on Thursdays'. She knows the difference between wrong and right, how to treat others, how to behave and carry yourself. She values trustworthiness and bases her life and relationships on it. This trait seems to cut across the family and those whose values and beliefs are suspect stand out. These include two of his uncles, one 'who is an alcoholic and the other who lives a lifestyle he cannot afford'. This uncle has had to resort to being unreliable in order to feed a lifestyle he cannot afford.

Much as Wandi believes in the church and attends all activities associated with the church, she however does not agree with everything that the church preaches and what her parents say to her.

> For instance, they don't believe in transgender people and that they are born like that. They believe that it is just an excuse. They just have an old fashioned way of thinking and haven't really adapted to the new world we leave in.

Wandi on the other hand believes that transgender people are born like that and that it is not just an excuse but who they are and must be accepted as such. 'It is not our place to judge, like in the bible it says God will judge them, not us. We shouldn't treat them any differently'.

Wandi is very passionate about issues of the vulnerable, poverty stricken, rural and marginalized. Her values and beliefs are grounded on the premise of pulling the poor and marginalized back into mainstream society. She for instance feels that transgender people were born like that and should not be marginalized and ostracized by society because 'who are we to judge?' She also feels that there is no need for her to bear children of her own when 'there are so many poor and marginalised children without parents'. She sees the future of South Africa as a more equal and non-racial society where the poor, rural and marginalized will be equally cared for.

She sees her father as her role model due to the work and hours of dedication she has seen him put into a rural KwaMhlanga community, caring for the sick. Politically she identifies with the EFF's calls for land and economic freedom and feels that much as their policies are similar to those of the ANC, they are more likely to change things as 'they have the right people to drive change and the ANC has wrong people'. All this mainly due to the fact that her own parents suffered a lot from poverty and marginalization; they couldn't afford 'textbooks and everything, not even lunch. They went through a lot and wouldn't want to go back to that kind of lifestyle'. 'My grandfather also wrote an autobiography about how he brought up my father and the struggles they went through'. Thus the influence of both the grandfather and the father is prominent in Wandi's life.

Wandi hopes to go to a

> ...university in America. It started with my dad wanting me to go. But now I feel like everyone stays here and if I also stay here and go to the same universities here with the same people I will not grow and meet new people and cultures. I also have family in Florida and I want to go and stay with them for a while and a lot of my dad's friends moved there.

Also,

> ...if I go and study in America, when I come back it is going to be much easier for me to get a job here. People will see that I have gone to a higher ranked university and made it there.

Especially with the

> ...university I want to go to, which is the University of Florida. They have the best engineering faculty in the whole of Florida. So that is a good thing as I will have better facilities and better teachers.

The conversations with her parents and other members of her family seem to be succeeding for Wandi because at her age she seems to already have a personal sense of exposure to different people and cultures, she seems to be alive to the unequal society we live in, she seems to be alive to the rankings of universities and what it means for her, she seems aware of her choice of university and how best the faculty she intends to study in is – these are key maps in her life. But they also have navigational tools, which include 'family in Florida' closer to her university of choice. She plans to become an outdoor Architect, designing buildings.

Wandi knows a lot about the work her father does and the communities he serves because 'when I was young he used to take me to his practise and I used to like his secretary'. He would also tell her stories about his patients and their difficulties and the relationships he has been able to build with the community.

She does not plan to have to have her own children when she grows up,

I just think ohh my God, my own biological children? No. I want to adopt. Why should you bring another person to the world when there are all these children out there without parents when you can adopt and be their parent?

She has friends at school,

...but we are not a big group of friends, we are like four. So if we have an activity planned and one of us cancels at the last minute then we end up not doing anything that weekend. But maybe once a term we go out together to the movies.

One of Wandi's friends is Karah, who was born in the Democratic Republic of Congo and has since moved to South Africa. They study at the same school and stay in the same estate attached to the school. Wandi's friendship with Karah is influenced by a number of factors beyond the shared estate and school. She feels that what attracts her most to Karah is that

...she is very motivated, she doesn't let things irritate her that much. She believes in overcoming obstacles and I like to keep those kinds of people around me. Also she is very funny.

Wandi does not have a boyfriend and has never had one because 'I am living for myself now'. She however feels that there

...isn't a set right time to have a boyfriend, if you can handle it now on top of everything, then go for it. But if you are already struggling with what you have now you can't add something [else] on top of that.

Wandi's sense of community has come through groups of Nigerian expats who also hail from his parents' locality in Nigeria and have moved to South Africa. Some of these expats are located in Pretoria whilst others are located in Johannesburg. They tend to come together over weekends with their families which have over time created a sense of community. However, this sense of community has increasingly become very fluid as some of the expats have moved on, some increasingly to Johannesburg whilst many others have subsequently left South Africa and moved to Canada. 'It is better for their children there and education and having a house is much cheaper and safer there'.

Wandi's first role model is her aunt. This is because

> ...she grew up not very privileged but did very well for herself despite all odds. She now owns apartments and owns shares and is very successful. She was then struck with cancer and her husband was not very supportive. But she survived on her own including the cancer and she continues to live and do well for herself.

Her second role model is her father. This is because 'he works so hard and doesn't really need to. But he does so because of his patients and the need they have for his help when they are sick'.

In reflecting about South Africa and its future, Wandi feels that the country should dedicate more of its resources to poor people and those in the rural areas. 'I feel like one day our economy will be better than it is today'. She expressed great delight in the 2016 Local Government elections held in South Africa. She feels that

> EFF is the party for the future. The fact that they are doing so well, in such little time, that means they are doing something right. The thing with ANC is that they have such good ideas of the future but they don't have the right people to put across their ideas. The EFF has better people to communicate their vision of the future, which is almost similar to that of the ANC. The only reason the ANC is still winning is simply because they are the party that brought freedom to South Africa. But I don't think people should vote just because of that.

Virtual Space

Wandi watches television, mainly 'cartoons with my sister'. There isn't anything specific that she watches on TV because she is 'not much of a TV person'. This is largely because she has problems with her eyes and they irritate her if she watches too much TV. She prefers 'reading books and novels in the main, such as Catcher in the Rye'. She is also not really a music person, so mainly she listens to 'what my sister plays'. She likes 'Beyoncé, and Rihanna and Alicia Keys'. She also watches a lot of funny videos on YouTube with her sisters whilst worrying about the glary screen.

Wandi also has an Instagram account and 'follows a lot of people'. 'I don't post a lot of pictures. I don't have a Facebook account'. However, upon running a thorough search on Facebook, I discovered that Wandi had an active Facebook profile that I was able to trace back to her. Much as the profile does not offer much information about her, the information that is on her profile such as her date of birth correlated with the facts she had given me during the interviews. She mainly uses Facebook to post pictures of herself and various pictures of the art she draws. The art displayed online is identical to the art that she had provided me with as part of the interviews conducted. Much as she has a Facebook profile and posts pictures, she is not very active on Facebook, with no opinion and/or word based posts – just her pictures and her art. Even with her pictures and art, over the years she has posted three pictures and two pieces of art. Few as these posts are, she is aware of her online Facebook profile and does access it periodically as these posts are spread over many years with some posted a few months after my interviews with her.

What was however interesting is that as part of my continued research online I later discovered that Wandi actually has two Facebook profiles. Whilst the first above is properly profiled with profile pictures and has many pictures of her, the second Facebook account does not have a profile picture and seemed anonymous. What is further misleading in this second profile is that even her date of birth does not correlate with the dates she gave me. This account also seems to have been opened earlier than the first one; in 2012. The first account covered above seems to have been opened in 2015. These accounts seem to have been opened and active despite Wandi being prohibited by her father from having any cellphone until recently. What is also very different on the second Facebook account is that, unlike the one earlier, this account has a lot of status updates and written posts from her, including a post of her exact residence on Google maps which, if her father's fear of ISIS and terrorists is anything to go by, flies in the face of all that scare tactics from her father's side. Anyone anywhere in the world could come to her exact household and ask for her by name whilst never having met her before. Her earlier posts on Facebook where simply: '*bored*', '*miss all my friends at Woodhill hope ur ok*', '*Gwd night and sweet dreams*' and the like. Nothing more than that. There are however no pictures and/or art postings as is the case in the earlier Facebook profile.

The Case of Naledi

Personal Family Space
Naledi is a South African female youth in Grade 11 at a middle class private school in the east of Pretoria. Unlike Wandi and Karah, she does not reside at the estate linked to the school, but rather at another estate less than five kilometres

from the school. She was born and grew up in South Africa, with parents born and raised in South Africa. Naledi's father comes from the Limpopo Province and her mother from the Eastern Cape Province. She has a younger sister and brother in Grades Nine and Four attending at the same private school. She thus comes from a family of five, with three children and two parents. Naledi has also been elected into the school committee leadership.

Naledi's parents are well educated, both educated overseas, with her mother currently studying for her Doctorate degree and her father intending to follow suit. With her mother busy with her Doctorate, Naledi is 'so proud of her'. Her paternal grandparents are also well educated. Whilst her grandfather is now a preacher at the church they attend, he is also a respected author of Sepedi books that have been published and used in schools. Her grandmother on the other hand is a retired teacher. Naledi has had opportunities to engage about her future with her grandmother, whilst her grandfather is 'more of a boy's person'.

Naledi is very active in various extramural activities both at the school and outside school. She plays netball at the school and does dancing outside school through a dancing academy in the city. 'Dancing for me is like a sport, something to keep me fit. It is not something I want to do like a profession'. When her parents arrived in the Gauteng Province from Limpopo, they used to live, just like Karah and Wandi in the Sunnyside area in town. Sunnyside, just like Hillbrow in Johannesburg, is a convenient city-based area with affordable accommodation mainly through flats with closeness, proximity to workplaces in the city. Like Hillbrow, it is generally a low income group area attracting all manner of South African and foreign nationals. The area tends to attract all manner of activities such as prostitution and drugs and thus a hype of police activity.

Though Naledi and her siblings were born and grew up in Pretoria East, they do at times pay visits to their parents' birthplaces in both Limpopo and Eastern Cape provinces.

The subjects that Naledi studies at the school are Science, Biology, Geography, Life Orientation, Afrikaans, Mathematics and English. She understands Xhosa and Sepedi but does not necessarily speak the languages, 'it's like they talk to me in their language and I answer them in English'. But 'I am more comfortable in Sepedi than Xhosa, so I would say my fluency in Sepedi is like 60% and maybe 10% Xhosa'. It is however very interesting that even though she is 60% fluent in Sepedi and the school offers Sepedi and Afrikaans as additional languages, that she chose to study Afrikaans at her current school.

> This is because I have been doing Afrikaans for so long and had to learn it and write in it in my earlier school years. But now things are different. Like my brother, he started doing Sepedi earlier on in Grade Five so he will be choosing Sepedi in Grade 10. If I had the choice like him already in Grade Five I would have probably taken Sepedi.

With the rest of the subject choices, Naledi had initially chosen Biology, Science, and Accounting.

> Because I felt safe but as time went on I didn't enjoy Accounting and then I changed it for Geography. I also took advanced Mathematics initially but I dropped it for Mathematics because you see, they teach less for advanced Maths, just once a week; so I dropped it for Pure Maths.

Naledi has been playing around with various options of what she would like to be when she grows up. 'I change my mind all the time, mainly because of the influence of TV and stuff'. She used to be a TV addict but 'ever since Grade 10 I have cut down the shows and I don't watch much during the week; I record them to watch over the weekend'. It was however Naledi's decision to cut down on watching TV during the week even though 'it was sad to cut down but I decided it had to happen. I used to do my homework whilst watching TV'. Therefore due to increasing school and extramural workload, TV had to take the back seat so that she could focus on her academics to improve her performance at school.

So initially, Naledi aspired to become a Forensic Scientist, 'and be like a Pathologist and work with bodies and stuff'.

> Then I wanted to be a Lawyer because I watched Suits on TV. Then I wanted to become an Orthopaedic Surgeon because of Grey's Anatomy, then I wanted to become a Neurologist, then marketing and business, then I was like let me go back to being a Neurologist. Then I work shadowed in neurology at Steve Biko Hospital and I actually fainted during the work shadow process. Then I realised that neurology is not for me.

She is now aspiring to do business management. What is however interesting about Naledi, is that in the midst of all the confusion and changing of minds, she nonetheless remains focussed on her future. The changes are more about preferences, trials, and making choices. Thus she is making different choices about her future options and not necessarily switching off or disconnecting. All of this with a great deal of enthusiasm and excitement about the possibilities that the future holds for her. Thus the map of her future is constant, but the navigational tools change very often.

Naledi's parents seem to play an important in role in guiding her towards the future she aspires for. Her mother is a Microbiologist – who is studying for her doctorate at the moment, and her father owns a company focussing on micro finance. She thinks that her interests in neurology was influenced by her mother being a microbiologist and now her focus on business management stems from her father's influence as a businessman. She wants to have her own business in future, even though her father indicates that 'running your own business is very hard'.

Naledi has had opportunities to trial her future over and above the work shadow that the school provides, one of which she fainted during. Since she has decided to progress towards business management, she has been asking her father to expose her more and more to the business world and has accompanied him to his work place and those of some of his partners'.

She has had conversations with her parents about her future and the options she is exploring,

> ...especially my mom because like she is into it. She is more like ohh, and calls us together to ask about what careers we want to follow because she wants to help us and stuff and she wants us to know now and be sure so that we can have time to ready ourselves. My mom also wants to expose us to the right people and find connections.

On the other hand

> ...my dad is more like ok, whatever. If you change your mind today he just says ok, and if you change your mind tomorrow again he is like – ok. He won't like ask questions as to why you are changing your mind and are you sure.

Naledi points out that when she wanted to drop one of her subjects and she informed her father,

> ...he was like ok. On the other hand my mom was like why, are you sure; and you must make sure it is the right choice and stuff like that.

Naledi enjoys the detailed conversations she has with her mother about her future because 'it gets me thinking and makes me realise that I am growing up and need to make the right choices sooner because time is like running out'. She is used to having such detailed conversations with her mother especially since moving from Grade Nine to Grade 10 when the subject choice space opened up. 'Now we do not talk about it as much because she is more certain about where I am going and is focussing more on my siblings'.

Naledi is intending to study business management overseas because 'my parents also studied abroad. It will be a change of scenery, a new lifestyle and different experience'. But in essence Naledi 'wants to do so many things, many things, but my focus now is being a Neurosurgeon or something in business'.

Naledi serves on one of the school leadership committees and indicates that it assists her to prepare for the future in terms of practicing her future possibilities. She further feels that black boys at the school

> ...are not so serious about their own future and you can see it in their academic performance, which tends to be below that of girls. It is not necessarily that guys are not focussed, we just put more effort and study longer for our academics than the boys do. We

make our notes meticulously and better. We put more effort into the work we do.

Community Space

Naledi and her family attend church services every Sunday and are part of the broader church community. Her grandfather is also a preacher, which has significantly influenced the family. As part of the church, they do a lot of outreach programmes and visit various communities to support and build.

Naledi values 'honesty, prayer, and respect for everybody, and not to look down on people and speak up for yourself because life is short; and be loving and caring'.

Naledi sees herself living overseas as an adult and running her own business. Her desire to live overseas is generally driven by her anxiety over 'safety issues in South Africa'. She has travelled overseas a lot and has realized that 'the world is so big with so many cultures and so much to do. If things don't work out here, you can always try out elsewhere'.

Overall, Naledi feels very happy with her life.

> I see myself always with a good job, a good education, my family happy and joyful. I also see myself helping out with charity and stuff and helping out with building schools and stuff. In South Africa I am not sure. Depending on where I find a job and all that I might not even be based in South Africa.

She feels that part of the improvement towards a positive future for South Africa will be driven by the youth of today. 'Because older people grew up in that era, they are bogged down by their own baggage and try to impose it on us'.

What worries Naledi about South Africa is 'the corruption and poverty' which is not helping the country move forward, and

> I just feel like we are a very angry nation as a result. We have a lot of road rage and this anger and we need to be happier. If they were to spend the money they are spending on Jacob Zuma's house to uplift some rural community somewhere it would be better.

Virtual Space

Naledi does not seem to have any kind of online presence. Various attempt to trace her online proved fruitless. Attempts to trace her even through her friends equally proved fruitless. What further convince me that she probably does not have any form of Facebook, Twitter, or Instagram accounts was that even when her friends would refer to her on their online posts, hers would just be a name and not an account. Ordinarily when you post and refer to someone who also has some online presence, you refer to her through her account (also known as tagging) so that they can see what you have said about them. In Naledi's case, the various references her friends made to her on all online accounts simply referred to her name which did not provide a link to any account of hers.

Naledi's online absence did not really come as a surprise because, of all the youth interviewed, she was the only one who confessed to watching TV the most. She knew all kinds of shows that are running on TV, especially the latest series that DSTV was running at the time. She of all the youth, was also the only one who seemed to be so deeply influenced by TV in her options and choices for her future. She could trace each choice she made about her future to a specific TV programme that she watched at a particular time in her life.

The Case of Nelo

Personal Family Space

Nelo is a female black township youth in Grade 12 at a local school. Her subjects at school are Mathematics Literacy, Science, Economics, History, Life Orientation, English and South Sotho. She plans to go to a nursing college to study nursing because 'I love nursing'.

Nelo has however not yet applied to study at her envisaged college, but plans to still apply at a private nursing college in the city. She is not aware of any closing dates for applications but hopes to find the application process still open and space available. A few weeks before writing her final year Grade 12 exams, Nelo had not made any post school applications to study.

Nelo's mother, who was a single mother, passed away some few years ago. She however continues to live in the same household that she always shared with her mother, grandparents, aunts, uncles and cousins. It is a household of 12 family members. She has a father that she is aware of, who stays elsewhere in the neighbourhood, but is not really involved in Nelo's life. Both her father and mother have however never really taken an interest in her life and her future. She indicates that

> I don't know why, but my mother, even when she was alive, never really took any interest in what happens to me. I have relied on my aunt from even when in was young.

She thus considered herself some kind of an orphan even when both her parents were still alive. Her mother's passing did not change anything in her life because she was in any case indifferent to Nelo's life prospects whilst alive. On the other hand, her father remains alive and lives a walking distance from Nelo's house, but he has never shown any interest in Nelo's life prospects either.

The passing of Nelo's mother has not changed much of her life as 'my aunt is still there and she talks to me about my future and has been encouraging me since I was young'. Nelo has also been trying to reach out to her father. She has even been broaching the subject of her post school future with her father and informing him of her intensions to study nursing. 'He supports me verbally and says I must go for it, but does nothing to help in a practical way'. 'He always makes promises but never keeps them'. Thus Nelo's life seems to have been a life full of promises and disappointments from both her parents. She has had to rely on her aunt, and over time grown accustomed to banking on her for support. The aunt lives in the same household with Nelo and all her other uncles and cousins. The aunt herself is also a single mother with children of her own, some of whom are the same age as Nelo. One of her cousins, who is the son to Nelo's aunt, is also in Grade 12 at the same school as Nelo.

Nelo is confident that she will pass matric, 'because I believe in myself'. However, she is not sure what marks she got in the June mid-year exams which would give her the confidence that she will be able to pass the final exams. However, the subject in which she vaguely remembers to have scored the highest in June was 'History, where I got sixty something percent'. Faith and hope, and most importantly, self-belief seem to be the main driving forces behind Nelo's outlook for her future. Besides that there does not seem to be much for Nelo to hold on to. She had not applied anywhere to study post matric – which was less than two month away at the time. She seemed aware that she had not been performing well in Grade 12 at the time, but seemed unaware of the exact percentage marks she scored and what would they demand of her final year exams.

This is probably why Nelo 'worries about the future every day'.

> What if something goes wrong, I ask myself daily. I worry most about the financial issues and where my life is going. I am always thinking about the risks I must deal with every day, like what if I meet a guy who is going to spoil my future, before I know it I'll be pregnant and having children with no career and no money?

It was very telling that Nelo seemed to know where she comes from – drinking alcohol and having boyfriends – and made a decision to change her life and vowed not to go back there, but however remains very worried about the allure of her past life and how easily she could simply drop back. The strong possibility of 'something going wrong' did not give her the comfort she needed for her future. To safeguard herself from these risks, Nelo 'feels vulnerable'.

> I mean when a guy comes in a VW Citi Golf Velocity and charms me I might end up feeling safe with him. Then before I know it, I will have fallen head over heels in love with him. There might be nothing I can do about that.

> So I try hard not to be committed in any relationship and try as much as I can not to be involved so that I don't have to beg a man. So at this moment I don't drink and I don't have a boyfriend. I started drinking and having boyfriends since I was fifteen, but stopped drinking a year or so ago and I have also been without a boyfriend for a few months now.

She has made the change in her life thus far, but remains at risk of falling back. 'It is not that I don't want to have boyfriends anymore, I just don't want a serious commitment for the sake of my future'. Nelo has also decided 'not to have any friends in the township, her only companions are her school mates'. She has also decided to put aside 'all other negative spaces surrounding me as they tend to distract me from focussing on my future'.

Nelo however remains in the 'negative spaces surrounding' her. Her reliance on her aunt is itself very thin, the township 'City Golf Velocity' charmers remain lurking, and the friends around the township remain in her face – even though she is keen to extract herself from that space. As will be shown later when looking at her virtual space, it would seem that the uncles who share the same dwelling as Nelo and her aunt, are luring her into a life of alcohol.

Community Space

Nelo believes that she, and most of her friends, do not want to fall pregnant because 'we all worry about our parents and also because the boys deny it when they make the girls pregnant'. But the problem is that when 'girls get involved in serious relationships with boys, even though we might use protection at the beginning, the boys end up demanding that protection not be used over time'. Thus there is always an element of vulnerability in Nelo's outlook on life. From the fear of falling in love and being misled, to the fear of moving from protected sex to later being forced into unprotected sex. Her sense of agency in her outlook on life tends to take the backseat in most issues she is confronted with.

What was however interesting was that Nelo believes it is a good thing for youth to be sexually involved from an early age 'because you learn a lot about yourself and others from an early age and you are able to manage relationships better when you are older'. She thus sees nothing wrong with having been sexually active and drinking since she was 14. This is all part, according to her, of gaining the necessary life experiences one might require later on in life.

Even though Nelo drinks alcohol, 'but I don't really enjoy drinking alcohol, I just drink a bit to socialise, because I was trying to fit in'. But she has avoided drinking alcohol 'since I was 15'. She experiences a lot of pressure to fit in in her life 'because everyone around me drinks alcohol. Almost all of my friends drink alcohol and codeine (a mix of cough syrup, Sprite cold drink, and marijuana)'. Thus the pressure to 'fit in' seems to be constant in Nelo's life. She is also not comfortable with her level of resolve to resist the temptation to 'fit in'.

Nelo also believes that money is important to her and her friends, and wants 'a man who gives you money (*o bechang*)'. This is where her vulnerability in the charmer driving the City Golf Velocity becomes more pronounced. This is because it is usually the guys who can afford to drive such cars who are likely to afford providing the money that she is looking for. Such money however comes with a lot of other pressures that Nelo is trying to avoid – alcohol, unprotected sex, and ultimately unplanned pregnancy.

On the socio political front, Nelo feels that 'the problem with our government is that they like to lie and are corrupt. In other instances however they try and us as the community we just like complaining'. She feels that the government

> ...also tends to lower standards too much, like lowering the pass rate in schools the way they have, they should not have done that. It makes us fail even more because we are now relaxed and know that we do not have to aim high as with just 35% you can pass.

Nelo's marks have themselves been very low at school. The fact that she does not seem to recall her exact June exam marks seems to indicate very worrying levels of performance at school. The silence about her matric performance on her Facebook postings observed in the New Year also signalled a possible lack of success in her Matric final year exams.

Nelo's favourite music is Hip-Hop and her favourite artists are mainly American. Her role model is however a local celebrity, Bonang Matheba. 'Because she is ambitious and independent and going places. She was doing a fashion show in New York recently. She is used a lot by other companies like Revlon'. Nelo herself seems to be drawn a lot into the beauty industry, with most of her postings on Facebook observed later suggesting this and that she seemingly joined a certain modelling agency. Thus her identification with Bonang Matheba and fashion and beauty did not come as a surprise. What is however worrying about such role models is the extent to which their success can be duplicated on a wider scale. There is no standard way of following in the footsteps of someone like Bonang Matheba and succeeding equally if not exceedingly. It requires no education, no specific funding, no specific skill and/or ability, and no specific trajectory. Nelo does not know whether Bonang Matheba has gone to school or not, if she has any educational qualifications, or how she got to be successful for that matter.

Nelo's second role model is her aunt.

> She is independent and a go getter. She is very committed to the right things and is very caring. I also feel that she is successful despite all the odds she has encountered in her life.

Consequently Nelo attaches a sense of independence and personal drive to role modelling. It is the same independence which she hopes will allow her 'not to beg a man' in her life. What worries her however, is how she will be able to get to the stage where she can be independent herself and not have to 'beg'.

Nelo attends church frequently, as do most members of her family. She goes to church most Sundays as her aunt does. She however does not regard herself as 'necessary religious'. It is just that

> ...that is how I have been brought up. Everybody goes to church at home on Sundays. Church also teaches you certain things that you cannot find elsewhere. So it is not necessary useless.

Nonetheless, she feels parents tend to overplay the role of the church and the difference it makes in one's life. This is because 'parents do not understand us, they call us the *X generation*; they expect us to do things the way they did them, and we are different'.

Virtual Space

Nelo's desire to become a nurse was largely influenced by what she saw on TV in a number of series that show nursing and what nurses do. That is what has influenced her most in her pursuit of a nursing career.

Nelo has an active Facebook profile, even though it is misleading with modified names, missing employment details, and missing details of school attended. It also depicts her status as being in a relationship. She is fairly active on Facebook, with most her postings being pictures of herself in model-like poses. She activated her Facebook profile in 2012, when she was 14 years old. As she indicated during the interviews, it would seem she had already been drinking alcohol by then given one of her posts in 2012 which refers to '*eish mic ma toxicated chicks nd my bf*', and another which simply indicated that '*Lol ysterdae my uncle got us drunk*'. This was on New Year's Day in January 2013. Around the same time, Nelo confirmed something we discussed in the interviews, which is that she had been sexually active since she was 14 years already in a post that said '*Bathong bare ke yentse thobalano* (people are saying I had sex)'. This was further confirmed two weeks later when she posted that she was '*missing my man*'.

Whilst in the first two years of her Facebook activities, in 2012 and 2013, Nelo was posting a lot of comments related to her personal life – in subsequent posts from 2014 onwards she seemed to simply be posting pictures of herself. From 2014 onwards, Nelo was only posting various pictures of herself without any captions. She would however only respond in the comments thanking people for complementing her beauty in the pictures she has posted. This shift in her online activity on Facebook seems to correlate very well with the interview discussions we held. There seemed to be a certain level of maturity and soberness creeping in with her which I picked up during the interviews. She did admit during our conversations that she 'used to drink alcohol' and that she 'used to have a boyfriend'. But by the time she was in Grade 12 and during our interviews, she had decided to stop having both the boyfriend and drinking alcohol so that she could focus on her future in nursing. For her to achieve her dreams, she recognized that she needed to focus on her schooling and making sure that she passed Grade 12 properly. Thus, in many ways, her Facebook life seemed to be a true reflection of the narratives she had provided during our interviews.

Conclusion

In this chapter I provided a descriptive case of the black urban female youth sampled, both middle and working class. Whilst each of the individual informants is different, they also share a number of traits that are shaped by their space and context. The middle class females tend to possess the maps and navigational tools that Appadurai talks about as against their working class counterparts. These can be found in both their personal and external spaces and are also reflected in their virtual spaces. The opposite tends to be true for the working class. For all the youths however, both middle and working class, the role of agency seems limited as against that of society. There are dynamics that seem common among the middle class female youth that seem absent with the working class youth. There are also dynamics that are present among youth born of foreign nationals that seem absent among youth born of South African parents. The online space of the female youth is also interesting in many ways. Much as their online activity does not seem as active as initially thought, there seems to be age dynamics that vary between the working class and middle class youth.

Narratives of Black Male Youth

Introduction

In this second part of my descriptive cases I focused on male urban youth, both middle and working class. I utilized the same three categories of personal family space, external space, and the virtual space as I did with the female youth in the previous chapter. In this chapter I will be dealing with five male urban youth.

The Case of Thabang

Personal Family Space
Thabang is a 19-year old black male urban youth based in Soweto. He is in his final year of schooling – Grade 12. At the time of the interviews he was two months away from writing his final Matric exams. He is an only child to a single mother who resides with her own parents – Thabang's grandparents, in a four roomed house in Soweto. Thabang, his mother, his grandparents, three of his uncles, and his cousin all live in one household – a total of eight people. As an extension to the four roomed house, they have three additional rooms built outside, which are mainly used by Thabang's uncles. He has recently been able to occupy one of the outside rooms which was used by one of the uncles who was imprisoned for car theft crimes. This uncle was recently released from prison and is a taxi driver in the township.

Thabang was undecided as to where he was going in January of the following year (four months' time) but 'I have options of the things I can do'. 'My options are around business. I could further study marketing and business management so that I may start my own business in future'. He applied to various institutions to further his studies, but they all told him that he did not qualify to study with them based on his subject choices and his performance at school at the time. Two issues immediately emerged for Thabang. First, he was 'undecided' about where to go when he completes Matric. Secondly, he was unsure as to what he wanted to become in life. All of this uncertainty and indecision, two month before he was due to begin his final exams.

Thabang does not have a present father in his life, he however does not

...feel his absence as I have uncles who fill the role that a father would have filled. I don't really miss him because my uncles help me when I need their support.

He believes he will 'succeed in life'. This is because he has 'commitment'. The commitment that Thabang espoused for himself and his future seemed a tough call in the context of his current situation. Because he does not know what the presence of a father could have meant for his life, he has chosen 'not to feel his absence'. He has nonetheless replaced this absence with his uncles. However, the uncles that he is stuck with, who serve as a replacement of a father, are themselves in a difficult space of crime and imprisonment. More interesting was that Thabang believed strongly that he knew what to do for him to succeed in life. This is by making sure that 'I stand for what I believe, doing my own thing and being different'. These are very noble principles for any human being to live by, the question however, is whether these principles work in the absence of maps and navigational tools.

Thabang plays soccer and belongs to a soccer team in the township. He however decided to stop playing soccer since he was in Grade 12. 'I just decided to stop playing soccer this year on my own so that I can focus on my studies'. His participation in the soccer club stemmed from his attempt 'to avoid doing the wrong things'. He played soccer to both keep fit but more importantly to 'occupy his mind with something that will take me away from all the bad influences'. Thus the agency that Thabang is exercising within a space of poverty, crime, delinquency, and failure became interesting. He seemed to be making a lot of choices and decisions about his life, all on his own, which would be a definite recipe for success in the presence of proper maps and navigational tools. He initially used soccer to 'hide from all the bad influences'. When soccer stopped serving this purpose and he was in Matric, he stopped playing soccer so that 'I can focus on my studies'.

Thabang however confessed that 'I do worry too much about my future, seeing that I am about to finish school in two months'.

> I mean it is my life on the line, I am depending on being given access to study at university, despite all my applications being rejected thus far. So it simply means if I don't succeed in studying at university, then I must start looking for a job.

Thus despite all the good principles he was using to guide his life, and despite all the good choices he was making about his life, Thabang remained alive to the constraints his current space imposed on him and the related prospects for his future.

> I see many people before me struggling, and I don't want to struggle like them – that is my worry. The aim is like, in my life, I don't want to be rich, I just want to be happy and not have to

worry about other things, if I become rich then that would be a bonus.

As a consequence, he has set his own goals about his future at a fairly low level. His focus is on escaping the current space and everything else after that 'is a bonus'. Thabang felt that he had done what was fair for him to succeed that far in his life. He studies Accounting – for which he averages 'the highest, forty-something percent', Business Studies – for which he averages 'somewhere above fifty percent', Mathematics Literacy – for which he averages 'around 40 percent'.

Thabang has his own room at home, which is an outside room. He 'sometimes takes advantage of this setup to bring girls to my room'. He has a 'steady girl-friend whom I bring to my room to visit'. For Thabang, 'girls are just normal, and not complicated. There are just things you need to understand about them, and then you will be fine with them'. His current 'steady' girlfriend is 24 years old whilst Thabang is still 19 years old. The girlfriend started working at the Spur Restaurant in Southgate as soon as she finished Grade 12 because 'she didn't pass well and wanted to work first and consider upgrading later'. Thabang felt that both boys and girls in the township are serious about their futures. The fact that he had a 'steady' girlfriend who is five years older than him and could not move much after finishing Matric except work as a waitress at a local Spur restaurant seemed to be enhancing his own fears about his future.

He felt that

> ...starting a business will be difficult because I will have to find someone to invest in the business and I will have to also prepare a business plan, all of which will be difficult for me to achieve.

He therefore knows what getting into business will require of him, but simply does not know how he will be able to accomplish such a goal. Therefore starting a business for Thabang if he does not gain university access for further education 'is out of the picture'. Resultantly, if he does not get university access, then 'I will have to start looking for employment and hopefully I will get a job'. This will put Thabang in exactly the same space as his current girlfriend.

> There are also these learnerships that they do for about six months. I have a friend who did one on diamond polishing somewhere in town. So I might attend that if everything else fails.

This option seemed to be the second last option for Thabang, who seemed keen not to just give up and collapse into the world of youth who are neither in employment, education, nor training.

Thabang's view on the *#FeesMustFall* movement was that 'the government must just compromise and pay all costs for young people who can't afford – everyone who can't afford. Just like NSFAS, they should do the same'. He however felt that the disruption and chaos around the protests 'is not good', and might distract from the cause of those who are 'really in need of this money'.

Thabang is not planning to have any children in future. This is because children are 'too much responsibility, it is an expense that I am trying to avoid'. Some of his friends however already have children with their girlfriends. He is also not planning to get married. This is because 'marriage is a big step, and committing to a marriage is not child's play, is not easy. It is a big step'. His views about marriage are largely influenced by the soap operas he watches on TV portraying divorces and men losing everything after divorce. 'We can settle in together, I don't mind, but marriage…no'. Thabang's views about marriage and family as 'too much responsibility' might have also been influenced by the difficulties he has experienced in his own life as opposed to just what he had seen on TV. This is so because Thabang acknowledges that the township environment in which he is growing has many challenges that are not easy to overcome. He believes 'you have to be true to yourself to not fall into the bad habits that surround us'. This is because

> I can see the effects of the bad lifestyle and what they due to people. Those who throw themselves into these lifestyles do so at their own peril. Everybody has their own choices.

This includes youth around him, whom he sees drinking and smoking and misbehaving from a young age. 'Every weekend it is happening at the parks with drinking of alcohol and smoking of marijuana and *nyaope* which make us fail more and more'.

Community Space
Thabang felt that he would raise his family the same way he was in terms of 'support and love'. Thus he felt that he was sufficiently supported by his mother and family and was given enough love in his upbringing. This seemed to have been an important element of Thabang's upbringing which built him to have the kind of thinking and outlook he had. He seemed to have held onto the love and support he received from his family to guide his own map creation process and the building of his own navigational tools. This 'love and support' seemed to have come from everyone in the family, including the jailbird uncle of his. What was interesting in our long conversations about the support and love he has received from his family is that even the uncle who misbehaved seemed keen to support and enable Thabang to succeed in life.

> My uncle tells me, don't be like me and end up stealing cars. You will be arrested and end up in jail like me. Look at me now, I am driving taxis, you must be something better.

His uncle further shares with him that going to jail is not an easy thing and is not as romantic as some of the boys in the township make it out to be – it is tough and bad. Thus Thabang promised himself that he would never get himself arrested and for him to do this 'I will have to avoid all the bad spaces and influences'.

Seemingly, Thabang's family supports and loves him – something that drives him to succeed. It is obviously poor, township-based and surrounded by bad influences – something he wants to escape. He feels that 'the environment I grew up in is fine, everything is there. I don't have to struggle to go to school'. But there is another thing he does not want to absorb from his family. 'The only thing that I would change in bringing up my family if I were to have one is the mind-set'. He indicates that,

> I was raised to be stereotyped and focus on one thing all the time – like church. When I was brought up I was told that church is the only way to be on the right path, which is not true and I don't want my children to be stereotyped like that. There are many people who do not go to church but are on the right path, and many others who go to church but are on the wrong path.

This difference in thinking seems to have informed the choices Thabang made on his own about his future path and how to traverse it. On the other hand, as a regular church goer, there are things that Thabang feels he learnt from church which have helped shape his outlook on his future in a positive way. He feels what he learnt from church includes 'faith and trust and how to share with others'. These are aspects of his church life that he continues to embrace.

Thabang's role model is his mother. His mother, who works at a local Shoprite store, 'has been my inspiration and does everything in her power to support me'. 'My uncles also guide me and teach me to do the right things'. One of Thabang's uncles works as a police man in the township, whilst the other '*ke le gintsa*' (a criminal). The criminal uncle gets in and out of prison as a result of various offences he commits. 'They are both supportive in their own way'. 'They do talk to me about stuff and girls and how to avoid the wrong stuff'.

> They also talk to me about education and encourage me to study hard and be myself and not be like him (the convicted uncle), and not to chase material things.

He thinks if he fails in everything he will 'just chill out and wait. See what will come my way,' With both grandparents still alive and living with them, both in their 70s, Thabang only ever talks about his future prospects with his grandmother rather than his grandfather. 'She would ask me, how was school today? How was church and you must go more often'. Even though both grandparents are roughly the same age, Thabang believes that he never communicates about his life with his grandfather because 'my grandfather is too old'. Thus even in the absence of a father, his grandfather has not attempted to occupy the space in Thabang's life that the grandmother seems to be conscious to occupy. The uncles on the other hand seem to be present in his life and provide guidance 'in their own way' to him. Thabang seems conscious of the fact that his uncles themselves are not shining examples of success in life, one of them being a criminal, but their 'own way' of advice seems to be helping him avoid 'bad influences'.

Amid all the confusion and indecision surrounding his life, Thabang has big ambitions of becoming a human resource specialist. However, he has never met and/or known anyone who works in that field.

> But on TV in soap operas like Scandal and Isidingo, they talk about business. Like when Sechaba (a character on the series) and this other guy were fighting for a job on the drama series. That is the closest I have come to understanding and seeing a human resource specialist role.

The school Thabang attends, even though he feels it has done everything it can to prepare him for the future, does not have any programmes (such as job shadowing and/or expos) to expose them to their prospective careers. Thabang is happy with what life gives him. What he knows is the bare minimum and he is happy with that.

Thabang believes that he has everything he needs in his life to build his future and succeed in life. He believes that he has the tools to succeed in life and that 'everything is there, I just have to use it to my advantage'. Looking and reflecting on the role the school has played in his life, he feels that 'it has done everything to help me succeed in life'. On the home front, he believes that 'I get a lot of support from my mother and grandparents and my uncles help me whenever I need their advice'.

> It is also easy for me to study at home. I have my own space, my own room, which was a spare room and no one wanted to use it at home.

Thabang has never had a conversation with his mother about his future,

> …because everything I do I do for myself, *yena* (she) just supports me. If I say to her I want to go to college she just says fine, she will not choose for me. She said I must ask for whatever support I need and she will support me going forward.

Thabang's mother was born in 1976. She passed her Grade 12 and later dropped out of college where she was enrolled for a Small Business Development Course. She has however asked Thabang about his career plans; 'asking me, Thabang, what do you want to become?'

> I gave her the options of what I want to study at university like Human Resource Programmes, Business General Management, Economics as a tourist agent, as well as Marketing. Unfortunately all these fields are not scarce in South Africa, they are just average and everybody studies them. I actually

want to become a human resource specialist because it is a simple programme, and wants someone who is fair and honest which I believe I am.

Thus Thabang's commitment and determination is admirable. He has done his best to understand his current space and prospects for his future, including the career choices and their scarcity levels in terms of job prospects. He however remains vulnerable with regards to his overall maps and navigational tools, which seems to be a result of the absence of guidance a youth his age still requires in life. The school has not bothered to educate him about his possible options and prospects for his future, so he has relied on television and believes that is enough. His mother is only willing to support and love him – no guidance, no exposure, no deep and meaningful conversations and no real engagement. The uncles and grandmother have also offered him love and support, but mainly by doing the bare minimum. All the grandmother is ensuring is that Thabang attends church and school and does as he's told in these institutions; nothing more, nothing less. All the uncle can do is say 'look at me and don't be like me'. The mother unfortunately is also just passively waiting for Thabang to ask what he needs and all she will do is her best to provide. Whether such provision is in the right direction or not, no one seems to know, including Thabang himself. To Thabang's credit however, he seems to have some sense that the direction he is taking might not result in the intended outcomes. He knows that his intended field of study is not a scarce skill area, and he knows many people in the township who have similar qualifications but remain without jobs. The best response he had to these unfortunate realities was to lower his expectations.

Whilst Thabang does not have a favourite political party, his socio-economic and political outlook on South Africa is largely bleak.

> Everybody in our politics wants to have power, and they want this power for their own personal use, they don't want the society to benefit. Everybody in Parliament wants the money and the tender and only wants to give his family a job. Nepotism and corruption is rife. There is also a lack of management.

Though Thabang acknowledges that not all political leaders fit the description he has given above,

> ...the good ones are not given a choice and do not have influence. Those that do are blackmailed by the bad politicians. People who should be our role models are the ones always involved in scandals. Like our President, I should be looking up to him, but every day is scandal, Nkandla, President this, President that, you cannot be looking up to such a person.

As a consequence, much as he sees a future for himself in South Africa, he however feels that 'the only problem is the people who rule our country, there are too many people sitting and doing nothing and unemployed'. He feels that, 'especially *mo kasi* (in the township), we don't get the same opportunities as the guys in the north (suburbs)'. He however sees the problem as not being one sided because

> ...the problem is that we all want to do the same things. Every boy in the township is studying music and being a DJ. So there are too many DJs producing all kinds of stuff that nobody wants to listen to, which does not make sense.

What is interesting however is that, even with his own choice of human resource speciality which he upfront points out 'is not a scarce skill area', he faces the same risks as the DJs he laments. This is an informed choice because as Thabang points out, 'it is easy'. This in Thabang's view is also caused by the

> ...career limiting choices we are given by the school. During career guidance, we are shown very few career options that we can follow, so we do not know what is out there. They never come to our school and show us options we have never heard about, it is always the same old things that everybody has done. Even the teachers do not seem to know more than us, as long as you can get a job; that is all everyone is worried about.

'Even our elders are struggling and have no idea what options are there'.

When coming to the broader community within which he is located, Thabang believes that the broader community's role is negative on his life. 'The community is just waiting for you to fail, *ke yona ntho'e ba e shebileng fela* (that is all they are looking for)'. He attributes the prevalence of failure in the township to this. 'Because everybody else fails in the township, they want you to fail too'. This is the reason Thabang seems to occupy himself differently from typical youth his age – to avoid the trap of failure. He of course wants to make sure that he denies those who wish for him to fail an opportunity to realize their wishes.

Virtual Space

Thabang watches TV 'maybe until 9pm, but usually sports and some soapies'. To some extent, TV has influenced him in relation to the career choices he is considering for his future, in particular, his choice of human resource specialization. Thabang is also a big fan of 'Hip-Hop' music. His favourite artists are American Hip-Hop star 'Nas, and locally I just listen to them because I must support local music'.

> Because if we spend our money to support local music, we will be spending our money on our own people and helping in circulating money amongst us and creating jobs, developing our own people and the like.

'But at some point I do enjoy local artists a bit'. Thabang is a big fan of Nas'
because

> ...he raps about life and things that happen around us; the
> hardships we all go through and the circumstances of black kids
> like lack of money; he also raps about when you see these white
> kids having plenty of stuff but you can't get them. Nas is trying to
> tell us that we must keep calm and do our own thing. Nas is also
> Tupac's fan.

He feels that

> South African artists only rap about money, how they get money
> and how they spend it, I am not interested in that. Ok, at some
> point they can rap about money, but just let that be one song. The
> other songs must at least give us direction.

Similarly, at times he listens to House music and his favourite South African
artist is DJ Kent, 'because he makes great music that accommodates everybody'.
Thus music for Thabang must do more than just provide sound, it should be more
about the message. What I found very telling was his attraction to Nas' music
'telling us to keep calm', when they see 'white kids having plenty of stuff but you
can't get them'. It is about deprivation and inequality, but keeping calm about it.
This calmness permeates all of Thabang's life and informs his acceptance of many
aspects of his life. These aspects include the family, the school, the government
and society at large. The bragging by South African artists about money and girls
also does not get to him; maybe because it might enrage him when he needs to
keep calm. What was also very telling about Nas' music, some of which I listened
to myself and enjoyed, is that it is very sparse on instruments. There is usually one
beat that is consistent in the song from beginning to end and usually is not varied
much throughout the song. What drives most of his music are the lyrics, which of
course most Rap music is based on, but his are deeper and more importantly,
somehow uninterrupted. Nas is also a much older Rap artist and like Tupac, I
would not have expected a 19-year old youth to listen to and enjoy his music.

Thabang was found to be active on social media, specifically on Facebook,
where his profile is a correct reflection of who he is including his name and surname. There are various kinds of persona that he takes online, some of which are
in line with the issues he raised in the interviews to somewhat varying degrees.
Amongst those include '*positive thinking is half the work done*'. His online persona
also reflected his deep black consciousness, which was unsurprising considering
his love for Tupac and Nas' music. This was evident in posts such as '*young &
black*', '*niggas with attitude (NWA)*', '*Chubby Niggas **Compton***' and '*I'm a
villain M16 **COMPTON***'. Reference to Compton is also telling but not
surprising in relation to Thabang's attraction to Tupac and Nas. Compton is a
township in the Unites States of American which is largely regarded as the
birthplace of Rap music as we know it today. Most Rap artists such as Tupac,

Snoop Dogg and Dr Dre were born and grew up in this area which was a crime haven back in the days. Thus the association and affinity that Thabang has with this place and its now multibillionaire artists resonate with his outlook on his present life and the possibilities that it holds for his future. Therefore Compton seems to be one of his maps of the future. Much as there has recently been a movie released about Compton, I remain unsure whether it could constitute a sufficient navigational tool for Thabang.

The need for him to keep calm about his circumstances, as he shared with me during the interviews in relation to Nas' music, equally permeates his Facebook posting. He seemed to be looking for this calmness not only from Nas as an artist, but from other avenues too. One of his posts refers to, '*Paranoid Stoners -_- Just be calm and ride along*'. However, upon checking this group online, it appeared to be a strange Facebook group that encourages smoking of marijuana, with their motto being '*smoke weed. …. Make money*'. The message of this Facebook group titled *Paranoid Stoners* is not very different from some of the other posts by Thabang which painted a picture different from the one painted during the interviews we had. Much as I had understood from our interviews that he does not smoke marijuana, in one of his posts he says that, '*we are not lazy, we are just stoned*'.

Equally, like most other youth his age, he often posts status updates about where he is and what he is doing, and comments on various other societal developments such as new song releases by his favourite Rap artists and soccer related developments. He also uses the space to share current political issues in the country and his views on them, such as his comment on the State of the Nation Address as: '*Zupta must Fall!!! Zuma and Guptas!!! 2016 STATE OF THE NATION ADDRESS!!*'

The absence of a father figure also comes through on his posts. Much as during the interviews he expressed indifference to a father-figure absence, on international father's day he posted '*happy father's day to my mom*'. In another separate post he seems to be proud to have been on a '*road trip with mommy*'. Thus his sense of pride in his mother and the role modelling that she seems to provide to him finds its way into his social media space.

Post the interviews and during the write up of this case study, based on his latest Facebook posting, it would seem that Thabang was able to pass Matric with a university entrance pass. It however remains unclear as to what subsequently happened to him as there were thus far no posts updating his situation.

The Case of Akhona

Personal Family Space
Akhona is an 18-year old boy from Soweto in his last year of schooling, He was born to a single mother with two siblings, one younger brother and an older brother. He lives in his grandmother's house, which is a typical four roomed house in Soweto – Phiri Location. The complete family unit comprises a grandmother, his mother and two brothers as well as his aunt with her two sons and a

daughter – thus the complete house hold comprises nine people. The house has been recently extended with an additional bedroom which now makes it a three bedroomed house accommodating nine adults. He grew up sharing his bedroom with his brothers.

Akhona did not to have a distinct sense of purpose and is not sure what the future holds for him. He is generally shy and somewhat reserved. He keeps to himself, attending school and listening to music in his room. Talking to him a day after he wrote his final Grade 12 exam paper, Akhona was neither sure what he was going do in the new year nor was he sure about his performance in the final exams. All he could tell me was that 'we will see'. From his current space, it was clear that Akhona did not see a bright future, if any future at all for himself.

Akhona however had a vague idea of what he would like to become, mentioning 'something in media and arts'. He had however not applied for study opportunities anywhere to pursue such a possibility. In one of our first interviews discussing his future, it so happened that on my way to the interview I had picked up on Metro FM that one of the DJs, Mo Flava, was giving out bursaries to deserving students in Akhona's chosen field and encouraging applications on his show. Quizzed about such opportunities, Akhona had no clue as 'he never listens to the radio'. 'I prefer listening to music on my phone and be in my own space, there is too much out there that I have to block off'. There seemed to be a lot that Akhona had to 'block off' in his life. First was his mother, who lives with them but is struggling to keep up with the costs and duties of raising three boys as a single mother. Whilst his mother does find work at times, most jobs she finds are generally intermittent, temporary, and low paying. This has placed a lot of stress on the family as they have to make do with the little that their mother is able to raise, when she is able to raise it. Unfortunately the lack of money in the family tends to spill over into behavioural aspects with the mother tending to show erratic behaviour and impatience with her children. As a consequence, there is tension between the brothers (Akhona, 18 and his elder brother, 24) and they are resultantly not that close to each other. They stopped sharing the bedroom as Akhona moved into the girl's bedroom. Furthermore, there seemed to be a lot of tension between his mother and his grandmother, which at times spilled over to the aunts and cousins.

Akhona is a typical township boy who does not trouble anyone but largely keeps to himself. His father passed away many years ago, although he was never present in Akhona's life when he was alive. Thus Akhona has never really known his father, he just knew that his father was alive and well somewhere, and later got to know that he passed on. His mother on the other hand lives with him in the family household and due to lack of education and job opportunities, is sometimes employed and at other times not. As a consequence, Akhona has had to rely on his grandmother for support at various stages of his life and continues to live in her house. The household tends to elicit a great deal of conflict between Akhona's grandmother and his mother, something that seems to have had a great deal of negative impact on him, which seems to have largely contributed to him closing off the world from his space.

Akhona however remains a typical township boy like any other decent township boy who does not get into much trouble. He has been attending school throughout his life and has been passing all his grades up to Grade 12. He has reached Grade 12 at the age of 18 and has a general feeling that he will pass as 'I have never failed a Grade in my life'.

Over and above attending school, Akhona spends most of his time with friends or at home playing music and/or studying. He currently does not have a girlfriend, does not drink alcohol, but smokes marijuana. However, a year later Akhona indicated that

> I don't smoke dagga anymore, I have moved on. It is just that the township environment is not good. That is why I will not raise my children in this environment, because I know what happens. Parties and the like, there are just like a lot of things that pop up randomly in the township which pull most people down.

It would seem that during school days Akhona entered a space which was not good, something which he attributes to the 'township environment'. Within a year of interviewing Akhona, he transitioned from schooling phase (Grade 12) into a post-schooling phase and started attending at a Further Education and Training College; he felt that he had 'moved on'.

Even though he later transitioned to an FET college, Akhona initially felt that he did not have any parental support and consequently no means of financial support to realize his goals and ambitions. This was one of the reasons he had not applied at any institution of higher learning because 'how will I be able to pay them? My mother tells me that we don't have money all the time and that we are poor'. Thus not only does he see and feel the poverty that surrounds him, he equally hears it every day through constant reminders from his mother. These reminders have somehow shaped his sense of giving up and 'not to bother'. He thus seemed to have muted himself in relation to his future prospects. He has an idea of what he wants to become, which is in the arts. He however never bothered to check possibilities for him to realize this future.

One of the key ways Akhona manages the space he finds himself in is through art. 'I spend a lot of my time in my room an'. So he draws all kinds of things using a simple pen and paper to pass time; something that he enjoys and 'I feel I am good at, but helps me escape from my family space'. Akhona shared with me a number of drawings that he did over time on his notebook, and I was fascinated at the quality and detail of his drawings, taking into account his age and resource limitations. The drawings are so accurate that when I tracked him and his friends online, I could immediately recognize faces of some of his friends from the drawings he had earlier shared with me. Thus he seems to be extremely talented in art but does not see any future in it.

A year into our interview sessions, Akhona managed to pass Grade 12 and qualified for Technikon and/or College entrance. He registered at a Further Education and Training college and was able to pursue his talent by studying art.

Interviewed again at this time (after Matric and during college), Akhona's outlook on life and his own prospects for his future had changed dramatically. He informed me that

> I have been reading this book, *The Secret by Ronda something*. It comprises of philosophers who tell you about the human mind and that your thoughts create a frequency. So if I want to have a car, I must say I have a car, I must not say I am going to have a car. I must say I have the house, instead of saying I am going to have a house, and then I am likely to get it.

The Secret is a self-help book by Rhonda Byrne. The book reflects on the law of attraction and makes claims that positive thinking can create life changing results. Akhona tells me that

> I bumped into this book when I was surfing the internet and bumped into some quotes by Michael Beckwith, who is a philosopher and I liked his quotes, which were so inspirational. So I discovered that he has a book and I downloaded it and saved it as a PDF file. I was shocked to discover the things he has written about.

Michael Beckwith is an American minister of religion, author, and founder of the Agape International Spiritual Centre. It was however very interesting that Akhona did not see Beckwith as a religious leader, but rather as 'a philosopher'. Akhona himself has not and continues not to be spiritually inclined. He does not attend church and grew up not attending any church. At no point during our yearlong interviews did he show any inclination and/or knowledge of the church and its rituals. His mother and grandmother however tend to vacillate from one church to another across various denominations, from the Christian faith based churches to spiritual Zionist based churches. Somehow Akhona has managed to insulate himself from all these church influences, an inclination further abetted by the absence of any push or insistence from the elders in the family.

> Triggered by these two books by Rhonda Byrne and Michael Beckwith, Akhona has 'since been reading books and they have changed my life and helped me to grow as a person'. He felt that he was becoming assertive, *'gore motho ga a mmametse a nkutlwe, wabona? (when someone is listening to me he must understand me)'* He also seemed to be understanding himself better. He seemed tuned on to who he is, what he represents, and more importantly, what he wants. What he wants is not only something that he seemed to have discovered, but something that he felt very passionate about and was decisive about realizing it – almost with an element of anger which he did not acknowledge. 'I have been discovering inspirational quotes that guide me and lead me to

books. Everybody should have that book. People degrade themselves and have too much anger which brings more evil to them. Like my mother always reminds me, "ahh my son we are poor" and *shit* like that, and there is nothing we can do and if you keep on saying that, the universe will say yes, yes, yes. Since I have read that book my life has changed and I have self-belief and I now know where I want to go'. He felt that he had 'been frustrated for too long living under somebody's shelter, I want to have my own house, own family, own everything'. Thus Akhona's inspiration seemed to carry a lot of anger from his past which has remained his present. Much as he did not openly acknowledge this anger, he saw the anger that remained with his mother. What remains very disappointing to Akhona is that 'my mother has too much anger, and my brother also has too much anger and they bring more anger to themselves. It is like they are all inside the box now, and I am outside the box and I am watching them. It is like I am watching the zoo'. He believes that 'my talent and opportunities are unlimited and I am exploring all of them and not degrading myself. I am driven by successful people and my destiny is in my hands and I will make it'.

All of Akhona's lessons and attitude were triggered by the usual surfing of the internet, bumping into a few inspirational quotes online, discovering books by specific inspirational authors and reading them. A year later,

This is what this book has taught me. We all have a choice, everyone has a choice, you just have to make your own choice and follow it. Everybody must read this book, it changed my life. Everything is a choice in life. The thoughts people have now are just under one thing and they don't realise who they are and their capabilities, which are endless and limitless.

There was a total mind shift in how Akhona saw the world and the opportunities that lie before him. This mind shift made him more determined to succeed and realize his dreams. It was not just about the mind shift and the dreams he had, it was also the steps he had taken to achieve those – passing Grade 12 and enrolling for art at a Further Education and Training college. There are however risks and dangers that remain lurking. He remains without the resources and tools to adequately practise his art. He has to use two taxi transport systems to get to the college, of which he tends to use only one and walk for over an hour to the college. He does not seem to have any idea what prospects his career choice holds for his future.

The total mind shift in Akhona's head however did not trigger itself, it seems to have come about as an unintended consequence of earlier interviews conducted with him when he was still doing Grade 12. Whilst the intention here is not to create maps and navigational tools, but to simply investigate their presence and/or absence in these youth and how they get constructed – the result seems to have inadvertently created maps and navigational tools. In Akhona's outlook,

> ...to be honest, to be really, really honest, I take motivation from everybody, so when we spoke, you fed me with motivation. And I told myself I want to do this and I am going to do this. To know that there is someone who cares about what you do, where you want to go, how you are going to get there is a big motivation for me. Just to have that conversation and share where you are going with someone who listens and cares. No negativity. That really got me thinking and going. You get one opportunity in life and this was one such opportunity for me, and I started with myself by removing anger from my heart.

Although he is of the view that he has 'removed anger' from his heart, his constant reference to it seems to indicate remnants of this anger remaining. It would also seem that where Akhona is at this stage is more about perceptions becoming realities. Thus when I spent time with him, what he saw was 'caring'. When I asked questions and simply listened to his answers and just continued asking more and more questions, what he felt was 'motivation'. When I probed deeper and gave examples of options that exist out in the world, what he saw was 'opportunity'.

Akhona however remains intimidated by his past, which remains his present; and he remains alive to the constraints that it brings. This has informed his own shaping of his future, in which he is 'planning to get married and have many children'. This is because he believes

> ...it is a legacy. I just want to have a bigger legacy. My family only has three children. I want to fill that space. I want to have six children; that is what I want. Little *me's* running around in my house, big house. I won't have the children before I have a mansion though. I must have a mansion first.

Akhona points out that

> I want my kids to grow like rich people. One thing...I would not raise my children the way that I was raised. I was not raised the right way. I was raised in a family with too many family feuds, and family feuds damage a young mind. I will surround my kids with people who are deserving; good people with a good mind-set. I would change my children's surroundings and environment.

The future that Akhona envisions for himself and his children is therefore totally different from his current space, but he does not seem to have the tools and/or maps to make it a reality. Thus far, the tools he has discovered for himself, the online books, have allowed him to jump 'out of the box' and look at it from the outside 'like I am watching a zoo'. He needs more tools for him to move from just standing outside the box.

Community Space

Akhona is not active in any political party and is unsure how and where to become a member and be active in a political party. Much as he knows about the ANC as the ruling party and most dominant since 1994, he feels that it does not talk to him. 'I feel that they are just doing their own thing for themselves and have forgotten about us'. He also knows about various other political parties in South Africa, but is equally 'not interested in them'. He seems not to think politics do anything for him, he thinks politics are just something that happens out there that is unrelated to him and/or his life and where it is going. Akhona is aware of dance and social clubs in the community, but does not belong to any of them. This is because they are more about 'dancing and drama, those things', and he is not interested in those kinds of clubs. There are also exercise clubhouses in the township which he also has not joined. This is because he believes 'you have to be a social person to join and participate in some of these activities', something that he regards himself as not connecting to. In the absence of all other avenues of external maps and navigational tools to help guide and shape his future, Akhona 'holds to my mentality'. 'What I see now in my life is not what I want in my future, so I am holding onto that and it drives me'.

Virtual Space

There are free Wi-Fi hotspots in the township, but some are said to not be working. But Akhona does not use even the ones that are working because he 'prefers to buy data'.

> The money that I get to go to school is for two taxis, but I usually
> don't take the second taxi and rather walk the remaining distance
> so that I can save some money to buy myself data.

On average, Akhona spends about R40 per month on data. On an average day, Akhona spends about three to four hours on the internet – including social media and all other internet based activities. When his data is about to expire, he uses the remaining amount of data to download documents and music. He however did not feel that the internet helped him with anything much in relation to his life and future, except looking for jobs that are available. Most of these jobs related posts are more pushed into the social media space when *liked*, and therefore tend to pop up more frequently. Much as he did not seem to attach much value to the internet and the impact it had on his life, it would however seem that the key mind shift he has had relate to what he found on the internet. The books that he discovered online and downloaded seemed to have significantly shaped his thinking, yet he felt that the internet played no major role in his life. If anything, it would seem that the internet became the most important navigational tool in his life – albeit mainly for changing the way he sees life and his space in 'the box'.

Akhona also has accounts on social media, specifically Facebook (where he has two different accounts) and Instagram. However, overall he did not seem to be that much active on social media. One of the reasons that could have contributed to this inactivity is the incident that happened with his mother when he was in Grade 11. He had a heated disagreement with his mother when he was in Grade 11,

> ...and she said it was the new phone that she had just bought me that was driving me crazy and making me disrespectful and she took it back as punishment.

His mother never gave him back the phone and he stayed for the remainder of his schooling years without a phone, unable to engage in any manner online.

Akhona's limited online presence was interesting. Whilst on Instagram he used his real name and surname on his profile, his Facebook profile on the other hand was very misleading. On Instagram, he posts various pictures of himself which are simple, albeit artistic with messages such as *'photography without art never expresses the true meaning of the photo itself'*. On Facebook he goes by various names, again with simple yet artistic pictures and posts. Such posts include, *'don't let them in ur head or else nothing will ever be achieved'* as well as *'she not really BAD till she fuck with art'*. One of his profiles depicts him as born and living in the suburbs of Johannesburg whilst another profile depicts him as a US citizen living in Florida. Both profiles denote his year of birth as being much earlier than it actually is.

The Case of Mercury

Personal Family Space

Mercury is a 17-year old black boy from Soweto, who is in Grade 11 at a school in the township. He comes from a family of four siblings with a single parent – a mother. He shares his grandmother's home with his sisters, their mother, uncles, aunts, and cousins in a household of 10.

Mercury's home comprises a normal four roomed house with three outside rooms. He comes from a family of four comprising two girls and two boys. Apart from attending school, in Grade 11, Mercury used to belong to a brass band for many years. He would use his spare time over and above schooling, over week-ends and holidays, to practice playing the trumpet with members of his brass band. However, since he began doing Grade 11, he stopped his participation in the band because 'my marks at school where dropping too fast, so I realised that I needed to focus on my studies'.

Mercury has also participated in various arts and culture groups and has auditioned on various occasions as an actor and a poet. He writes his own poems and has continued to do, and published some of them on Facebook. This is because his secondary goal, below that of becoming a philosopher, is to become an actor. He thus spends most of his time looking for audition opportunities from various casting agencies hoping for a break in the acting industry. He has three goals in life, the first is to become 'a philosopher', the second is to become a poet 'which is like being a philosopher in another way', and the third is to be an actor. He believes that none of his dreams require him to be educated beyond the schooling phase.

Mercury's mother works for *Telkom* and his father, who passed away in 2010, was a caretaker at the local school. His father passed on when he was 10 years old.

Mercury's main aim in life, as indicated earlier, is to become a philosopher, because 'I want to give people the ideas of life and the philosophy of how they can be'. He thinks he will be able to do this because his understanding of philosophy means 'love of wisdom and is about how people can live in a better way and how we can change things in life'. He feels he can succeed as a philosopher 'because I like writing poems during my spare time, maybe before I sleep I write about two or three poems'.

When Mercury's mother first saw the poems he was writing, she encouraged him to do more and he felt that 'maybe I can achieve more in life if I become a philosopher'. Mercury believes that 'a philosopher is someone who gives people the advices of life. Like an adviser of how people should live, by doing good'. Thus in the main he sees himself advising society about life and the lessons thereof and ensuring that society at large does the right things. Mercury feels that he has been inspired by the work of 'Niccolò Machiavelli, from 1652; he wrote books and that is what I plan to do; write a lot of books'.

The absence of a father figure for Mercury 'does not affect me that much because we are good in life'. 'All I do is hold on to his words to me when he was still around, to be real and do my own thing'. He believes he will 'succeed in life'. This is because 'I am a hardworking person and I invest a lot of my time doing my school work'. More interesting is that Mercury believes that he knows what to due to succeed in life. 'By making sure that I tell myself that whatever I do, I will succeed. By just maintaining a good attitude'. Thus key maps and navigational tools for Mercury are threefold. First he holds on as much as he can to some of the things his father used to tell him when he was young. Secondly it is hard work and belief in himself. Thirdly, it is a good attitude.

Mercury had a girlfriend 'since last year January (when he was 15), but I want to dump her'. But the problem is that 'girls are complicated, today you are hot and tomorrow you are not; you are cold. They are like the weather. And they have expectations'. 'Most of the girls expect a lot from me and that is why I prefer to dump them'.

> I am used to girls; I am always with them and they like me a lot. I have a lot of girlfriends, but there is one that I am serious with, but lately... *ahh*, I want to dump her as well.

He sees himself as a girls' man and that girls are always after him. He entertains their interests in him, but to 'avoid complications', he usually dumps them early to avoid being pulled into such complications. He sees nothing wrong with being involved with many girls at the same time, nor does he see anything wrong with having girlfriends at such an early age. He indicates that he 'prefers to be in the company of girls' than that of boys.

Community Space

Mercury's role model is Tupac Shakur, whose music and movies 'I like a lot and like to watch and listen to'. The reason he is such a big fan of Tupac Shakur, an American Hip-Hop artist who was shot dead in the 1990s, is because

> I think my life of being a philosopher is related to his. Tupac believed in fighting for the States (USA) and what he did not like about how they treated people. He was always thinking about the community and the people.

Thus in his endeavour to become a philosopher, there seems to be a strong philanthropist element permeating through Mercury's wishes. His goal is closely linked to a notion of society, a drive to do good, and a responsibility to fight for the downtrodden and marginalized. He however does not see himself realizing these 'fights' in any way besides through writing. Equally, celebrities and artists and music are not just that for him, they are about the projects they pursue and the extent to which they mirror his own projects and future prospects in life. Kendrick Lamar is another one of Mercury's favourites and role models because

> ...he is also a philosopher, a visionary and a politician in one. He wants to change the life of black people today, and that is why I listen to him.

The role models that Mercury looks up to, and the artists that he follows, are all American Hip-Hop artists – some of whom died probably before he was born. This is so because Mercury feels that 'South African Rap artists are not inspiring. They are always rapping about girls and money. I like people who give advice to the community, not people who destroy'. 'I don't like their lyrics'. 'Like Cassper Nyovest; he only sings about money and girls'. Mercury believes that 'music is not just music. Music means a lot, to be honest. I don't feel comfortable supporting local music when I don't get what I expect'.

Mercury believes that part of the reason most township youth and his friends misbehave is because of the influence of the local Hip-Hop music.

> These local musicians glamorise these bad behaviours and since everybody is listening to music... they are destroying the community to be honest. That is why youth these days always go to parks and smoke marijuana and buy beers, busy with girls always. It is because of these musicians, they glamorise these things because there is no one who is not listening to music.

'Most youth are going to these parks drinking *codeine* and smoking, like 80%. This happens from an early age'. 'I don't take *codeine* anymore because I once had a bad experience – that thing nearly killed me'. 'I don't know how I got home that day and since then I stopped drinking'. 'Codeine is a mix of cough syrup you can buy from the Pharmacy like *Bronclear*, *Cetirizine*, and *Stilpane*, but must have (the ingredient) codeine in it'. 'You then mix the cough syrup with *Sprite*, and marijuana'. 'If you mix it the wrong way it can kill you. It nearly killed me and I stopped drinking alcohol since then'.

Mercury seemed amusingly surprised at my ignorance about this drink, which has become the main choice of narcotic for most youth in the township. There are three main reasons why they create and drink this alcohol based narcotic, even though it could kill them. First, it is cheap to put together. Therefore in the working class context which these youth find themselves, this drink makes access to alcohol easier. 'It costs less than half of what *nyaope* costs'. *Nyaope* is a competing drug, and not alcohol, which is the cheaper version of cocaine. Mercury tells me a stash of *nyaope* costs R70 and 'you have to keep on buying more of it to remain high', which is why 'it makes people addicted to it and they start stealing from the community to feed their addition'. He feels that *nyaope* is not the way to go and he is very scared of it. Codeine on the other hand, 'is not addictive'. Secondly, codeine 'really gets you drunk and knocks you off'. Lethal as this concoction sounds, it 'either kills you or knocks you to a drunken stupor'. The various articles I read on this concoction, which are all over the internet, attest to this reality. Third and most importantly, it does not smell like alcohol. 'It makes you drowsy and drunk quickly, it's cheap, does not smell, tastes nice and you can disguise when you get home'. The third reason is very important for these youth because it helps them avoid parental supervision and suspicion. Even when knocked out, as it did with Mercury, the others can simply carry him home under the pretext of falling ill and having given him medication, which of course the parents would be able to smell – correctly so.

A deeper enquiry of codeine with Mercury however revealed that its origin is not in South Africa, as it is 'something all over the internet'. It would also seem that Mercury was correct in pointing out that 'most American Hip-Hop artists sing about codeine and call it "purple drank" in their lyrics and it has also killed a number of them'. Such lyrics from Hip-Hop artists like Lil Wayne include '*smoking purple in a black tee, I love weed...Kush and codeine, now I lean like the Italy*';

> I buy a bottle pop, drop some syrup in it, get on my waffle house...
> one more ounce will make me feel great... me and my drank.
> Sippin on some drink color purple like sili. Really they say I should
> chill before it kills me. Drink got me moving slower than a retard.

It is understood from an online blog *Arts.Mic* that '*it's well known that rapper Lil Wayne has an addiction to the popular Southern adult beverage Purple Drank*'.

Mercury believes that youth who smoke and drink at the parks do these things in front of their parents because the parents 'do not know what their children are doing'. Mercury believes however that the parents ordinarily 'should know that their children are drinking alcohol and smoking marijuana at the parks but the problem is that we are two faced'. 'When we are at home we are children but when we are in the parks we are adults'. Thus much as the parents should be knowing that their children are doing these things, it is not their fault that they do not know, but the fault of the youth themselves. It is an attestation of the youth's ability to disguise and fool their parents.

Mercury's outlook on South Africa's socio-political and economic health is quiet negative because for him

> ...the parliament has turned into a mess. There is a lack of leadership here in South Africa and we are all watching as the youth. Many people are watching and all that politicians are looking for is power so that they can benefit themselves and they don't want anybody else to benefit. They are selfish in other words. The one who is in power right now, our President, Jacob Zuma – I don't see any importance of him being the President. First thing, and I cannot blame him, but he is not well educated. Second, his leadership skills are too low. He looks like he is being influenced by other people. He is the one on top, but he is influenced by the people who are under him. Now that he is in power, he is spending the money like it is his personal money. He is corrupted.

This was a very interesting take on South Africa's current political space by Mercury, which is not necessarily common. He is clear that President Zuma is 'corrupted', and not corrupt. To illustrate that he knows what he means and it is not just a language ignorance issue, he elaborates further by indicating that 'he is being influenced by other people', and 'he is influenced by the people who are under him'. He further justifies why it would have been easy for 'other people' and 'those under him' to corrupt President Zuma because 'he is not well educated' and 'his leadership skills are low'. But even for this reasons of lack of education and low leadership skills Mercury is clear that 'I cannot blame him'.

This analysis of President Zuma and South Africa's current socio-political environment by Mercury sounds deeply conflicted. First he seems to recognize that there is a problem, but is keen not to apportion blame. He is at the same time disillusioned about the state of affairs. Similarly, even when assessing his parent's roles and responsibilities in his life in relation to his future prospects, he is keen not to apportion blame as he believes he has everything. With regard to the role of the school, he is keen to take responsibility and not apportion blame. The only component of his life for which he is keen to apportion blame is the community. In the midst of all this, he feels that his 'favourite political party is DA (the Democratic Alliance)'.

Mercury believes that he has enough tools and support structures that support him to be able to succeed in life and in the future. The school amongst these tools he believes 'is doing everything it can to help me succeed in life'. He is also able to use the local library in the township to study and prepare better towards improving his marks at school. The local library, Phiri Library, he believes

> ...is properly equipped with study materials that I sometimes borrow and take home or use inside the library because it is quiet and nice in there, very easy to study in the library.

Mercury also believes that his family, 'especially my mother is doing everything she can to support me realise my dreams'. 'I also have my own room at home which I use when I need to study'. More importantly, for Mercury to realize the future he envisions for himself, he believes that

> ...God is great. God has a plan for all of us. Sometimes you have to go through tough situations for you to realise your future. If that is what God has planned for you, then that's it...

Whilst Mercury is very positive about both the role the family at home and the school are playing in his life, he is however very negative about the role of the broader community on his life and future prospects. He believes that because of the abundance of failure in the township, every other member of the community

> ...wants everybody else to fail because they themselves have failed. Because their children are failures, they also want and wish that I should fail just like their children. If you are doing a good thing, they will still just have something negative to say about you just to bring you down.

Thus he feels that the community is not supporting him as 'they are only supportive in terms of their issues'.

Virtual Space

Mercury likes watching movies, 'especially Tupac's movies', and only watches 'TV occasionally'. He also has a Facebook profile whose details are misleading as they present him as having already studied at the University of Johannesburg and currently living in New Orleans in the United States of America.

Most of Mercury's postings seem to relate to the issues we discussed in our interviews, including his love of poetry and admiration for Tupac Shakur as his role model. In one of his posts depicting Tupac's face in the background it says,

> I see no changes / wake up in the morning and I ask myself / Is life worth living? / Should I blast myself? / I'm tired of bein' poor and even worse I'm black / My stomach hurts so I'm looking for a purse to snatch / Cops give a damn about a negro? / Pull the trigger.

In a separate post by him in his own words he posts: '*death gudda be easy coz life is hard*'. Whilst the first post seemed to be a copy of something that Mercury might have taken from somewhere, given the language that it uses, the second one seemed to have been typed and posted by himself on Facebook. What seemed consistent in both posts was the depiction of life as being hard. Secondly, there seemed to be a toying, in both posts, with death and/or suicide – either through an act of '*blast myself*', or '*pull the triger*', or '*death gudda be easy*'. These are deep reflections which are on the dark side of other posts by the same Mercury as shown below.

There are on the other side highly aspirational posts on Facebook by Mercury, posting some of his poems online such as the one titled '*The Rose that grew from concrete*'. In this poem, that he says is 'autobiographical', it reads –

> Did u hear about the rose that grew from a crack in the concrete | Proving nature's laws wrong it learned 2 walk without having feet | Funny it seems but by keeping its dreams | It learned 2 breathe fresh air | Long live the rose that grew from concrete | When no one else even cared!.

The poetic aspects of this post are a different matter. . It is the sentences and the messages that they seem to convey that are of importance here, including their relation to the presence and/or absence of maps and related navigational tools. It is firstly interesting that he refers to this poem as autobiographical – which denotes a reference to himself. Thus it is safe to assume that it is a poem about self.

Secondly, the title of the poem, and most of its essence, seems to be about achieving the impossible in the face of adversity. A rose is a beautiful product, but for it to 'grow from concrete' is almost unimaginable – but this one does so through a 'crack'. This rose does many impossible things, including 'proving nature's laws wrong', it even learnt to 'walk without feet', 'it learnt to breathe', and lived for long. This rose achieves this by 'keeping its dreams' and did not mind that 'no one else even cared!' It is equally important to note that the last part of no one caring is completed with an exclamation mark. This talks directly to aspiration, and what Appadurai calls the 'capacity to aspire'. The aspiration by Mercury to become this rose is there, but for it to be realized he will have to achieve the impossible and grow through concrete. What this rose is in real life, and how it fits to Appadurai's notion of rich versus poor maps and navigational tools, remains open to question.

What was consistent however, across all the Facebook posts by Mercury – both dark and aspirational, is the depiction of life as hard. Thus even when aspirational and looking forward to a brighter future for himself as 'a rose', Mercury has to 'grow through concrete' to achieve this.

Mercury also has an Instagram account, but did not to be active on Instagram yet as he had not posted anything at the time. He however has a number of followers on Instagram already, most of whom are female youth. On the other hand, it seems as if he does not have a Twitter account.

The Case of Vuvu

Personal Family Space

Vuvu is a Grade 11 pupil at a middle class school in the east of Pretoria. His chosen subjects are History, Geography, Biology, Life Orientation, Mathematics Literacy, English, and Afrikaans. Vuvu is neither in any leadership activities in the school, nor does he participate in any sporting activities. I was informed by the school that of the 60 pupils who applied to become leaders at the school for the following year, only one black boy applied. Vuvu is one of the boys who had been coaxed into participating. None of the black boys attending this school had come forward with feedback on their participation.

Whilst Vuvu does not specifically know where he was born, he thinks it is 'somewhere in Gauteng and grew up in Pretoria East'. He lives with both his parents, a South African mother and a Kenyan father. He claims to be 'lazy to run in athletics but believes if he tried he would be good at it'. He attends the most elite private school in Pretoria East and lives in one of the adjacent estates less than five kilometres from the school. His first choice of subjects at school was Biology, and then he dropped Biology for Science, and then again dropped Science for Biology – because 'it is my first love'.

Unlike Mzwandile (a friend of Vuvu's interviewed separately), Vuvu is not part of the Rap group because 'I am just too uncool and Rap is just not my thing'. He prefers to 'listen to R&B (rhythm and blues)'. As long as Vuvu is allowed 'to do whatever I want without hurting anyone in the process', then he is happy in that space. He attends a church located in the east of Pretoria every Sunday with his parents, though there is 'nothing I am getting from the church'. Vuvu only attends church 'because my parents say we must go. I would have preferred for my parents to only force me to attend school and not church on top of that'. Even though Vuvu would indicate his preference for school rather than church, his apathy towards school nullifies his preference of school over church. As will be shown throughout this case study, Vuvu generally seemed as less interested in school as he seemed to be in church. His involvement in the school, academic or otherwise, showed a general lack of interest. This covers all facets of his life including where he comes from (not knowing where he was born), where he is (not participating in any activities surrounding him including the Rap group (*Usual Suspects*), and more importantly where he is going by not knowing what he wants to do in future except chill. At various points during the interviews I even wondered if he was okay and would repeatedly ask him if he was. He would at times just seem out of it and disconnected, which I was not sure what to attribute to as the interviews were voluntary and at times fun.

Vuvu had no idea what he wants to be, or what he was working towards. Even though he was finishing Grade 11 in a month's time and would be in his last year of schooling in three months' time, Vuvu did not 'know what I want to be'. He plans

> ...to just use my hobbies to succeed like stocks, like investing in stocks. Not as a job, but like something on the side. This is

something I can even do now and I am going to start during the coming holidays. I got money from my parents, like R4000, and I will just invest from there on an App. You just invest on the App.

'When the sun rises, I will just wake up and check on the App how it is going, I don't know, watch TV or something'. The application Vuvu plans to use is *MetaTrader*. *MetaTrader 4* is an online trading platform widely used by speculative traders in the finance sector. This is however not the only trading platform available online. There are various others that do similar work such as *Ninja-Trader*, *TradeStation*, and *cTrader*.

These platforms mainly trade in binary options. As part of research I registered myself to trade in one of these platforms, referred to as *Binary de Blanc*. The essence of these platforms is that they sell themselves as allowing their clients to trade and become rich overnight without any education, experience, or skills. To register and open an account with them usually requires a minimum of around 200$/Euros. In South African currency, depending on the exchange rates, this is between R3000 and R5000.

Once an account is open, trading in what is commonly referred to as binary options is then allowed. It is fairly simple and straight forward and the platforms provide guides and manuals on how to trade successfully. The binary options themselves are also simple – first the commodity to trade in is chosen. This could be any currency such as the Dollar or any other, it could also be crude oil, or gold, or a listed company. Secondly, one then decides whether that commodity is going to go up or down in value by a specific date and time. Such date and time could be within two minutes or two weeks. Lastly a decision on the amount to trade in is made, which is usually in Dollars or Euros, depending on the platform chosen.

The amount used to trade in is the amount that will have already been deposited as per the minimum amounts stipulated. Then one simply waits and can win or lose. In case of a loss of course the amount chosen to trade in is lost. If one wins, the profit margins (which are often stated upfront when you bet) range between 60 and 80%. This is what Vuvu is planning to do with his future as he will just 'wake up in the morning and check how things are going on *MetaTrader*, then watch TV and stuff'.

Vuvu is setting himself up to embark on this journey and seems to be held in high regard by his peers because of this. When I asked one of the male youth about who his role models are, he mentioned Vuvu as his role model. Probed further on why he saw Vuvu as a role model he indicated that,

> I respect him for the fact that he is already trading and he is very serious about it. Even during lessons in class, he would be busy on his phone trading and checking economic trends so that he can bet and make money.

Thus the fact that Vuvu would use time in class to check on his phone and trade is regarded as something to look up to by some of the black male youth at the school. The distraction it causes for Vuvu and the impact it could be having on his studies and lessons seems to escape them, despite Vuvu's poor performance at school.

However, when he passes matric, Vuvu thinks he 'will study something, but I don't know what'. He is not sure what guidance he will get from where, as he reckons that

> *I guess I sometimes have conversations with my dad, like once a month. It usually starts with my dad saying 'Vuvu you need to study and improve your future', something like that. But I don't enjoy such conversations with him because he says that so that he can start complaining about me and my marks. I think he assumes that I don't study simply because he does not see me study, but I do. But with my mom we don't usually talk about that.*

At the time though, Vuvu was not interested in participating in any of the school's activities, be it sports – 'because I am lazy' or 'I am not fit', or school leadership activities – 'because I don't want to give up my lifestyle. I don't want to give up chilling with friends and something like that'. He however regards his academic performance at school as being 'good'. This is despite that in my reading of his marks at school, Vuvu and almost all other black boys consistently performed way below average. Most of the black boys, Vuvu included, performed below 50 percent with Vuvu hovering in the 30 to 40 percentage range. When Vuvu compares black girls' performance at school to that of black boys, he feels that 'girls perform better than boys'. According to Vuvu, the reason for this discrepancy between boys' academic performance and that of girls is because 'girls are more focussed in academics and boys are not. Boys are busy thinking about other stuff, like partying and girls'. Vuvu felt that the way things were with black boys' performance at school and outlook on their future 'is not okay, but it doesn't bother me'.

That is the general sense I got with Vuvu – nothing seemed to bother him. He was however aware of good and bad, wrong and right. He knows that 'girls are more focussed', which can only mean boys like him are not focussed. He knows that he 'has to study something' in future, but is just not bothered at this stage as to what field of study it should be. He knows that he will need to make money in future in order to survive, but is not bothered at this stage about how he will make the money. All these whilst he's left with only 12 months of schooling.

Whilst his peers believes he is the coolest boy in school, Vuvu otherwise mentioned others as cool, some of whom he referred to as being a 'guys' guy'. According to Vuvu a 'guys' guy is somebody you prefer to chill with and do stuff together outside school'. Among all the youth at this school, Vuvu was the only youth who admitted to having a girlfriend whilst others did not have girlfriends and/or boyfriends due to not knowing 'how to get a girlfriend', among other reasons. He indicates that this is because 'I do not like to be lonely. I just like talking to somebody about stuff. I feel more comfortable talking to my girlfriend rather than my parents'.

Community Space

What became telling about Vuvu and his current and future space was when we began to talk about role models. Throughout the interviews with him, Vuvu was generally switched off and uninterested, to an extent that I had to ask myself why I was interviewing him, during some of the interviews. Here was a male youth in front of me in a rich suburb, a rich school, and by all calculations a rich family, not interested in anything. He thinks her mother 'might be from Atteridgeville (a township about 10 kilometres to the west of Pretoria)', he thinks he was 'born somewhere in Gauteng', he does not know 'what I want to study' when he finishes school. He does not even intend to work at all in the future except 'trade online using the App'.

Vuvu looks up to his grandfather, 'because of the money and he is rich. He is a successful structural engineer and has made money out of it'. So he is keen to make money and be rich, which explains the focus on trading in binary options online. What was more interesting however was Vuvu's second role model. Interestingly, Vuvu's other role model is Gordon Ramsay, the world-renowned Chef. This is because, for Vuvu, Gordon Ramsay 'is just straight up. Says it like it is and tells it like it is and is the best Chef'.

Upon enquiring about this unexpected interest in a Chef and whether it in any way reflects any maps for him, Vuvu indicated that, 'I did have an interest in being a Chef but culinary school is too expensive'. Apparently because 'my parents told me it is too expensive'. Vuvu's parents said what they want for him is to 'go to a normal university'. He has taken the time to check culinary schools out and 'there is one in Menlyn and I think it costs just over a hundred thousand'.

This turned out to be a critical revelation about Vuvu, which explained his current space, and similarly carried huge implications for Vuvu's future. I realized his interest, ambition, and more importantly aspiration to be a Chef. This aspiration seemed to be so deep that it shaped a role model for him, and he spends a lot of time online watching videos about cooking as will be further elaborated. This aspiration of Vuvu's is so deep that, in my view, its non-realization has muted his interest in any other life activity. This is partly because, as he indicated, his main interest is to become a Chef – he 'does not want academics'. He has raised this matter with his parents, and asked that they remove him from an academic school and send him to a 'chef school here in Menlyn' (about four kilometres from his current school in the same locality).

> But my parents said chef school is too expensive and I must finish Matric first. But I am just wasting my time here, I would already be far as a Chef.

Whilst I might have initially dismissed these claims as mere diversion, I later found out in a separate discussion on the role of media that Vuvu does seem to have a genuine interest in being a Chef due to the amount of time he indicated to be watching YouTube videos and TV programmes about Chefs as well as his choice of role models who happen to be Chefs too.

I had to consequently assess how unrealizable this aspiration of Vuvu is, especially in relation to its financial implications. I then conducted an online assessment of culinary schools in terms of their location, what they offer, and most importantly, how much they cost. This is because Vuvu had indicated that the cost issue was the main reason his parents did not agree with the culinary school option and that he had indicated that they cost around 100,000. From my online assessment, a culinary school cost is, as a matter of fact, cheaper than Vuvu's current school. Vuvu's current school, from Grade 10 to 12, costs around R120 000 per annum. If culinary school costs R100 000 as indicated by Vuvu, then it is R20 000 cheaper than his current school. However, having checked all the culinary schools in the east of Pretoria, I found it interesting that the chef school that Vuvu's parents indicate as being expensive costs less than his current school at R74 000 for a fulltime registered diploma over 12 months of theory and six months practical. Furthermore, the entry requirement for the culinary school is not Grade 12, but Grade 10 that he would need to have at least completed to be accepted.

This is however what Vuvu wants in life, 'because I don't want to work in an office, I'd rather just do that than work in an office'. It then suddenly emerged, that this seemingly indifferent Vuvu with no ambition and purpose, does have ambition and purpose, knows what he wants in life, knows the people who are doing what he wants to do and regards them as role models – but that his chosen path does not mirror that of his parents'.

As a consequence, Vuvu does not feel he gets opportunities to practise his future because the things he wants to do in future are not the things the school and his parents are teaching and preparing him for. So he seemed to have consciously decided to switch off because his main interest was to become a Chef – he does not 'want academics'. Furthermore, he felt that he was

> ...not really getting enough opportunities at school to practise my future because there is no application in what we study now for the future. Like when we study English, I wish there was a mobile application through which we could learn English and be able to practise it.

Nonetheless, Vuvu felt happy with his life and the direction it was taking, even though this happiness appeared tentative. The future he saw for himself in South Africa at the time was mainly 'I don't know, I see myself just chilling'.

Vuvu likes South Africa, his country of birth, 'because it is interesting'. The interesting part of the country for Vuvu is 'the politics. I just find it entertaining sometimes, mostly parliament'. On a more positive and serious side, Vuvu also believes that 'if fracking in the Karoo happens it might provide a lot of jobs and stability in the country as the economy will grow' Vuvu's political role model is the second Prime Minister of Egypt, Gamal Abdel Nasser. This is because 'he got stuff done and built a dam, the Aswan Dam. I learnt about him from our History lesson'. In South Africa, Vuvu's political role model is 'Thabo Mbeki', whilst 'Jacob Zuma and Angie Motshekga are the worst politicians for me'. Vuvu feels that 'Angie is not qualified and probably does not understand most of the policies she is supposed to implement'.

Much as Vuvu could see advantages of his school and the good facilities, he however felt aggrieved that

> ...the school got rid of camp. Now it is everybody for themselves and we don't know each other anymore. Camp allowed for some bonding among us and brought us closer together. But now that the school has gotten rid of it, we are distant from each other.

This relates to another issue that seems to be troubling Vuvu, the need to bond, and as displayed earlier, not being lonely. The presence of camp at the school seems to have been a big thing for Vuvu, despite all the black female counterparts indicating their happiness at its cancellation because 'it introduced all kinds of fights which were not necessary'. But for Vuvu it was about the bonding opportunities it provided which he missed. Similarly, he attributes his need to have a girlfriend to not wanting to be lonely. Thus there seems to be a void in Vuvu's life which has led him to seek companionship outside his family through both boy and girlfriends.

Even though Vuvu was initially not keen to participate in the study, he later indicated post the interviews that the conversations

> ...made me think about my future and that I need to focus more. Hearing other people knowing what they want to do with their lives in future made me think.

Thus Vuvu seems to have the ability to think about his future, it just seemed to have been muted at that stage.

Virtual Space

Vuvu does not watch normal Television that much, 'maybe less than 30 minutes a day'. He 'prefers streaming rather than TV'. The main channel that he tends to stream is '*buzzfeed*'. *Buzzfeed* is a news and entertainment media which posts news, entertainment, and video material. This is the site Vuvu indicated he uses to 'watch videos about food and how it is cooked'. Vuvu also has a Facebook rather than Instagram account.

Vuvu's online profile is however more diverse than just Facebook, but also very complex. Of all the learners I had to track online, Vuvu's online presence was the most difficult to identify. Firstly, he had not shared with me that his other name is Joseph, with his online profile utilizing this name. Secondly, he had not shared with me that before coming to his current school, he was a student at another private school in Waterkloof. Waterkloof is also one of the rich suburbs in the east of Pretoria renowned for being home to dignitaries such as Ministers and Diplomats from all over the world. I was able to consequently trace back Vuvu's life to 2011 when he was doing Grade Six at another school. It would seem that the disengaged and uninterested Vuvu I was seeing then was completely different from the Grade Six pupil at the Waterkloof School. The Vuvu in Grade Six seemed to be active and participating in school initiatives, though the money making bug had already bitten. I reached this conclusion based on an article Vuvu wrote and was posted on the school website on one of the key fundraising initiatives of the school as shown below,

> Go-Kart and Market Day at WHPS
>
> by Vuvu Sadik (Pretoria)
>
> The Market Day began with choir and then a parade. I was looking forward to the Market Day, so that I could make lots of money for Wet Nose. The first minutes were very busy. I didn't take part in the Go-Karting but it was very exciting to watch. 5T beat 5N by one lap! Market Day was a brilliant day and I hope we made lots of money for Wet Nose.

From another different website I came across Vuvu's drive to make money beyond the binary options and the school fundraisers – the www.olx.co.za website. *Olx* is a company that was established a few years ago mainly for online trading with second hand goods between consumers. It is open for anyone to register an account for free and place any obsolete items for sale online. Vuvu has an open account on www.olx.co.za which he uses to sell some of his used *PlayStation* games.

Vuvu's Facebook presence began in 2012, when he was in Grade Seven and started attending his current school. His first post was about starting at a new school. It does not contain any pictures of him, except some pictures of an armoured warrior. There are not many posts on his Facebook page, less than 10 in total, and all ending in 2013 when he was in Grade Eight. But by then something strange, and dare I say some change in mood began to shape up. His last two posts on Facebook, both in 2013, were sad, if not ambiguous. The first post, in January 2013, simply said, '*really annoyed with someone*'. The second and last post, also on the same day, declares '*gonna go to gr.8?!?!? Should I be happy or sad?*' This is a very unusual question for a young boy, who had just passed Grade Seven and was to about to start with Grade Eight, to ask. It is even more worrying when it is asked on the 2nd of January – a day after New Year's Day and weeks before the schools reopen for the new academic year. No open accounts of Vuvu's on both Instagram and Twitter could be found.

The Case of Mzwandile

Personal Family Space
Mzwandile is a black 17-year old boy in Grade 11 at an elite middle class private school in the East of Pretoria. He has been studying at the school since Grade Eight having come from a public school in the area. He had previously been

studying at a public school also located in the same middle class area. His chosen subjects are Information Technology (IT), Drama, History, Mathematics Literacy, Life Orientation, Afrikaans, and English. He had initially also chosen Science, 'but then I dropped it and took History as the main subject'. This is because 'they were learning chemistry and I didn't want chemistry. I only wanted physics. I thought learning chemistry would be useless for me'.

Mzwandile's aim when he finishes school is to become a writer or an actor, on 'TV or on the stage'. So far he has done a number of school shows. Mzwandile however intends to also study IT at university 'just in case my writing does not go well then IT will become my fall back'. He believes that 'you don't really need school to write, so I intend to go to the University of Cape Town to study IT'. Mzwandile's primary goal in life is to become an actor and/or writer. But he is worried that acting and writing might not be sufficient for him to survive as an adult. He thus intends to pursue IT as a career so that he can fall back on it should he need to. His choice of the University of Cape Town as the place to study post Grade 12 is because he understands that 'through UCT it is easier to branch out to overseas institutions if you want to further your studies abroad'. This is because as an adult he wants 'to live in London, Canada, or New York'.

> I want to travel a lot and maybe live there, especially New York because there's a lot of popular writers over there. In Canada, some members (aunt) of my family already reside over there.

Mzwandile comes from a family of four with two children and two adults – a father and a mother. He is the eldest of the two children. Mzwandile's aim in life 'is just to be happy, I just want to be happy'. He attends church every Sunday with his parents in the same area. He also reckons that

> ...church helps me define my relationships with others and how to respect and nurture them; also with my family. These are the kinds of teachings I take with me from attending church.

Mzwandile and all his black male friends at the school had not initially volunteered to participate. This is due to their claims that they either 'did not attend the session' when I addressed all Grade 11 and 12 pupils, or they 'did not hear what I said', or 'they did not understand what I was saying'. I was consequently keen to understand whether they talk about school amongst themselves as black middle class boys? Whether they reflect on what is happening in their current lives, and whether they reflect on their futures and what they need to due to move forward.

What was clear in their decision-making process was peer influence, 'one of my friends said that if three other friends of ours participate in the study then he would also join in'. He indicated that he and his friends at school

> ...only talk about the things we don't like, because it is natural. We talk bad about the school. Like my friends play hockey and they

won the league but only received half colours from the school instead of being given full colours. We also talk about life and our dreams and talk about girls and parties, and sometimes school.

From the variety of issues that these youth talk about, in order of priority, they 'spend about 15% talking about school, another 15% talking about parties, 30% talking about girls, and 40% talking about their future'. Thus nearly half of these black boys talking time when chilling is about girls and parties.

When reflecting on their dreams and futures, Mzwandile and his friends talk about 'a lot of things'. Like my other friend wants to go into movies and we even have like a Rap group. So we talk about how to get equipment and what we will need to start recording. We can see ourselves performing on stage and the like. All of us are Rappers. We already have a group called *Usual Sxspects*. The Instagram page of the group is *usualsxspects*, which promises '*new music coming soon*'.

> For me that group is going to be like a plan B for my future as
> well. But for some of my friends it is their plan A, their main plan.
> Most of us don't really like want to go to university, our dreams
> are like movies and music.

Thus Mzwandile's and his fellow male youth dream entails going into movies and music – this is their map. They equally realize that their navigational tool for achieving their goals is different from the one they are currently using. They are aware that they could start realizing their dreams immediately and do not have to go to university as such.

Mzwandile and his friends continue to attend school 'because of our parents'. Amongst themselves they always

> ...talk about how nice it would be if our parents could divert all
> the school fees they pay the school directly to us so that we could
> use the money to jump start our intended careers in the music and
> movie industries. Then we just drop out. We could even invest
> some of the money.

Mzwandile has attempted to have the conversation about dropping out and being given his school fees to pursue his intended acting and music career with his parents but

> ...they weren't having it. I specifically spoke to my mom about it
> and I told her school is so expensive and if you could give the
> money to me I will make good use of it and be able to even leave
> the house soon.

But Mzwandile's mother 'was like angry and told me I am going to end up leaving in Plastic View (an informal settlement), she was dissing me'. 'I thought she would think I was joking a bit, and I said it jokingly, just to put the idea in her mind'.

Mzwandile on the other hand has not had such a conversation with his father.

> Because I just tried it with my mom and it didn't work out. My dad also does not really like to talk about my future. My parents just want to make sure that my school is okay and that I will finish and like go to university. I only talk to my dad sometimes, like I don't really stay with him much, I am always in my bedroom and I spend more quality time with my mom and I speak more with her. I don't know, that is just how it is. She enjoys talking more.

Thus whilst Mzwandile's father is 'present' in the home, he is at the same time somewhat absent, and Mzwandile has made peace with that reality.

However at school, Mzwandile is not interested in participating in any sporting activities and/or school leadership responsibilities because

> I don't need it. Most people do those things because they think these things will help them with access to jobs and/or universities, but I don't need that in my life. To write and act and be a music icon I don't need school leadership or sports.

Mzwandile also believes that his academic performance at school is 'good'. However when he compares black girls' performance to that of black boys, Mzwandile feels that

> ...some girls perform better and so do some boys, so maybe 51% v/s 49%, with black girls performing better than boys at 51% compared to 49%. But I don't know why it is like that.

This discrepancy between black boys and girls performance 'is not okay, but it doesn't bother me'.

Mzwandile feels that he has had sufficient opportunities to practise his future and receives what he needs from his parents. He downloads a number of books to read about writing and gets to practise IT at school through his subjects.

Of all the black youth that needed to be interviewed, middle class black male youth were the most difficult to persuade. These youth offered various reasoning for their reluctance to participate. Some claimed that they were coloured and not black, others claimed that they are not in the targeted Grades, thus are not needed. Amongst these youth was Mzwandile, who upon his parents consenting to his participation in the study, simply indicated that he and his friends 'never bothered to think about it and whether they want to be involved or not'. Thus it was not that there was a conscious decision on their part not to participate, but simply that it was something that they just did not think about and consider. This lack of thinking and consideration seems to be permeating through various other aspects of their lives – impacting specifically on their own maps and resultant navigational tools. Mzwandile further claimed that during the meeting for all Grade 11 and 12 youth, at which I addressed them about the study and requested their involvement, he 'was sitting at the back and didn't hear anything'.

This was very telling about his personal space in that he would see nothing wrong with being physically present at an occasion but being comfortable with having no clue what the occasion was all about, nor its intended outcome. Mzwandile further claimed to have 'forgotten to give consent forms to my parents', making it difficult for them to commit to the study. The main reason for Mzwandile's (and his friends) apathy to participate in the study is because they were very keen that 'we just want to chill, and don't want anything too serious'. Post the interviews however, for those who had ultimately agreed to participate such as Mzwandile, he felt that through the conversations

> I realised also that I need to focus more on the current affairs of the country. And it also made me think about what I will do if I was an adult and unemployed.

Community Space

Mzwandile is 'not sure' who his role model is as he

> ...would have to think about that. I don't know, maybe my cousin. He is somebody I grow up around and he is the guy I try to watch closely and see how I can be able to do what he does. Now he is doing writing. He writes poetry and even performs it. He is always happy. I have never seen him unhappy or stressed and I want to be like that, always happy and no stress and no debt.

What is interesting about Mzwandile's role model is that he's already doing what Mzwandile wants to do and does not seem to offer much in role modelling except happiness. It also sounds like he is more of a carefree guy who does not seem to be much bothered by whatever surrounds him, which is the map Mzwandile has in his head.

Furthermore, Mzwandile felt happy with his life and the direction it was taking towards his future. He affirms that 'I am happy with my life and feel like it is going in a proper direction towards writing and doing music and studying IT at University'.

Mzwandile also felt very positive about South Africa and indicated that it was going to improve with time.

> I just feel that with the youth things will get better because we view things differently than older people. I feel like older people are more racist than us the younger generation. In the past black people and white people didn't hang out but now we hang out

with each other more and this will improve the country moving forward.

Mzwandile however does 'not follow politics and I don't follow any politician. So I don't really have any role models in the political space'. However if he had to choose one, 'Nelson Mandela would be my political role model'. On the other hand, 'I regard Jacob Zuma as the worst politician'. This is because 'Jacob Zuma is corrupt and built Nkandla with our money. I heard that he stole money from the country'.

Whilst there are many things that Mzwandile considers good about the school, he is nonetheless 'not happy that the school got rid of camp and removed sweets from the Tukshop'. He feels that 'camp was the opportunity for them to bond and come together'.

Virtual Space

Mzwandile does not watch much of television, limiting it

> …to less than two hours on a typical day. I prefer to stream videos on the internet through YouTube and *Buzzfeed*. The channels I tend to watch on *Buzzfeed* are those that do various kinds of experiments. For example you can go to a person and recite lyrics and see if they can recognise them.

He indicated that he has Facebook, Instagram and Twitter accounts. But 'I don't really post on Instagram and Facebook, I just look at other people's posts and videos'.

Mzwandile's Facebook profile correctly reflects who he is and where he studies. There are however no personal posts or pictures, except for a few pictures of sports cars. Most of his *likes* are mainly Hip-Hop artists. These artists are both local and international, with largely local artists that he seems to identify more with. Mzwandile also seems to have a liking for movies and TV shows. He seems more inclined to action comedy in movies. His liking for books is also clear in his online profile, with comic books featuring amongst his *likes*. PlayStation games also feature amongst Mzwandile's *likes*, which comes as no surprise for a 17-year old boy. Mzwandile also belongs to groups, which are related to his aspirations of being a writer. One such group is the *Young South African Writers Circle*, and the other called *Book of the Day*.

Mzwandile's Instagram profile on the other hand turned out to be very mysterious with the profile name of '*speedster_bangz*'. Its profile picture is identical to that of his Facebook profile, featuring the same red sports car. As he had indicated during the interviews, there are no posts from him whilst he has 220 followers and follows 446 people.

Mzwandile's Twitter account was even more difficult to trace since it is titled '*youngzer authentic*' and belongs to '*speedster_bangz*'. The '*speedster_bangz*' name picked up from Instagram is the one that led me to the '*young authentic*' Twitter handle. Further confirmations of this handle, and their link back to Mzwandile was the email address provided for the Twitter handle. It further confirms the account owner as based in Gauteng Pretoria East, which is where Mzwandile is currently based. The account profile also indicates that *'born in Durban/ raised in Pretoria/ A real nigga/ trapaholic/ Jesus is my King #Enoughsaid/'*. The final detail linking Mzwandile to this profile is based on one of the tweets *'couldn't believe that Woodhill has talent'*, which was his new school at the time. All these tied very well with the Mzwandile whose narratives are captured here. The handle was very active until 2014, when the tweets tricked down. A lot of retweets were posted on this handle, but I focus only on Mzwandile's own tweets at the time.

Of course at the beginning, in 2013 when the account was opened, Mzwandile was mainly concerned about getting followers. Tweeting that *'guyz plz follow back when I follow you'* and *'I really need followers'*. He provided a lot of constant updates on the number of people following him and those that he was following. This is not unique and/or surprising because most youth that age are keen to be followed and tend to follow as many people as they can.

His tweets however take on a more personal tone when he begins posting tweets such as *'"I need to talk to you" is the one sentence that has the power to make you remember every bad thing you've ever done in your life'*, and *'I notice everything. I just act like I don't'*. He posts further that *'I lose interest when I get ignored'*. A related post from him also indicates that *my parents when I was 8 'go to your room'. My parents now 'please come out of your room'*. These last two posts seem related to another similar post, which in itself is linked to Mzwandile's earlier narrative, *'I fake sleep when my family members come in my room so they don't talk to me'* and *'my mom blames everything on my phone. "you failing?" cuz that phone'*. Thus it would seem that there is a lot of reprimand Mzwandile gets from his parents, but it seems to come only through his mother. Of all Mzwandile's tweets, whilst there are a number of them referring to his mother, there was not a single tweet referring to his father. Mzwandile also seems keen to avoid talking to his family, rather preferring to 'fake sleep' in his room. This is something he also indicated during the interviews. Some of Mzwandile's tweets seem to connect with his ambitions of being a Rapper, with posts such as *'Dumb niggas hustle for hoes. Young niggas hustle for clothes and sweets. Real niggas hustle for goals'*. Posts with pictures of artists like Tupac are also common in both his Instagram and Twitter accounts, even though he never mentioned Tupac in any way during the narratives.

Mzwandile also has a number of tweets that talk more to his spiritual side, as he seems to be religious like *'Dear God. Today I woke up. I am healthy. I am alive. Thank you, I apologize for all my complaining. I'm truly grateful for all you've done'*. In most of his tweets, it seemed that Christianity has had a major influence on his life and that there are aspects of him attending church that he carries with him beyond the church.

Conclusion

Whilst much of the concluding remarks can be similar to those dealing with their female counterparts, the story of the male black youth is however different in key respects. The unexpected part of this story is that which dealt with middle class black male youth. Whilst in many respects the story of the working class male black youth could be expected, that of the middle class black male was unusual in many respects. At the crux of the unusualness of the middle class male youth's story seems to be missed opportunities, whilst that of the working class male youth is expectedly that of no opportunities. The missed opportunities of middle class male youths seem to negate Appadurai's notion of the capacity to aspire as being more communal than individual. Middle class male youth are located in an environment rich with maps and navigational tools that their female counterparts seem to be absorbing, but the male youth seem not to be absorbing these. They seem to be exercising their agency much more in defying the established protocols, maps and navigational tools. They are choosing to do their own things separate from what has been laid out for them. So instead of participating in the various school activities such as sport, they chose to establish their own Hip-Hop band and do Rap music. Instead of paying attention in class, they chose to go online and engage in online trading. Their parents are choosing middle class academic paths for them with related schools such as the one they are attending, yet they believe that the money would be better spent elsewhere (in a band or attending a Chef school and learning how to cook). These are all agency based aspirations that are happening among the middle class male youths separate from the maps and navigational tools that they might be provided with.

Chapter 3

OATS: A New Conceptual Framework

Introduction

In this chapter I reconnect with Appadurai's notion of the capacity to aspire more intensely, with the aim towards developing a conceptual framework of the concept.

I begin by tracing the origins of the capacity to aspire and what had informed its initial conceptualization. I then provide a critique of the concept and its tenets as initially proposed, appreciating its strengths and identifying the gaps. Whilst I believe that the concept carries a lot of meaning and possibilities for changing lives for the better, I am also of the view that its power has not yet been fully explored – and its richness thus remains somewhat vague.

It is in this context that I propose a conceptual framework of the capacity to aspire with the intention to mine deeply the power it possesses.

The Conceptual Framework

The Genesis

The notion of the capacity to aspire was coined by Arjun Appadurai, an economist anthropologist, in his quest to engage with the slum dwellers of India's Mumbai village. Appadurai's engagement with the slum dwellers of Mumbai was shaped by an attempt to find ways and mechanisms available for the poor that could assist in pushing themselves out of poverty and slum life. Thus since 2004, Appadurai has been doing a lot of work in this area shaped by the key question of 'the poor (to) contest and alter the conditions of their poverty' (2004). This is the question that gave birth to the notion of the capacity to aspire.

Over the last decade, Appadurai has further elaborated on the notion of the capacity to aspire in various key ways, many of which are applicable here. Initially, Appadurai's notion of the capacity to aspire (2004) was tabled as a notion that talks to more than just the concept of aspiration – from the verb aspire (and not inspire) as commonly utilized in our everyday conversations. Thus in his attempts to 'alter the conditions of their poverty', Appadurai wondered as to whether those living in conditions of poverty (such as the slum dwellers of India's Mumbai village that he studied) have any aspirations, will and/or wishes to get out of such conditions of poverty and deprivation. In wondering about the existence of such will and/or wishes among the slum dwellers, Appadurai was

Black Youth Aspirations, 87–111
Copyright © 2022 Botshabelo Maja
Published under exclusive licence by Emerald Publishing Limited
doi:10.1108/978-1-80262-025-220211003

compelled to confront the question of what goes into possessing such will and/or wishes – which helped deepen the notion of the capacity to aspire as elucidated by Appadurai. It forced more of a focus onto the 'what and how' of aspiration, and more importantly, the enablers and constrainers of aspiration among the slum dwellers of Mumbai India.

Key Tenets

Appadurai thus defined the capacity to aspire and gave us a number of tenets of this concept that take us beyond the everyday life of appreciating the notion of aspiration. He defined it first as a cultural capacity – culture again understood here differently from its everyday meaning. The capacity to aspire is a 'cultural capacity' and not an 'individual motivational trait', and it is consequently shaped by knowledge and experience (Appadurai, 2004). Appadurai agrees with the notion that knowledge and experience, as shown earlier by Bourdieu and others, is not equally distributed amongst member of society. Appadurai's linking of culture to knowledge and experience must also be understood in the context of his redefinition of culture as not just being about the past and present, but more importantly as futuristic – an aspect largely ignored by most literature on culture thus far. Appadurai's conception of culture is not just culture as we ordinarily know it – practices and traditions inherited from our ancestors – but is mainly about the future and thus aimed at altering the conditions of poverty. It provides for 'real progress on the relationship between culture, poverty, and development' (Appadurai, 2004). For culture to provide for such a relationship with poverty and development, according to Appadurai, it needs to be understood in a manner that brings a change in the way we look at culture in order to create a more productive relationship between anthropology and economics, between culture and development, in the battle against poverty. This change requires us to place futurity, rather than pastness, at the heart of our thinking about culture (Appadurai, 2013). As a consequence, 'culture is a dialogue between aspirations and *sedimented* traditions' (Appadurai, 2013). Whilst recognizing the role and value of culture in understanding past practices and traditions, and thus identity formation, if understood only in relation to the past and present, it will stunt our aspirational capacities and allow us to fail in our attempts to 'change the terms of recognition'. Thus at the core of the notion of the capacity to aspire is the quest to change the terms of recognition, and alter how social class is reproduced to the detriment of the poor and marginalized. It is not just about sedimented traditions as is commonly regarded. Therefore 'by bringing the future back in, by looking at aspirations as cultural capacities, we are surely in a better position to understand how people actually navigate their social spaces' (Appadurai, 2013). It is on this basis that the capacity to aspire needs to be understood as a 'future-oriented cultural capacity', and not as is commonly understood, 'an individual motivational trait' (Appadurai, 2004).

It is also about aspirations, however not looked at narrowly from an individual perspective, but understood in its broader socio-economic context – the political economy of aspiration. Thus, according to Appadurai, an individual's capacity to aspire is shaped more by the socio-economic context – what he refers to as 'social spaces' – within which they find themselves, rather than an individual's inborn trait. Appadurai goes further to define these 'social spaces' that shape one's capacity to aspire. He argues that these social spaces are not equal. Thus suggesting that those who are located in superior social spaces – mainly the rich and privileged in our societies, tend to have more aspirational capacities than those coming from poor and impoverished backgrounds. Privilege in these social spaces opens windows to see outside one's immediate space; it brings with it opportunities to trial the future and provides for the necessary social safety nets to not only fall, but to rise more than you are falling. These are what Appadurai refers to as maps and navigational tools. For those whose social spaces are deprived and impoverished, the opportunities to see outside, trial and have the advantage of safety nets, are more limited and in some instances unavailable. These poor spaces, such as the slum areas of Mumbai that Appadurai studied, are the ground on which the notion of the capacity to aspire is born – in our attempt 'to alter the conditions of poverty'.

The future oriented logic of Appadurai's theoretical construct, is also premised on hope, aspiration, and anticipation – what Appadurai terms 'the ethics of possibility'. It is these ethics of possibility, under Appadurai's umbrella term of the 'politics of hope', that pinned my focus on aspiration. This is so because 'it is only through some sort of politics of hope that any society or group can envisage a journey to desirable change in the state of things' (Appadurai, 2015).

Central in the theoretical construct of the capacity to aspire is also that, in the main, it is a social and collective capacity – 'a meta-capacity'. It is not that the capacity to aspire cannot be possessed by individual members of society, such as the youth here. It is however always shaped and informed by the broader society within which individuals are located. Equally, as a meta-capacity, it is not about the 'immediate objects of aspiration' (Appadurai, 2004). It is more about 'the complex experience of the relation between a wide range of ends and means', 'the relationship of aspirations and outcomes', and about linking 'material goods and immediate opportunities to more general and generic possibilities and options' (Appadurai, 2004). Both the township and suburban youth are in various ways shaped by their immediate localities and the global space which they access through media in shaping their own capacities to aspire – whether as future Hip-Hop stars and/or as Chefs. These youth are also grappling with this meta-capacity in various ways, with the working class youth and the middle class males fairing differently to middle class female youth. As correctly pointed out by Appadurai (2004), the most immediate, visible inventory of wants has often led students of consumption and of poverty to lose sight of the intermediate and higher order normative contexts within which these wants are gestated and brought into view.

Equally, it is premised on what Appadurai refers to as the 'ethics of possibility', which can offer a more inclusive platform for improving the planetary quality of life and can accommodate a plurality of visions of the good life (Appadurai, 2015). What Sen refers to as 'capability set' is as much about the 'ethics of possibility' as it is about the 'politics of hope'. Thus the 'capacity to aspire, is also a collective asset that is clearly linked to what Amartya Sen has referred to as capabilities. They are two sides of the same coin…' (Appadurai, 2015).

Last and most importantly, it is a navigational capacity with maps and navigational tools 'through which poor people can effectively change the terms of recognition' (Appadurai, 2015). The capacity to aspire gives meaning to words such as 'empowerment', 'voice', and 'participation' (Appadurai, 2015). This is similar to capability, which is essentially one of freedom (Dreze, Sen, & Hussain, 1995). In so doing, it changes the terms of recognition for the poor and marginalized groups of a society within which they are generally trapped; terms which severely limit their capacity to exercise voice and to debate the economic conditions in which they are confined (Appadurai, 2015). In changing the terms of recognition we will need to shift focus from the present to the future, as Appadurai sees the capacity to aspire as one dimension of culture – its orientation to the future – that is almost never discussed explicitly. Changing the terms of recognition in this regard would require building the future on a different platform. In this regard, key elements of this new platform are capabilities according to Sen, capacities and aspirations according to Appadurai. All the elements of the new platform have two things in common – they are all intangible and their realization cannot be guaranteed. This is because, as Appadurai puts it, we have not yet found ways to articulate how anticipation, imagination and aspiration come together in the work of future-making (Appadurai, 2013).

Towards a Conceptual Framework of the Capacity to Aspire

There are various things I would suggest are required to enhance the work of Appadurai. Firstly, what Appadurai, Sen, Nussbaum, Fataar, Bok, Walker, Fraser and Honneth all have in common is that they locate capacity/capability in a class based society with clearly defined boundaries. What I have shown is that these boundaries are not as clearly defined as one would assume. Black middle class youth studied here, located in a suburban context, have other sets of constraints that impact on their capacity to aspire. There is a variety of other key factors that impact on their capacity to aspire in ways that neutralize the class based argument as presented thus far. Therefore the capability/capacity class nexus is not as linear as previously assumed.

Secondly, working class youth transition patterns, and the aspirational capacities that shape them, seem to be driven by a stronger sense of desire as defined by Aristotle. This 'desire' tends to be informed by different sets of value systems such as the presence of community as part of the extended family, and a stronger drive to 'reach valuable states of being' (Sen, 1993). As a consequence, I demonstrate is that the 'hope to achieve' that Appadurai (2015) talks about can be inverted; the engagement 'with own future' (Appadurai, 2015) is not linear and most importantly, not only can the 'capacity of imagination' (Sorabji, 1974) be assumed to be class based but its link to 'immediate objects of aspiration' against the 'wide range of ends and means' (Appadurai, 2015) is not predictable on any class basis. Working class youth seemed to see and possess a wider array of options and possibilities (ends), but do not seem to possess the capabilities and/or freedoms to realize them (means). Middle class male youth on the other hand seemed to neither be in possession of the ends nor the means that would enable them to transition into a more sustainable future. Middle class female youth, whilst they seemed to possess the means, were very thin on the ends themselves, as these seemed to be driven mainly by parents.

Thirdly, what seemed to drive the presence of the means, what Appadurai calls navigational tools, is what I would refer to as the network of possibility. This network of possibility (borrowing on Appadurai's ethics of possibility term) tends to emanate from the youth's immediate 'social arrangement' – family members, friends, school, church and community. In Karah's case for instance she would have benefitted from this network of possibility due to her father being a Science Professor and businessman, her mother being a specialist in Accounting, her brother being a businessman in mining, and her sister being an Industrial Engineer. This is a very rich network of possibility that provides the necessary means for her to realize her goals from possessing what Appadurai refers to as navigational tools.

Fourth and lastly, it would seem that Appadurai's theoretical construct – the capacity to aspire – focusses more on the aspect of aspiration rather than that of capacity. In all of Appadurai's work and further elaborations of the concept thus far, the concept of 'aspire' seems to be more explained than that of 'capacity'. Much as these two concepts are inter-linked, they also bring into the framework their own respective energies. There can be no meaningful aspiration without a capacity to realize it. Similarly, capacity on its own is meaningless if it is not embedded in aspiration of the kind that alters the terms of recognition. If aspiration requires maps and navigational tools, what does capacity on the other hand require? Thus the real contestation and/or problem in Appadurai's conceptual framework relates to the notion of 'capacity' versus 'incapacity' – an area which has thus far not been adequately addressed. What elements feed into the black female youth's capacity to aspire, which do not seem to be feeding into the other black youth's incapacities to aspire?

To deal with this problem adequately, we need to first define what capacity is in the first place. Capacity is will, or drive, or motivation, or intention or ability. It is about agency in all its three modes – direct personal agency, proxy agency that relies on others to act on one's behest to secure desired outcomes and collective agency exercised through socially coordinative and interdependent effort (Bandura, 2001). It is about all the three modes of agency and not just about the personal agency that Fataar refers to with regards to Fuzile Ali, nor just about the collective agency that Appadurai refers to as a meta-capacity. To make their way successfully through a complex world full of challenges and hazards, people have to make good judgments about their capabilities, anticipate the probable effects of different events and courses of action, size up socio-structural opportunities and constraints and regulate their behaviour accordingly (Bandura, 2001). For this multidimensional capacity to be realized, what does it require? To answer this question, the conceptual framework proposed here focusses more on the *objects*, *agency*, *tools*, and *spaces* (OATS) that are analytic tools to unpack the socio-logical aspects that enable and constrain the capacity to aspire – the OATS of the capacity to aspire.

Conceptual Framework – Objects, Agency, Tools and Spaces (OATS)

Inherent in Appadurai's conceptualization of the capacity to aspire are two key concepts – capacity and aspire. In further elaborating on this conceptualization, Appadurai provides some deeper analysis of one concept and very little on the other.

The concept that Appadurai defines a bit further is that of aspire. Appadurai uses what he refers to as a 'navigational metaphor' to further elucidate the concept of aspire. He sees the concept of aspire as entailing what he calls maps and navigational tools. According to Appadurai, the presence of maps and navigational tools – which are not equally distributed – is a form of capacity that is central to shaping aspirations.

Appadurai's navigational metaphor helps us deal with the notion of aspiration at its basic level. It allows us to know where to go and how to get there. Maps show us the picture of the landscape from a helicopter view with all its physical and political features. Maps however do not help us to navigate our travels from one point to the other in the map. This is where inequality emerges. Navigational tools on the other hand provide us with the instruments to enable us to move from one point to another, but they are neither the same and nor are they equally distributed. A sexton is a navigational tool which can provide you with a precise position in the landscape, which is different from a compass – which is also a navigational tool that only helps to point you in the correct direction.

For the youth sampled; they will know what subjects to choose, for what career options and what pass and entrance requirements are linked to their future trajectory. Maps and navigational tools however don't help us with higher order information, such as why we need the careers we have chosen (why we must go there) and what likely impact they will have on our lives and those of others (the consequences of us getting there or not getting there). To further enrich Appa-durai's conceptualization, I propose that we need more than just the navigational metaphor of maps and navigational tools used thus far (Fig. 3.1).

I first and foremost would like to suggest that we take a step back and attempt to define the concepts of capacity and that of aspiration a bit more deeply before we utilize them. I suggest that we need to define in more detail what I call ele-ments of capacity, as against elements of aspiration, both of which are central to 'altering the terms of recognition' (Appadurai, 2013).

I am proposing key elements of capacity we need to be able to alter the terms of recognition. The first relates to the tools we need. We need the maps and navigational tools that Appadurai posits as core to the navigational metaphor he utilizes. The additional tools that we need however, as I propose here, are win-dows and social safety nets.

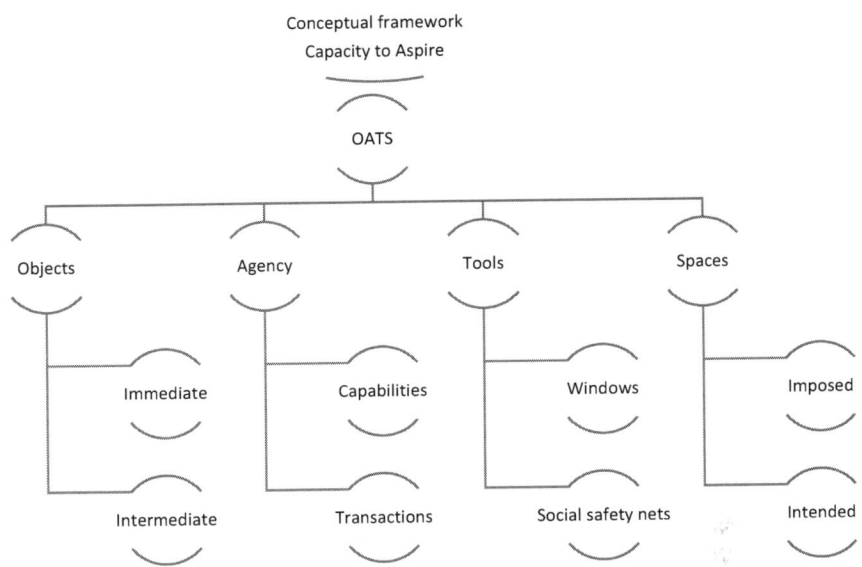

Fig. 3.1. Conceptual Framework: Capacity to Aspire.

Appadurai only deals with tools as part of his navigational metaphor. I am further proposing that capacity must also deal with a second element, that of agency. Fataar refers to this as the individual's 'active self-formation and disciplining' (Fataar, 2010). Agency as a form of capacity must in essence deal with two key aspects. The first is the aspect of what I call agentic capability – which is more inward looking, and the second focussing more on what I refer to as agentic transactions – which is more outward looking.

Similarly, I also believe that with regards to aspirations, we should take a step back and refine our definition of aspirations more before we can utilize it in our attempts to grapple with the process of altering the terms of recognition. I propose two key elements of aspiration that will assist us in this regard. The first key element has to do with what I refer to as spaces. These are both what I refer to as imposed spaces and intended spaces. Imposed spaces are the inheritances of today and the realities they present to us either as enablers of future trials, or as efficiencies that they either create or block. Intended spaces on the other hand look to the future in a manner that opens and/or closes our eyes to hope and imagine. Accordingly, spaces form one element of aspiration.

The second element of aspiration has to do with what I refer to as objects. I differentiate between two types of objects – immediate objects and intermediate objects. Immediate objects are the kind that emerge only as specific wants and choices: for this piece of land or that, for that marriage connection or the other, for this job in the bureaucracy as opposed to that job overseas, for this pair of shoes over that pair of trousers (Appadurai, 2013). As Appadurai has correctly pointed out, this last, most immediate and visible inventory of wants has often led students of consumption and of poverty to lose sight of the intermediate and higher-order normative contexts within which these wants are gestated and brought into view (Appadurai, 2013). Intermediate objects on the other hand focus on what Appadurai refers to as 'higher order normative context' (Appadurai, 2013). Put differently, intermediate objects are about a more complex experience of the relation between a wide range of ends and means, because they have a bigger stock of available experiences of the relationship between aspirations and outcomes, because they are in a better position to explore and harvest diverse experiences of exploration and trial, because of their many opportunities to link material goods and immediate opportunities to more general and generic possibilities and options (Appadurai, 2013).

Objects

The concept of objects, whilst tentatively introduced by Appadurai, is not further developed beyond its mere mentioning. This, I suppose, is as a result of the subjects of Appadurai's work, who are in the main working class adults in the slum of Mumbai, India. The subjects of this study however, are youth as opposed to the adults in Appadurai's work. Thus the concept of objects derives a new importance. Appadurai simply distinguishes between what he calls 'immediate objects of aspiration' and the complex experience of the 'relation between a wide range of ends and means'. He further elaborates on this distinction by differentiating between what he calls 'material goods and immediate opportunities' and 'more general and generic possibilities and options'. It is this distinction that I shall refer to as immediate objects (i.e. immediate objects of aspiration and its related obsession with material goods and opportunities), and intermediate objects (i.e. appreciation of the relation between a wide range of ends and means which tends to provide for more generic possibilities and options.

Secondly, my focus on objects is informed by a different lens from that of Appadurai. Appadurai's lens is informed and shaped by the community of slum dwellers in India and other countries who are struggling with how to alter their terms of recognition in a manner that could extricate them from poverty and all its negative elements. My focus is different. First it is informed by young black South Africans who are about to enter the world of 'own life making'. The space of possibilities is still ahead of them, even though their respective spaces are different. Similarly, they are not slum dwellers, but are located in both imposed and intended spaces that vary – from working class to middle class. Therefore the altering of their terms of recognition takes on a slightly different focus in this context. Appadurai's altering of the terms of recognition is from a deficit point – triggered by slum life. This study's altering of the terms of recognition is from a vantage point – triggered by the opportunities that 'youthness' and its related energies provides. Even though the working class youth were born and are growing up surrounded by the kind of poverty that shaped Appadurai's conception, their full lives still lie ahead of them, they still have opportunities to shape and define their own lives. Their futures still lie ahead of them. Their hopes, their desires, their wishes, and more importantly, their aspirations are in their prime and have not yet suffered the test of life – the ethics of possibility surround them.

It is in this context, different from that of Appadurai that the notion of objects derives a new level of importance. It helps us differentiate between wants and needs, between the immediate and the intermediate, and as Appadurai puts it, our understanding of the capacity to aspire as a meta-capacity.

Immediate Objects

Immediate objects of aspiration tend to be more visible, and provide for an immediate reward with minimal effort. They are more about wants, rather than needs. These objects however cloud the real meta-capacity that Appadurai posits as key to altering the terms of recognition. The immediate objects of aspiration do not alter the terms of recognition, instead, they are central to how social class is reproduced. This takes us back to the same question Bourdieu dealt with, of how stratified social systems of hierarchy and domination persist and reproduce intergenerationally without powerful resistance and without the conscious recognition of the members (Swartz, 1997). Thus these immediate objects of aspiration, the wants, encourage and perpetuate the same terms of recognition.

As a consequence, the working class – the majority of whom are black in South Africa – tend to be the targets of such immediate objects of aspiration such as designer clothing, latest top of the range cars, latest cellular phones and televisions. The main beneficiaries of such a consumerist culture are the middle class – the majority of whom are white in South Africa. This is the system that Bourdieu (1986) referred to earlier. It is the system that Appadurai also refers to as the antibook to a meta-capacity to aspire.

Intermediate Objects

Intermediate objects of aspiration tend to be less visible for today, but provide for long term rewards with sustained effort. They are not just about needs rather than wants, but they connect with goals and vision of purpose. These objects are what real meta-capacity is about, which Appadurai posits as key to altering the terms of recognition. The intermediate objects of aspiration alter the terms of recognition, open up the ethics of possibility, and take us closer to the attainment of freedom as described by Amartya Sen.

Young people generally tend to connect more with immediate objects rather than intermediate objects. The adolescence phase of growing up has traditionally been held as responsible for pushing young people's attention into the space of immediate objects rather than intermediate objects. It is when they are at the cross roads of transitioning from a life of general schooling to that of post schooling and subsequently adulthood that youth also need to begin transitioning from their adolescent focus on immediate object towards intermediate objects. The youth in are at such a crossroad, hence the importance of objects in understanding their aspirational capacities.

Agency

Agency is about the individual and his/her ability to make choices and act on them, what Fataar refers to as 'active self-formation and disciplining' (Fataar, 2010). This ability is impacted on in various ways, including own belief system, society, structures and circumstances of one's environment (Marx, Weber, and Bourdieu). Of course Marx, Weber, Bourdieu, and lately Sen and Appadurai have correctly contrasted the notion of agency as against that of structure, which is 'those factors of influence (such as social class, religion, gender, ethnicity, ability, customs, etc.) that determine or limit an agent and his or her decisions' (Marx, Weber, and Bourdieu).

Bandura (2001) takes the conversation on agency further by giving us what he calls three modes of agency. The notion of agency, at its basic level, has always been and will likely continue to be about an individual's capacity to act as they choose. Like all concepts however, it is used and understood in life in a more complex manner. The concept of agency brings with it various facets of life. Thus agency is about human beings, their capacities and their choices in action. All of these elements are not neutral, as Bandura points out, 'people are producers as well as products of social systems'. It is in this context that the notion of agency versus structure comes up. Agency refers not to the intentions people have in doing things but to their capability of doing these things in the first place – which is why agency implies power (Giddens, 1984).

In recognizing power, and its reproductive elements as espoused by Weber, Bourdieu, and Appadurai, I propose two ways of looking at agency. The first is that which proposes the concept of agentic capabilities, expanding Giddens (1984) notion of 'capability of doing things', Bandura and Walters (1977) notion of 'direct personal agency', and Sen's (1980) notion of capability as freedom. The bias here is on the person/the agent as the producer/doer. The second conception of agency that I propose refers to agentic transactions. This notion expands on Bandura and Walters (1977) two forms of agency – proxy agency and collective agency. The bias here is on the social systems and how they impact the power of the agent/individual.

Agentic Capabilities

Agentic capabilities talk to the very notion of agency itself. Here I use the notion of agentic capability to strengthen the capability aspect of agency or as Fataar calls it, 'active self-formation and disciplining' (Fataar, 2010). Without such capability, agency itself becomes non-existent.

I equally use this notion to bring the aspect of agency closer to Appadurai, Weber and others in recognizing the unequal distribution of the capability it requires. Lastly, I further infuse the notion of agency with capability to recognize Sen's argument that sees capability as freedom (1993).

Agentic Transactions

Agentic transactions do constitute, when utilized as part of a realization of one's capacity to aspire, some form of stepping stones. It takes the conception of Appadurai's navigational tools (2013) and that of Nussbaum's (1997) concern with function a step further. For Nussbaum's concern with function, it takes us beyond her listing of the most central human capabilities into specifying the conditions needed to realize these capabilities. Unlike windows – which allow us to see further and wider and inform the choices we make, or social safety nets – which give us the necessary assurance to jump knowing that we can fail safely, agentic transactions enable function in that we can immediately start moving forward and higher, utilizing them. To cross the river, or to climb a mountain, we are enabled by the presence of these agentic transactions. Unfortunately, as Appadurai (2013) has already noted, agentic transactions are not equally distributed.

Ball and later Bok use the notion of 'transgenerational family scripts or inheritance codes' to define how parents' own life journeys tend to inform and shape the paths their children ultimately follow (Ball, Davies, David, & Reay, 2002; Bok, 2010). These scripts, which Ball et al. (2002) links to 'social class related patterns', ultimately shape the capacities of youth from low socio-economic backgrounds to aspire (Bok, 2010). The main argument in the literature is that youth who are born and grow up in families that have achieved the highest levels of education, economic and social status are more likely to achieve levels commensurate with their family standing. The same would also apply to youth born and raised in families with low socio-economic status, in that their capacities to aspire are more likely to be stunted and so are their future achievement prospects.

All youth aspire for a brighter future and see themselves successful later in life. However, their capacity to aspire as defined by Appadurai differs – informed by their respective socio-economic conditions. What I have shown thus far, is the role of parenting, specifically the father, in relation to the black male youth's capacity to aspire. Bok talks about the 'intergenerational nature of aspiration formation' and tells us that 'transgenerational family scripts' are key to map formation and the capacity to aspire (2010). However, Bok assumes automatic provision of such 'scripts'. Amongst the youth studied here, as shown earlier, automatic provision cannot be assumed, even when present – as is the case with some of the fathers.

Agentic transactions can also be linked to presence. The people our youth spend the most time with are likely to form the basis of their agency and tools acquisition. What was common among both working class youth and their male middle class counterparts was the absence of fatherhood-based agentic transactions.

Equally important with regards to agentic transactions are social networks. The presence of agency and tools is not supposed to be narrow and limited to careers and finance. The role of rich social networking spaces seems to be key, as these feed into rich avenues for agency and tools. Their absence or negative presence provides for zero or minus zero agency and tools. Agentic transactions cannot be one-dimensional, but must be multidimensional – parents, community, friends and schools – all of which feed into a social network space for the youth.

Agentic transactions can also be historical. There seemed to be some difference between middle class female youth born of South African citizens and those whose parents are immigrants. Whilst the work of John Ogbu (2008), when looking at children of migrant families assists us here, the role of historical narratives cannot be overstated. This juxtaposition in the South African context is even more telling. The focus, dedication, and presence of agency and tools among middle class females of foreign descent seemed to be much higher, followed by middle class females of South African citizens, and lastly South African males. The key differentiator in this regard seems to lie in the agentic transactioning of historical narratives. Black youth of immigrant parents attest to the deprivation and suffering of the parents before they were born and/or whilst young vividly and in detail, whilst black youth of South African parents seem generally oblivious and/or unaware of an equal amount of such suffering by their parents from the apartheid days. There thus seems to be a practise/culture of knowledge sharing and experience transactioning and/or sharing within families of black youth born of immigrants as opposed to black youth born of South African natives. It would seem that black South African parents did not share with their children their own stories of hardship and hard work to trigger agency and tools as opposed to foreign born parents.

Agentic transactions are also about role modelling. It is evident that youth who see their own parents as role models tend to extract specific agency and tools from such parents. Thus there seems to be a correlation between the existence (and utilization) of agency and tools by black youth whose parents' and grandparents' levels of education and achievement is high. These youth seem to be feeding off parents' knowledge and achievement in shaping their own aspirations. However, this is not automatically a good thing, as it remains class based and does not seem to trigger inter-class social mobility. Thus working class youth whose mothers are properly role modelling will not necessary be able to extract such role modelling such that it can bridge them into the middle class. Middle class female youth on the other hand, seem not only able to extract such role modelling to keep them in their middle class status, but always seem to carry much higher possibilities than those of their parents.

Agentic transactions also relate to stepping stones which tend to be present for middle class youth and absent for working class youth. These are what I would like to refer to as *enablers and disablers* for the capacity to aspire. Middle class youth are surrounded by various enablers – career guidance and job shadowing opportunities, internet and computer access, wealth creation spaces and a variety of valuable regenerative resources. Working class youth on the other hand are surrounded by various disablers – poverty, unemployment, crime and a general absence of valuable regenerative resources. Whilst the enablers do not impose themselves and thus still require extraction, the disablers on the other hand impose and imprint themselves and leave little room for manoeuvre (imposed spaces versus intended spaces). The working class youth sampled are constantly faced with these disablers. They are however not indifferent to the presence of these disablers and seek to overcome them as much as they can. However, the imposition of these disablers on these youth, even with their attempts to overcome them, is such that they remain grounded. This leads to Willis' argument on 'how working class kids get working class jobs'.

Agentic transactions can be imposed on youth either through 'super natural' (inverted in order to recognize that such powers are not always supernatural but can be imposed by class based human action – diseases tend to inflict the poor, and lack of medical attention for the poor also results in unnecessary deaths from easily curable diseases; violence resulting in death tends to affect the poor the most and security for them tends to be poor or non-existent) powers such as mortality or human powers such as negligence. Much as it does relate to Marx, Weber and Bourdieu with regards to class as well as Sen's inequality focus, it is not entirely dependent on it.

Tools

I propose the notion of tools, triggered by Appadurai's navigational tools, to encompass more tools than simply navigational as per Appadurai's metaphor. Appadurai sees the capacity to aspire as 'a navigational capacity'. It therefore must be

> ...seen to consist of a dense combination of nodes and pathways...
> Where these pathways do exist for the poor, they are likely to be
> more rigid, less supple, and less strategically valuable.
> (Appadurai, 2013)

Thus in taking Appadurai's notion of maps and navigational tools further, it goes without saying that at some point we will have to confront the question of the kinds of pathways that build the necessary capacity to aspire amongst youth. These pathways, according to Appadurai, are rigid, less supple and less strategically valuable for the poor. They are 'rigid' in that they provide for only one route forward, which for the poor keeps them trapped in the poverty cycle. They are also 'less supple' in that they are not agile enough to open new pathways that are unchartered and context imposed. At the same time, these pathways are not 'strategically valuable' in that they do not open new doors to a brighter future.

As Appadurai correctly points out, the capacity to aspire, which is shaped by social, cultural and economic experiences as well as the availability of navigational information, is not equally distributed (Appadurai, 2004). Thus working class youth find themselves located in spaces and pathways poor with maps and navigational tools. Those with parents are usually in single parent households and/or child headed households and/or grandparent households, most of whom do not possess the required maps and navigational tools.

Firstly, I recognize the power of the navigational metaphor that Appadurai utilizes as feeding the capacity to aspire – maps and navigational tools. However,

I propose two additional tools which I believe are also key to feeding the capacity to aspire; namely windows and social safety nets.

Windows allow you to see outside from the inside. The more of the outside you are able to see from the inside, the better you can anticipate and plan ahead. This gives one what is called 'the heads-up', and an ability to see the future much better.

On the other hand, social safety nets are about the provision of varying guarantees and warranties. The stronger the guarantees and warranties, the more we are prepared to take risks and take our trials of the future to a higher level. This is because we know that even if we are to fail, the net will catch us and we will rise again and trial again – in the process enriching our maps of the future and building the necessary capacities through an accumulation of knowledge – experience.

Windows

Windows shape one's capacity to aspire in various key ways. Firstly, like a room in a house, they can provide a glimpse of the future. Houses for the rich tend to have bigger windows than houses for the poor. A house with bigger windows allows its occupants to see more of the outside – explore all the angles of the outside, ascertain risks better – if there is inclement weather approaching from the east; and to see further and over the horizon. Houses for the poor on the other hand, with their small windows, achieve the opposite. Those who are located in houses with smaller windows cannot see the future much further than the immediate and therefore cannot act in ways that alter their terms of recognition. Bigger windows allows for better sight of the future and plant the seed of aspiration beyond immediate objects, but more as the meta-capacity that Appadurai talks about which is a complex experience of the relation between a wide range of ends and means (Appadurai, 2004). The windows of life tend to be bigger for the middle class and smaller for the working class. But what this research has shown is that even for the middle class youth, bigger windows do not automatically translate into a meta-capacity to aspire.

Social Safety Nets

Social safety nets are instruments that have kept the circus industry going for decades and saved millions of beach goers from shark attacks for centuries. People prefer to swim in beaches that have safety nets for a reason – you can take the risk of swimming in such beaches because you know that there is a net protecting you from possible shark attack. Life in general is similar – thus the concept of social safety nets.

Those who enjoy the safeguard of social safety nets that are likely to be rich and privileged, are more likely to take higher risks, shaped by the meta-capacity to aspire. The presence of the social safety nets alone is enough to propel one into the pace of new boundaries and the opportunities they present. However, the presence of these social safety nets alone is not always a sufficient condition for the capacity to aspire. These social safety nets must be present, must be known, and must be tested. When tested, of course they must be able to prove their reliability. For black middle class South Africans, the testing aspect of these nets does not always prove reliability.

Social safety nets are also about custodianship. At the core of the concept of custodianship is responsibility. When you are a custodian you are responsible. It cannot be shared and/or delegated. Custodianship talks to the existence and/or extent of parental presence, guidance and influence on youth sampled. It is also an imposed space on a tight leash in that it does not provide options or choices. *Custodianship* is also linked to space in that it is about responsibility and ownership. Custodians own their space and take responsibility for it, providing the guidance and leadership that feeds the capacity to aspire.

Custodianship comes at two levels, as primary custodianship and as secondary custodianship. Primary custodianship is about what I would refer to as the 'aspirer'. The aspirer is the person beholden to the aspiration – the owner, the individual person – what Appadurai later refers to as the 'dividual' (Appadurai, 2015). Primary custodianship is located in this 'dividual' because, as Appadurai correctly puts it, s/he is the 'actant' – 'something that acts or to which activity is granted by others' (Appadurai, 2015). It is this actant, in whom primary custodianship is located, who possesses 'the eye (and its sensory-neural infrastructure) which is the materiality through which seeing – as a practise of mediation – takes effect' (Appadurai, 2015; Latour, 1996). Seeing is of course the key here. For you to develop either wants or needs, you must first see. It is when you are seeing that you become the primary custodian of either 'wants' – which will not alter your terms of recognition, or the primary custodian of 'needs' – which are critical to the development of a meta-capacity to aspire.

Secondary custodianship on the other hand talks to those around you who take responsibility for putting the key things you must see in front of you. These are in the main your parents and/or guardians. They are secondary custodians in that they, from birth, impact in one way or another on the objects, agency, tools, and spaces (OATS) that you experience. I deliberately do not define secondary custodians as 'mediants', even though they form part of mediants as defined by Appadurai – and they produce the same *materialities*. This is mainly because Appadurai's concept is not intended to deal with the issue of custodianship, but rather more of class reproduction. Appadurai informs us that we must recognize the 'dynamic materiality of mediants' which the concept of secondary custodians does. These mediants are 'dividuals that interact to produce various materialities, ideas such as class, interest group, multitude, mass and public' (2015).

Spaces

A space is a place where one finds themselves, both physical and hypothetical. Thus one can be in a physical space such as a room in a house. Simultaneously, whilst located in a specific physical space, hypothetically one can also be in a different mental space such as an upcoming wedding or exam, or any other forthcoming and/or previous hypothetical space. Thus space can be both real – see it, touch it, smell it and hear it, and imagined – an experience, a reflection, a wish or even an idea.

Spaces bring two key forms to the capacity to aspire debate which I propose here. The one form of spaces is what I refer to as *imposed spaces*. The second form of spaces I refer to as *intended spaces*. I characterize imposed space as the current space, over which one has little choice. It is here and now, it is real. It can either be good or bad, might feed the kinds of maps and navigational tools that alter the terms of recognition or might actually hamper them. It might provide for the additional tools that I proposed earlier such as windows and social safety nets or it might not. Whatever it does, it remains real. I further borrow from Gould's (1987) conception to refer to it as a 'tight leash', in order to signify the little movement it provides for. We can try to get out of the imposed space, we can try to reduce its impact on us as persons or we can even try to divert it – whatever happens, we are forced to deal with it.

The intended spaces on the other hand borrow heavily from the respective conceptualizations of Gould (1987), Bandura (2001) and Appadurai (2013). The intended spaces conceptualization combines an extrapolation of Bandura's notion of agency as three dimensional, Gould's notion of biology as having 'culture on a "loose leash"', and Appadurai's conceptualization of culture as future oriented. Intended spaces focus on the horizon, the spaces of the future and the ethics of possibility – hope and imagination that they feed. Imagine and hope are mainly about one's belief system, which shapes one's ability to see the future and develop the capacity to aspire.

The Two Forms of Spaces

Spaces present themselves in two dimensions. The one way of conceptualizing spaces attempts to acknowledge the work done by scholars such Marx, Weber, Bourdieu, Nussbaum, Sen and Appadurai on how social class is reproduced. The work of Willis (1977), on how working class kids get working class jobs fits into this field. These are the imposed spaces whose terms of recognition Appadurai intended to alter in his conceptualization of the capacity to aspire.

Equally important however, are what I refer to as the intended spaces. These spaces are created in one way or another by the variety of players coming through the imposed spaces – role models, media (through the internet, television, radio, print etc.), friends and family as well as school and community. They are intended in that they are by nature futuristic, as aspiration itself is. These spaces are about hope and imagine, and can thus allow one to impose him/herself on them. Their value however, and ultimately their realization, depends on trials of the future and the social safety nets that allow for risk taking.

Imposed Spaces

Race, class, age, gender and sexual orientation can result in different kinds of what I call imposed spaces. These spaces impose themselves on one's life at different times in any given society. Being a black woman in post-apartheid South Africa brings with it different kinds of imposed spaces to those of being the same colour and gender in apartheid South Africa. Thus imposed spaces vary according to time, location and the individual. It is these kinds of imposed spaces that Appadurai says shape the aspirational capacities of people. The fact that these spaces are imposed does not however mean that they cannot be altered, a matter I shall return to later. What it means is that they are present without our active individual endeavour to bring them onto our present.

Imposed spaces, like all other spaces, have their own individual and collective characteristics. Such characteristics vary according class, race, gender and age, amongst others. Thus the imposed spaces of black people are not the same as those of white people, same with men and women, same with the rich and the poor, same with young versus old people and so forth. It is these characteristics and their related imposition as spaces that shape the capacity to aspire. There are various spaces young people occupy, but also move in and out of. Representations of these spaces include the school, church, home and community, as well as the virtual space.

Intended Spaces

Appadurai locates his conceptualization of the capacity to aspire as being about culture, albeit with the concept of culture itself reconceptualized as futuristic. I would like to further locate the capacity to aspire as being about intended spaces. The intended spaces conceptualization is also located in the future, but more as space rather than just culture. It further locates itself better within Appadurai's utilization of maps and navigational tools. Space, maps and navigational tools are all about location. With these spaces conceptualized as intended, the role played by the tools that Appadurai's puts at our disposal – maps and navigational tools – and those proposed here – windows and social safety nets, become critical.

Intended spaces, whilst imaginary and intangible, feed hopes, provide a glimpse of the future, open up possibilities, and if adequately utilized, shape the capacity to aspire.

The Two Elements of Intended Spaces

Imagine

The capacity to aspire requires the ability to imagine and see a future that does not yet exist in reality and at present for yourself. Thus Appadurai's conceptualisation of the notion of mediants, materiality and normativity comes to the fore here which somehow connects with Einstein's theory of relativity. You can look, but not see. You can listen, but not hear. Thus 'the eye (and its sensory-neural infrastructure) is the materiality through which seeing – as a practice of mediation – takes effect' (Appadurai, 2015). To be able to imagine a future different from your current, in a manner that enables you to alter the terms of recognition, requires of you to not only look, but to have the ability to see the future as a practice of mediation taking effect. To look does not allow for this 'practice of mediation' to take effect, and thus stunts one's ability to imagine differently and thus aspire differently.

As a consequence, I suggest that the future is not as much of a 'loose leash' as one would assume, especially for the working class. One needs to have 'things' present in the visual space that feed the capacity to aspire. One must also be able to see these 'things', rather than just look at them, in order to imagine. The pressures and pain of the present do not seem to allow sufficient room or the luxury to imagine a future of a different kind.

Hope

The concept of hope borrows heavily from Appadurai's (2015) notion of 'hope to achieve', which is also about the 'politics of hope' (Appadurai, 2013). The concept of hope is also intrinsically linked to Amartya Sen's notion of freedom. It is thus not equally distributed, even though not an imposed but intended space. It is not determined, but influenced. Similarly, to hope without aspiring is the same as having a plan that you don't execute. Aspiration takes us closer to Nussbaum's (1997) concern with 'the exercise of function' or Appadurai's notion of 'materiality'. Similar to the 'meta-capacity' that Appadurai refers to (2013), the hope that I refer to here is also some sort of meta-hope. It is the hope which, as an intended space, allows one to 'reach valuable states of being' (Sen, 1993).

The youth fall into four categories on the matrix of hope and imagine as shown in the diagram below. Middle class female youth have developed the ability, as a result of various interventions and circumstances, to be able to look and to see. This 'materiality' has given these youth great hope for a future different from their current. They are able to imagine themselves in a future different from their current, aware of the paths (maps and navigational tools) that they will have to follow to get there (Sen's notion of freedom). The working class female youth on the other hand, are able to look but cannot see. She has hope but cannot imagine. Interestingly, middle class male youth are also looking but do not see. They have no hope and cannot imagine. Despite the fact that middle class male youth are looking at advantage all around them as opposed to working class youth who are surrounded by disadvantage, their inability to see and thus ensure that 'mediation takes effect' leaves them with no hope and not being able to imagine. Lastly, working class male youth are generally choosing not to look, so that they do not see. They also, like their middle class male counterparts, have no hope and cannot imagine (Fig. 3.2).

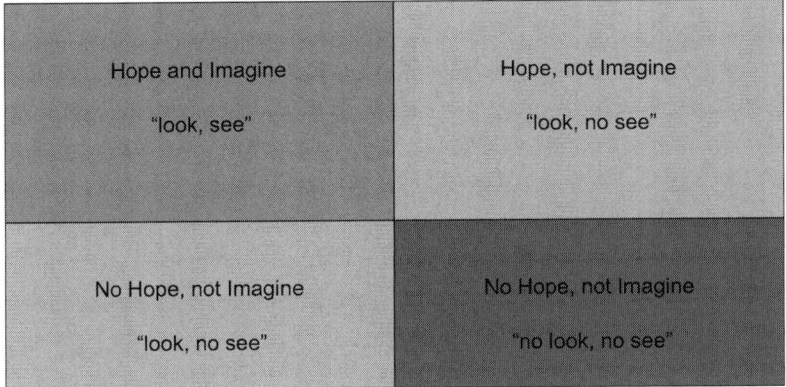

Fig. 3.2.   The Matrix of Hope and Imagine.

The Two Elements of Imposed Spaces

I further suggest that there are two elements of spaces. The first is the kind of space that provides or does not provide for future trials. Our reality of today may or may not allow us to test (trial) the future today. It is about practicing well before the actual match. For youth sampled, such trials of the future may include parent work accompaniments such as the *take a girl child to work day* campaign in South Africa. They may include job shadow programmes, internships and various others – in whatever shape or form they take, so long as they entail some practise of the future today. The second element of space is what I call time as space. Time and space are two sides of the same coin. Time as space talks to understanding and utilizing time in space. We all have a specific amount of time to live on this earth. It is the time we take to do the things we have to do whilst alive that talks to time as space.

Future Trials

In his attempt to explain how capacity to aspire gets cultivated, Appadurai points out that,

> ...to aspire, like any complex cultural capacity, thrives and survives on practice, repetition, exploration... the opportunities for such conjecture and refutation with regard to the future are limited for the poor.
>
> (Appadurai, 2013)

Thus the rich tend to have ample opportunities to practice, repeat and most importantly, explore the future they hope and envisage for themselves even before they reach it. These trials of the future consequently enrich the maps and navigational tools of the middle class than they would for the working class.

Aspiration is about desire, hope, longing, yearning and wishing – all of which are future oriented verbs. Thus the capacity to aspire as elucidated by Appadurai is future based. It is in culture that ideas of the future, as much as of those about the past, are embedded and nurtured. Thus, in strengthening the capacity to aspire, conceived as a cultural capacity, especially among the poor, the future-oriented logic of development could find a natural ally, and the poor could find the resources required to contest and alter the conditions of their own poverty (Appadurai, 2004).

Therefore opportunities to practice, repeat and explore – in the context of my attempt to illustrate the notion of the capacity to aspire – are all future oriented. As a consequence, the role and importance of trialling the future in shaping the capacity to aspire becomes critical.

Spaces can either inhibit and/or enable future trials. The future is today's pilot. The more of the future one is able to trial today, the better the chances of altering the terms of recognition. Opportunities to trial the future tend to be present and richer for the middle class than is the case for the working class. However, the presence of these opportunities in itself is not sufficient cause for a meta-capacity to aspire. Whilst spaces for future trials tend to be imposed, they can also be intended – opening the necessary space for hope and the ability to imagine.

Spaces for future trials vary in density, shape and size. Some spaces are more constrained than others, others are bigger and more frequent than others. Their density and richness may also vary according to time, location and individual. Despite these variations, two things are however consistent when it comes to the capacity to aspire. First is that, the more frequent and consistent the trialling, the more the building of pathways towards the capacity to aspire. Secondly, those who do not occupy the spaces to their own advantage by trialling their future, whether rich or poor, are unlikely to realize their meta-capacity to aspire and therefore are unable to change the terms of recognition in a manner that builds a better future for themselves.

Future trials also create stepping stones that enable the building of the future today. Just like trials, stepping stones are 'experiments' that enable the movement towards the development of the capacity to aspire. Stepping stones are like ladders, they allow us to climb higher and see further. They expose us to the space beyond the horizon, helping us to see beyond the immediate objects and more of the intermediate objects. The concept of stepping stones was informed by the work of Bok (2010). Similar to Appadurai's focus on the working class, Bok deals with the issue of how low socio-economic students' substantial aspirations can be restricted by their low capacities. Thus stepping stones are integral to a gradual climb that enables the movement towards the development of the capacity to aspire. Using Bok's analogy inversely, stepping stones are about doing a play with a script. Appadurai refers to this script as maps and navigational tools. This script however, is multi-class based.

Here we are dealing with stepping stones for middles class youth versus stumbling blocks for working class youth. These are what I would like to refer to as enablers and disablers of the capacity to aspire. Middle class youth are surrounded by various enablers for realizing their capacities to aspire – career guidance and job shadowing opportunities, internet and computer access, wealth creation spaces, and a variety of valuable regenerative resources. Working class youth on the other hand are surrounded by various disablers for realizing their capacities to aspire – poverty, unemployment, crime and a general absence of valuable regenerative resources. Whilst the enablers do not impose themselves and therefore still require extraction, the disablers on the other hand impose and imprint themselves and leave little room for manoeuvre. The working class youth were constantly faced with these disablers for realizing their capacities to aspire. They are however not indifferent to the presence of these disablers, and seek to overcome them as much as they can. However, the imposition of these disablers on these youth, even in their attempts to overcome them, is such that they remain grounded.

This leads to Willis' argument on 'how working class kids get working class jobs'. In these youth's various attempts to hustle and better themselves, they either utilize the wrong agency or the wrong tools. One of the youth (Vuvu) aims is to trade in stocks, but with the absence of agency and tools in this regard, he believes he can achieve this noble goal only with a Matric pass. All his mother can tell him is that she will support him. There is no attempt to understand and negotiate optional paths towards becoming what this youth seeks to be. Consequently, the paths that these youth see for themselves are neither traditional nor ground breaking, seeking to keep them as working class as possible.

Time as Space

The second kind of imposed space is what I refer to as time as space. Time does not happen in a vacuum, it moves within a defined space. Technically, minutes, seconds, hours, days, months and years move at the same pace in a predetermined manner. Sociologically however, time moves in different ways for different people. It is this variance that sees different people benefitting differently from the same technical countdown of time. Thus the concept of time as space relates to this sociological dimension of time. When you have nothing to do, time can move very slowly for you – time as space. When you have a lot to do with many of your goals not yet fulfilled, time can move very fast for you – time as space. Time as space is thus about the individual, what Appadurai (2015) refers to as the 'dividual', and not necessarily about time itself. Time as space is mainly about recognizing that

> ...the dynamic materiality of mediants, seen as dividuals that interact to produce various materialities, ideas such as class, interest group, multitude, mass and public will all need to be rethought.
>
> (Appadurai, 2015)

It impacts on the working class differently from the middle class, affecting the extent to which the terms of recognition can be altered, and the capacity to aspire.

The concept of time and its related impositions in relation to life transitions is a fact of life. How time as space and youth life transitions correlate is open to debate, safe to say that it is not a linear process. Secondly, time as space is linked to objects, agency and tools. In fact, they are as much a function of objects, agency and tools as they are of life itself.

In writing about space, time and gravitation, Eddington (1921) borrows heavily on Einstein's theory of relativity. Eddington points out that we need to separate the share of the observer and the share of external nature in the things we see happen. The perception of an object by an observer depends on his own situation and circumstances; for example, distance will make it appear smaller and dimmer. We make allowance for this almost unconsciously in interpreting what we see (1921). Thus the concept of time as space that I use here has its foundation in experimental physics, which I extrapolate into the social sciences and utilize to expand on the concept of the capacity to aspire.

Time is relative – both in experimental physics as defined by Einstein, and in social science as I shall show here. For the observer of time, who 'depends on his own situation and circumstances' (Eddington, 1921) as is the case with youth sampled here, time also becomes elastic. Equally, as they say, 'time is everything'. There is a time to sleep, there is a time to be awake, there is a time to do something, and there is a time to do nothing. All of this is time. Like a loose leash, you can stretch it as far as possible or like a tight leash you can also tighten it as close as possible. The more time is stretched, the less it feeds the capacity to aspire. The less stretched it is, the more it feeds the capacity to aspire.

As a consequence, time as space tends to function in different ways for boys and girls. They also seem to function differently for suburban versus township youth. The literature has documented sufficiently (Pattillo, 2013; Willis, 1977) how working class youth tend to transition at a much slower pace to their middle class counterparts. Both in the United States of America (Pattillo, 2013) and in South Africa (as this research and others show) and in the United Kingdom (Willis, 1977), these time as space youth transitions have also been race defined. In the main, I would argue, time as space youth transitions are about the capacity to aspire. When you don't have hope and the ethics of possibility are absent from your radar, time moves slowly and you only see today, and not tomorrow. This is the story for many black people in South Africa who avoid thinking about tomorrow and reflecting on what today means. They think that all they need to do is first finish school, and only afterwards will they need to think about the future, what to do next as well as what will be required. It is about time as space, which is lax for working class youth and middle class males and tight for middle class females.

The concept of time and its related impositions in relation to life transitions seems to function in different ways for boys and girls and for suburban versus township youth. Most township youth and middle class boys avoid thinking about tomorrow and reflecting on what today means. They think that all they need to do is first finish school and then only think about the future and what to do next and what will be required afterwards. This proves that time as space is loose for working class youth and middle class males and tight for middle class females. I shall refer to these phenomena as *tight time as space* versus *loose time as space*.

Take the cases of middle class male youth to illustrate the notion of loose time as space. These youth were very keen that 'they just want to chill, they don't want anything too serious'. For those amongst the youth that ultimately committed to the study, many of them did not 'know what (they) want to be'. This despite being in Grade 11 already and left with only one year of schooling in their lives. What is even more telling about these youth is that which informs their career choices and options for the future – which is mainly a zero role that they see for the school and education broadly. Thus they remain in school, spend time studying, but see not role for schooling in their futures. It is a very strong and almost resentful view of schooling and the education system and what it produces – which they do not identify with. They very often indicate the minimal and/or non-existent role that they see education and schooling playing in their future trajectory, and the absence of tools in that context. Similarly, working class youth showed similar loose time as space trends. Thus whilst such loose time as space for the working class youth is attributable to their socio-economic status, so is the capacity to aspire – which is not evenly distributed in any society. It is a sort of meta-capacity; 'the relatively rich and powerful invariably have a more fully developed capacity to aspire' (Appadurai, 2013).

Thus the capacity to aspire is more than just about maps and navigational tools, as posed by Appadurai. It is also as much about time as space. Black female middle class youth agonize about tomorrow and are alive to the reality that there is no tomorrow without today. By the time they are in Grade 10, these middle class female youth have made choices about their futures and are alive to the actions they need to take today in order for them to realize their choices of the future. In doing so, these female youth extract maps and navigational tools that are in abundance around them and utilize these to properly shape their futures. Thus, unlike Appadurai's assumption, it is not just about the presence and/or absence of maps and navigational tools, it is equally about the extraction of such maps and navigational tools when present.

How does one however explain the difference in time as space between middle class male youth and their female counterparts? Middle class males are located in similar settings to those of middle class females. Their settings are similarly rich with tools. Two factors seem to shape this phenomenon for middle class black males. First is their reluctance to extract these tools for own use. Therefore, again unlike in Appadurai's argument, the responsibility to extract available tools remains the responsibility of the aspirator. But this still does not explain why female middle class youth are keen to extract available tools whilst their male counterparts are reluctant to extract the same tools for themselves. This talks to the second factor for middle class male youth – what Ramphele refers to as 'the absence of valuable regenerative resources'.

In this context however, informed by the findings of the research conducted, I need to redefine the concept of 'valuable regenerative resources' differently from Ramphele. Ramphele's notion of valuable regenerative resources was largely societal and more specifically, community based. Her argument was township based and she indicated that the absence of such valuable regenerative resources in the townships robbed youth in these settings of role models and examples of what exemplary behaviour and standing looks like. Whilst I agree with this definition and I used it earlier in my literature review, my findings however point to a more nuanced outlook of this concept – which is more individualistic and family based. For middle class youth (where a sense of community it virtually absent) the notion of valuable regenerative resources tends to shape itself specifically around the family unit. Thus middle class males look up to their fathers for agency (specifically what I call agentic transactions) and tools whilst middle class females look up increasingly to their mothers for similar agency and tools. However, the black family units sampled had absentee fathers across class and setting – leading to loose time as space transitions for male youth.

Whilst the phenomenon of absentee fatherhood amongst the youth studied was more nuanced in the middle class and starkly pronounced in the working class – the effect it had on the black male youth was the same. Amongst the working class, fathers were mainly absent in all respects. In some cases they had passed on, whilst in other cases they were alive but leading their own separate lives elsewhere without any form of involvement with their biological children. Amongst the middle class on the other hand, fathers were in all cases physically present but absent in many other ways – without the provision of agency and tools. They were present but not intimately involved in providing agency and tools to their children. In some instances this phenomenon is linked to work pressures. In Karah's case, the father was running businesses mainly overseas with the mother as a stay-at-home-mom. The family seemed to be very rich as the comforts of wealth seemingly created by the father are being enjoyed by the family. However, as a consequence, the one female sibling in the family possessed tight time as space – despite bemoaning the fact that her father and the airport seem synonymous in her head. The male sibling of the same family on the other hand possessed loose time as space as a consequence of the father being predominantly away. There are however many other cases of middle class fathers who seem to work and live in the same way as the mothers, who nonetheless keep an agency and tools distance from the family – leading to the male youth's reluctance and/or inability to benefit from agentic transactions and their related tools. This seemed to be the dominant phenomenon and thus having loose time as space impact on the male youth. Either these fathers are said to 'not like to talk that much', or prefer 'to keep to themselves', or 'are not at home that much' and thus simply unavailable. Most of them nonetheless sleep and wake up at home on a daily basis. Their presence is however not felt by the youth and thus no provision of agency and tools or the extraction thereof takes place.

Conclusion

In this chapter I have sought to provide the conceptual tools that could help us make sense of the internal workings of the capacity to aspire. I have proposed four key aspects of these tools which include objects, agency, tools, and spaces – OATS. Each of the four conceptual tools provides various sub-elements that dig deeper into our sense making process of the capacity to aspire.

These are the tools that will now become central in my analyses of the descriptive case in the next chapter.

Chapter 4

An OATS Cross-case Analysis

Introduction

It is generally accepted that 'working class schools in the black African townships are likely to persist in reproducing working class school leavers, with a few exceptional cases of upward social mobility' (Robins & Fleisch, 2014). Bowles and Gintis referred to this as the 'correspondence principle, namely, by structuring social interactions and individual rewards to replicate the environment of the workplace' (Bowles & Gintis, 2002). The case studies of working class youth are not much different in this regard. The converse is also assumed to be correct, that as a consequence, middle class schools also persist in reproducing middle class school leavers, with a few exceptional cases of downward social mobility. This is the argument that is equally central to Arjun Appadurai's conceptualization of the capacity to aspire – which is mainly about the working class and how to trigger their upward mobility through them changing 'their terms of recognition' (Appadurai, 2014). This study is informed by nine case studies of black South African youth, four of whom are working class and the other five being middle class. Based on these nine cases, the research can therefore neither claim cases of generality, nor can it claim cases of exceptionality. What it has shown is that whilst it can largely confirm what the literature says about the reproduction of working class school leavers, the cases of all middle class male youth seem to challenge mainstream literature when it comes to the reproduction of middle class school leavers. The reproduction of black middle class male school leavers seems to not be as given as the reproduction of middle class female school leavers and that of the working class youth.

The problem statement was guided by Appadurai's notion of the capacity to aspire, and how maps and navigational tools play a critical role in shaping such capacity. Appadurai had used poverty stricken communities in Mumbai, India to explore how, by providing such communities with the necessary maps and navigational tools, they could alter their conditions of poverty.

I take this theoretical construct further by suggesting that what the capacity to aspire requires is more than just maps and navigational tools. Using both middle class and working class school going youth in South Africa, I propose the theoretical construct of OATS. In this construct, I suggest that we need to equally focus on *objects* and *agency*, as much as we agree with Appadurai on the *tools* that he proposes. I further suggest that we must appreciate the *spaces* that equally

Black Youth Aspirations, 113–169
Copyright © 2022 Botshabelo Maja
Published under exclusive licence by Emerald Publishing Limited
doi:10.1108/978-1-80262-025-220211004

inform the capacity to aspire. I shall illustrate the applicability of this theoretical enhancement based on the youth studied in the nine case studies.

Let me first expand a bit on the applicability of the OATS theoretical construct.

Just like the capacity to aspire, I am proposing OATS as a tool that could be used to realize such capacity, but more importantly, as a tool that is critical to altering the terms of recognition. Appadurai introduced the concept of the capacity to aspire as a way of understanding culture differently, as not only being about the present and the past, but more importantly about the future. I embraced this analysis and provided no further insight in that regard. Appadurai went further and introduced two concepts that he regards as the necessary tools to realize such capacity – maps and navigational tools. Whilst I accept the two tools proposed by Appadurai, I however argue that we need more than just those two as proposed by Appadurai, and require something more systematic.

It is in this context that I propose the OATS theoretical construct. In my OATS theoretical construct I subsume Appadurai's maps and navigational tools into the third aspect of my theoretical construct, which is titled tools, and further suggest two additional tools that we need to realize the capacity to aspire. These are *windows* – which enable us to see further and wider into the future, and *social safety nets* – which allow us to make the necessary jumps assured of a safe fall should we miss our landing.

The first aspect of the OATS construct is *objects*, in which I differentiate between two kinds of objects, *immediate objects of aspiration* – which refers to short term wants which tend to take the form of material goods, and *intermediate objects of aspiration* – which are medium to long term and tend to show an appreciation of the relation between a wide range of ends and means.

The second aspect of the OATS construct talks about *agency*, here I also propose two types of agency which include *agentic capabilities* – which focus on one's internal agency and the decisions and indecisions one is capable of making on their own, and *agentic transactions* – which focusses on the kinds of external transactions (interactions) one needs in order to make the decisions they are required to make.

The third aspect of the OATS construct is *tools*, which I explained earlier as proposing *windows* and *social safety nets* as further necessary to Appadurai's notion of maps and navigational tools.

The fourth and last aspect of the OATS construct is *spaces*, again proposing two forms of spaces which are *imposed spaces* – which are about the current and the possibilities it provides of trialling the future and managing time as space, and *intended spaces* – which are about the future and how it is shaped through hope and imagination.

In this section, I use the OATS theoretical construct to delve deeper into the nine case studies and provide a cross case analysis. The aim is to understand and explain these case studies in relation to the value and applicability of the theoretical construct, and the extent to which both the cases and the construct can enhance the notion of the capacity to aspire. The cross case analysis undertaken here is done both vertically and horizontally. Vertically in that an analysis of the four main groups studied will be provided as the first part. The horizontal element of the cross case analysis is in relation to youth's 10 main activities that are crosscutting. I therefore apply the OATS conceptual framework to my descriptive cases in two key ways:

(1) I first use the four main groupings of youth studied here as reflected in the descriptive cases in the earlier chapters. These categories include middle class female youth, middle class male youth, working class female youth, and lastly working class male youth.

(2) Secondly, I extract the 10 main activities undertaken by the youth and subject them to the new conceptual framework. These activities include their extramurals, role modelling, hobbies, peers, storytelling, prognostication, exposure, job shadowing, social media, and congregation.

Cross Case of Youth Groupings

This research was shaped by four groups of black urban youths. The first group comprised middle class females, the second group covered middle class males, the third group dealt with working class females, and the last group focussed on working class males. Each of these groups, though not necessarily homogenous, brought into the research its own dynamics and nuances.

The Middle Class Female Youth

The first aspect of the OATS theory is Objects. There are two kinds of objects proposed in the theoretical construct – immediate objects of aspiration and intermediate objects of aspiration. Middle class female youths tend to privilege intermediate objects of aspiration over the immediate objects of aspiration – which serve as an antibook to the capacity to aspire. Thus school – an intermediate object of aspiration – comes first for them. Every other thing they do gets assessed on the basis of whether it will contribute positively or negatively to their schooling – an intermediate object of aspiration. Even their choices of extramural activities and the role models they choose, remain linked to their vision of purpose and demonstrate what Appadurai (2013) refers to as an appreciation of the relation between 'a wide range of ends and means'. They also see boyfriends and marriage as not really priorities for them. What is important are their intermediate objects of aspiration such as, 'living overseas as an adult and running my own business'. They hold dearly to what they regard as their values and beliefs, which include trustworthiness and 'living within your means' – a key trait of intermediate objects of aspiration.

The second aspect of the OATS theory is Agency. There are two forms of agency proposed here – agentic capabilities and agentic transactions. Female middle class youth, whilst benefiting from very high levels of agentic transactions that come with their socio-economic status, also seem to exercise equally high agentic capabilities. Even in cases where such youth are exposed to the kinds of agentic transactions that might seem to suppress emergent agentic capabilities – such as their middle class parents telling them what to do and how to behave and what choices to make – these youth seem to transcend such limitations and continue to exercise their agentic capabilities. Agentic transactions are also about what I call custodianship. Custodianship talks to the existence and/or extent of parental presence, guidance, and influence on youth sampled. All the middle class female youth had the benefit of a consistent presence of their mothers – compared to constant absence of their fathers. This motherly presence to middle class female youth seems to have positively impacted on them and the choices they make about their futures. Though their mothers were all highly educated in excellent fields of education, they tended to be 'stay at home' moms. The comparative role of mothers as against that of fathers with regards to custodianship and agentic transactions for these middle class female youth is demonstrated through conversations with their parents about their futures and the options they are exploring.

Agentic transactions also provide what I call stepping stones. In all the cases of middle class female youth, there is a strong element of stepping stones that they are ascending as provided by their parents, family, and especially their mothers. Karah, Naledi, and Wandi have mothers that, even though some are currently stay-at-home-moms, they have studied in specific fields of education that they are knowledgeable about. These are the fields that the youth have tried and/or tested – even though in some cases they did not like. These however remain the necessary stepping stones that shape their capacities to aspire.

The third aspect of the OATS theory is tools. There are two additional tools proposed as key to feeding the capacity to aspire, over and above Appadurai's metaphor of navigational tools and maps. These are windows and social safety nets. Middle class female youth, mainly due to their position of middle class privilege, are surrounded by wider windows and protected by very rich social safety nets. Wider windows allow these youth to see further and wider, enabling them to explore options and make choices about their future which feed the capacity to aspire. The existence of these wider windows however does not automatically feed the capacity to aspire, as it still requires of the youth to not only 'look', but more importantly to 'see'. It is this difference between looking and seeing that negates the class based argument of Appadurai, as shall be shown later when assessing middle class male youth. Similarly, the rich social safety nets that surround middle class female youth allow them to explore, trial, and take risks, assured of a safe landing should they falter. You can only jump higher if assured of a safe landing even if you miss your intended landing spot.

Spaces constitute the last aspect of the OATS theoretical framework. There are two forms of spaces proposed here. The forms of spaces proposed are the imposed space – which is here and now and cannot be changed, and the intended space – which is on the horizon and in the future. Under the imposed form of space there are two elements, which are future trials and time as space. Future trials are an element of space which is largely imposed – aligning itself more with the class based arguments of Appadurai, Bourdieu and others. Time as space on the other hand is not class based, though also imposed. Under the intended form of space I am also proposing two elements, these are hope and imagine.

Looking at future trials as an element encapsulated under an imposed form of space, it is clear that all the middle class female youth have had rich future trialing opportunities through the school, their families, and their social networks. These future trials were both intended and incidental. They also provided options, which included future trials that were good experiences, and those that were not in their intended fields of study. But what these future trials were able to do is inculcate a capacity that these youth did not have before – that of test driving their options for the future. These trials helped these youth not only to know better what is possible and what is not, what they are capable of (as used by Sen in reference to freedom) and what they are not capable of – experience. Future trials are thus not only about knowledge – which can be gathered in various ways from various sources such as books, teachers, elders, media and the like. They are most importantly about experience – which can only be gathered through the act of doing. It is through the act of doing that we are better able to understand our capabilities (using Sen's notion), as well as our limits. The act of doing also gives us an opportunity to ascertain our enthusiasm for the act at hand, which is core to feeding aspirations.

Equally, as an imposed form of space, time as space as the second element in this regard shows middle class female youth's sense of time as tight and urgent. When talking about time, two considerations come to mind. Time can be absolute and independent of us as human beings. This could either refer to an exact time of the day such as 14:00GMT, day of the week such as Tuesday, date and month of the year such as 24th July, and even the year such as 2018. On the other hand, time can also be subjective and dependent on us as human beings. Our year, month, week, or day could have been too long, or our flight could have been too short. The notion of time as space is an attempt to nuance both these elements of time, the subjective and the objective, into our lives as human beings. The middle class female youth's sense of time is tight – too much to do in so little time. They stress and worry about tomorrow more than they do about today and yesterday. As a consequence, their futures have become clearer to them today – the distance between their present and their future is short and tight. They feel the pressures of tomorrow today – from their mothers who hold serious conversations with them about their futures. Therefore, middle class female youth see possibilities and options about their future because they consider themselves 'serious about their own future'. They 'put more effort and study longer' – thus making the arrangements necessary to realize the possibilities that lie ahead. The capacity to aspire, as a future oriented capacity, requires the kinds of tight time as spaces that female middle class youth have put in place to be able to alter the terms of recognition. Without these tight time as spaces, the future will not look or become different from the present.

Female middle class youth intended form of space, hope and imagine, seemed to be rich and feeding the kind of capacity to aspire that could alter their terms of recognition. The middle class female youth were able to imagine, and had hope – both of which are intended forms of spaces. As one of the youth indicated on what attracts her most to their friendship, they are 'very motivated', and don't 'let things irritate' them that much. They believe in 'overcoming obstacles'. The ability to 'overcome obstacles' is essentially about hope. This is one of the essential characteristics shared by the female middle class youth.

The Middle Class Male Youth

To recap, the first aspect of the OATS theory is Objects. There are two kinds of objects proposed in the theoretical construct – immediate objects of aspiration and intermediate objects of aspiration. The immediate objects of aspiration seem foremost in middle class male youth's mind, such as wishing for their school fees to be diverted into their personal accounts and doing movies and music immediately. These youth's focus was on

> ...thinking about other stuff, like partying and girls. The way things are with our performance at school and outlook on our future is not okay, but it doesn't bother me.

Some of them saw themselves as 'guys' guy – somebody you prefer to chill with and do stuff together outside school'. Their male role models were mainly about 'money and he is rich' – all featuring as immediate objects of aspiration. Their objects of aspiration are immediate in that they satisfy the today, instead of focusing on the tomorrow that the capacity to aspire is about. Their focus on the immediate objects of aspiration has denied them opportunities to see beyond their current. They are unable 'to produce various materialities' that allow them to alter their terms of recognition in relation to class, race, and gender (Appadurai, 2015).

With regard to the second aspect of OATS, agency – there are two ways of agency proposed– agentic capabilities and agentic transactions. Middle class male youth agentic capabilities seemed to be exercised in a counterproductive manner. There was too much tentativeness in their lives such that it was difficult to identify any form of agency that they could be exercising. The agentic transactions among the middle class male youth seemed to create some form of antithesisto the capacity to aspire. Since their inability to imagine, their stunted hope, and their preoccupation with immediate objects of aspiration seemed to be shared, this impacted on the agentic transactions amongst themselves. Their peer group agentic transactions did not feed their capacity to aspire. Thus their agentic transactions from their peers were not the kind that feed the capacity to aspire. At the same time, they did not experience the kinds of custodianship and the required stepping stones from their fathers to be able to alter their terms of recognition and see a future different from their present. Fatherly inspired networks and custodianship seemed to be absent for middle class male youth. There was a telling absence of fatherly involvement and guidance for these youth, even though these fathers were physically present in their lives. They have fathers who are married to their mothers, stay with them in the same house, sleep and wake up daily with them, but receive no form of custodianship beyond mere presence and financial security. This seemed to have been a big factor in numbing middle class male youth capacity to aspire.

The third aspect of the OATS theory is tools. There are two additional tools proposed as key to feeding the capacity to aspire, over and above Appadurai's metaphor of navigational tools and maps. These are windows and social safety nets. The middle class life that male youth are born into has given them bigger, wider, and higher windows. However, these youth only used the available wider windows to look outside without seeing anything. These bigger and wider windows fed their need to 'want to live in London, Canada, or New York', 'want to travel a lot and maybe live there, especially New York' – without any change to their terms of recognition. They were looking but not seeing through these bigger and wider windows – the windows were just like walls around them. What they were looking at they did not want. Nothing that surrounded them in this middle class life made any sense, as such they did not see. The middle class male youth also have, like their female counterparts, the second tool of strong social safety nets which come with their middle class life. They reside in a middle class suburb in families surrounded by siblings and both parents. They attend the best private schools and their parents have successful careers and jobs of their own. Their parents enforce a number of middle class traits such as ensuring that they attend the best schools and are consistent in their attendance of their respective churches. Their parents seemed to have insisted and expect of them to graduate into higher education of some form or shape leading to blue collar careers, even though this seemed to have been an unwelcome development for them. However, social safety nets are useless if they are not being tested and stretched – as is the case with middle class male youth. Without taking the risks necessary to change the terms of recognition, the need for social safety nets becomes unnecessary.

Spaces constitute the last aspect of the OATS theoretical framework. There are two forms of spaces proposed here. The forms of spaces proposed are the imposed space – which is here and now and cannot be changed, and the intended space – which is on the horizon and in the future. Under the imposed form of space there are two elements, which are future trials and time as space. Future trials are an element of space which is largely imposed – aligning itself more with the class based arguments of Appadurai, Bourdieu and others. Time as space on the other hand is not class based, though also imposed. Under the intended form of space I am also proposing two elements, these are hope and imagine.

Middle class male youth's imposed form of space, just like their female counterparts, are generally exposed to the element of various future trials that come with being middle class. The school, amongst others, runs a work shadow programme for all pupils from grade 9 to 11. Thus the school created the necessary space for them to test the future they would like to see for themselves. These trials of the future feed aspirations for the future whilst simultaneously building capacity for the realization of the same. This future trialing that these youth are exposed to is over and above available resources that give them exposure to their intended futures, such as internet access to 'books to read about writing'. The extent to which these future trials feed the capacity to aspire for middle class male youth is however suspect. The trials are imposed, but their uptake is not automatic. What the male youth are trialing is not linked to their desired paths, making the trials immaterial. There seemed to be a mismatch for the trials the middle class male youth would have liked, and those imposed by their parents and the school they attend. Thus some of the youth felt that they are not necessarily getting opportunities to practice their futures because the things they want to do in future were not the things their parents and the school was teaching and preparing them for.

As a consequence, the middle class male youth's second element of an imposed form of space – time as space – had a lot in common with working class youth. In many respects their time as space also differed from that of their middle class female counterparts, whilst they shared a lot with working class youth. These youth participation in any school activities outside academics was something they did not have an interest in. This is the direct opposite of all the middle class female youth, who participated and valued their involvement in various extra-curricular activities at school. The middle class female youth saw their involvement in various extra-curricular activities as critical to the building of their future selves. However, for middle class male youth, they felt that they 'don't need it'. Similar to working class youth, middle class male youth had no clear sense of their future trajectory, no passion for what to do next post matric, and they had not even adequately applied their minds to the things they need to have today to be able to achieve tomorrow. Time was not an issue to worry about for them.

Middle class male youth intended forms of space – hope and imagine – do not feed their ambitions of a future capable of altering their terms of recognition requires – which requires much imagination from them. The blocking of their avenues of a different future by their parents seemed to numb their capacity to aspire. Thus middle class male youth were struggling to imagine a future better than their present, consequently opting to 'just to be happy, I just want to be happy'.

The Working Class Female Youth

In terms of the first aspect of OATS, objects: Nelo's biggest fear about her future prospects was linked to the dangers of the lure of immediate aspirational objects. She believed that money is important for her and her friends, and 'wants a man who gives you money (o bechang)'. This is where her vulnerability to a charmer driving the Golf Velocity becomes more pronounced. This is because it is usually the guys who can afford to drive such cars who are likely to afford providing the money that she is looking for. Such money however comes with a lot of other pressures in the township that Nelo was trying to avoid – alcohol, unprotected sex, and ultimately unplanned pregnancy. On the other hand, Nelo's attempt to connect with the intermediate objects of aspiration, seemed to be cosmetic and not grounded on a strong foundation.

The second aspect of the OATS theory is Agency. There are two ways of agency proposed – agentic capabilities and agentic transactions. Nelo had, and demonstrated, agentic capabilities. However, her agentic capabilities were clouded in conditionalities. It was very telling that Nelo seemed to know where she came from – drinking alcohol and having boyfriends – and made the decision to change her life and vowed not to go back there. She however remained worried about the allure of her past life and how easily she could simply drop back. The consistent presence of 'something going wrong' did not give her the comfort she needed for her future. Nelo's agentic transactions are also not the kind that feed the capacity to aspire. Her stepping stones are weak and loose, leading her to trip and falter more often. In referencing her drinking of alcohol she indicated that, 'I don't really enjoy drinking alcohol, I just drink a bit to socialise and because I was trying to fit in'. Thus the transactions that Nelo is exposed to require of her to drink alcohol at a tender age (14 years old) as her only way to 'socialize' and to 'fit in'. She experiences a lot of pressure to fit in in her life 'because everyone around me drinks alcohol. Almost all of my friends drink alcohol and codeine'. These negative agentic transactions of Nelo's are not only inherited from her friends, as she had indicated during the interviews. They are also inherited from her uncles, as her Facebook posts depicted. In one Facebook posting Nelo posted that, '*Lol ysterdae my uncle got us drunk*'. Nelo's custodianship is also very weak. Whilst her mother passed on, her father is still alive and resides nearby in the same township, but is not really involved in Nelo's life. Both her father and mother have never really taken an interest in her life and her future.

The third aspect of the OATS theory is tools. There are two additional tools proposed as key to feeding the capacity to aspire, over and above Appadurai's metaphor of navigational tools and maps. These are windows and social safety nets. As is the case with working class male youth, working class female youth are also surrounded by walls, rather than windows. For Nelo, her desire to become a nurse was largely influenced by what she saw on TV and a number of TV series that show nursing and what nurses do. That is what has influenced her most in her pursuit of a nursing career. For working class youth, the issue of available social safety nets can also be as barren as they come. This is the case with Nelo. Unlike the middle class female youth, Nelo does not have a mother, and continues to live in the same household her mother left her in with her grandparents.

As a working class female youth, Nelo exposed herself to some element of future trialing, but not the kind that feeds the capacity to aspire. She has been sexually active and has experimented with alcohol since she was 14 years old. She believes these future trials (to be sexually active from an early age) are a good thing for youth 'because you learn a lot about yourself and others from an early age and you are able to manage relationships better when you are older'. Another element of an imposed space, which is time as space, is also loose for Nelo, similar to other working class youth and middle class males. Nelo's time as space is loose, which does not feed the capacity to aspire. Her attitude towards time, was that which did not necessarily carry any dictates towards her. In the last month of her final year of schooling, Nelo had not yet applied to study at her envisaged college. She was not even aware of any closing dates for applications, but hoped to find the application process still open and space available when she eventually applies. She could not tell what her marks half way through the year were or what that meant. She seemed aware that she has not been performing well in Grade 12 at the time, but seemed unaware of the exact percentage marks she had scored and what would they demand of her final year exams. Thus, her time as space is evidently loose with no pressure to ensure that she has a definitive place of study to proceed to after Matric.

As an intended form of space, the ability to imagine a future different from a current requires an element of freedom from fear. For working class youth however, such a freedom is more of a luxury than a reality. Fear surrounds them daily in a manner that stunts their ability to imagine. It is this ability to imagine, in my view, which serves as a precursor to the capacity to aspire. For Nelo, her not being sure of her school performance during the June exams does not inspire much confidence in the belief in oneself. Thus there is faith and hope, and most importantly, 'believe in myself' that seems to be the main driving forces behind Nelo's outlook for her future. Outside faith, hope, and belief – there was nothing much for Nelo to hold on to, let alone any capacity to imagine.

The Working Class Male Youth

The first aspect of the OATS theory is Objects. There are two kinds of objects proposed in the theoretical construct – immediate objects of aspiration and intermediate objects aspiration. Of the three Soweto youth, Thabang was the only one attempting to break away from the common narrative of immediate objects of aspiration. However, despite his attempt to avoid the immediate objects of aspiration, Thabang was still unable to crack into the intermediate objects of aspiration which feed the capacity to aspire. The trap of the working class is not easy to break. The immediate objects of aspiration impose themselves on them as young working class males. Some of these youth notice the traps of the immediate objects of aspiration and thus even despise the manner in which South African artists continually bombard them with such immediate objects of aspiration by 'rapping only about money'. Amidst the hardship, they crave for and are looking for 'direction' towards the intermediate objects of aspiration, but they are not getting it. First they see and recognize their current environment as limited and only providing them with immediate objects of aspiration. They however, which is my second point, are unable to break into the realm of intermediate objects of aspiration. Such intermediate objects of aspiration come with their own set of responsibilities, expenses, lifestyles, habits, and choices. They create 'a more inclusive platform for improving the planetary quality of life and can accommodate a plurality of visions of the good life' (Appadurai, 2015). Breaking into the realm of intermediate objects of aspiration further builds a bridge 'through which poor people can effectively change the terms of recognition' (Appadurai, 2015). All the male working class youth could do from their vantage point, was to 'keep calm and do our own thing'. Evidently because the

> ...most immediate, visible inventory of wants has often led
> students of consumption and of poverty to lose sight of the

intermediate and higher order normative contexts within which these wants are gestated and brought into view.

(Appadurai, 2004)

All three township youth had serious difficulties connecting with the intermediate objects of aspiration. This is because, as already argued by Appadurai, these are not equally distributed. It is thus easy for them to be comfortable in focussing on the immediate objects of aspiration, such as having 'little *me's*' all over the place, or having as many girlfriends as possible.

The second aspect of the OATS theory is Agency. There are two ways of agency proposed – agentic capabilities and agentic transactions. The three working class male youth demonstrated various kinds of agentic capabilities in their lives. These capabilities however seemed to have been seriously limited by the kinds of agentic transactions these youth were exposed to. Their exercise of agentic capability is not the kind that can change the terms of recognition that Appadurai (2013) talks about. Neither does it exercise any form of power that Giddens (1984) refers to. For the Soweto working class youth, agentic transactions are a luxury that does not arise for them. Thus the very notion of some form of transaction that could serve as a stepping stone or that could provide some form of custodianship did not arise. What was clear across all three working class boys was that the kinds of agentic transactions they were exposed to, served as an antibook to the capacity to aspire. Instead what they seemed to engender is the reproduction of no hope, no imagine, and thus zero chance of changing the terms of recognition. Their common agentic transactions were about failure and how to multiply it, 'because everybody else fails'.

The third aspect of the OATS theory is Tools. There are two additional tools proposed as key to feeding the capacity to aspire, over and above Appadurai's metaphor of navigational tools and maps. These are windows and social safety nets. All three working class male youth are surrounded by walls, rather than windows. They cannot see beyond their immediate space and confines. Their world is their present, and its scope is defined by the four walls surrounding them. They cannot see beyond their present space, let alone imagine and/or aspire to a better outside space, which is key to changing the terms of recognition (Appadurai, 2013). Thus whether it be the inattentiveness to radio that made Akhona miss the radio announcement on scholarships, or the listening to music that Mercury espouses, or the watching of television soapies that Thabang seems to be practising, these do not constitute tools of the kind envisaged in the conceptualization of windows. If anything, they constitute walls. They cannot see or grasp opportunities when they are not there. For these walls to become the windows of the type envisaged as tools, able to feed the capacity to aspire, it requires a different architecture of class for the working class boys. As working class youth, similar to Willis argument (1981), they are trapped in working class conditions. Like windows however, social safety nets are all about social class. This is the point made by Appadurai, as shaped by Bourdieu's views and those of Weber – 'they are not equally distributed' (Appadurai, 2013). All three working class youth do not have social safety nets, and thus cannot look further and take the kinds of risks that are future building. This is because, should they fall, such a fall would be catastrophic. When you live under desperate conditions 'falling' is not thought to be catastrophic. The logic behind the criminal behaviour is that there is nothing to lose. They all come from either single parent families (mainly mothers) and/or no parents – with aunts or uncles or grandparents as parents. They all reside in extended family homes shared with various other members of their families. They are working class, with all its disadvantages of no social safety nets.

Spaces constitute the last aspect of the OATS theoretical framework. There are two forms of spaces proposed here. The forms of spaces proposed are the imposed space – which is here and now and cannot be changed, and the intended space – which is on the horizon and in the future. Under the imposed form of space there are two elements, which are future trials and time as space. Future trials are an element of space which is largely imposed – aligning itself more with the class based arguments of Appadurai, Bourdieu and others. Time as space on the other hand is not class based, though also imposed. Under the intended form of space I am also proposing two elements, these are hope and imagine. As an imposed form of space, the working class male youth studied here had limited to zero exposure to one of the two elements of an imposed space – future trials, especially those that feed the capacity to aspire as espoused by Appadurai. In the absence of such future trials and/or experimentation, these youth 'trialled the future' in various ways. Thus for working class male youth, their context and reality – in terms of future trialing – is a tight leash. Even more, the different configurations of the varying spaces they find themselves in, as part of their current, do not provide any future trialing prospects other than what they see on TV. The home and family space, the school space, the peer group space – all are devoid of any options for future trialing. Thus, based on their agony, it would seem the very concept of 'future trials' is 'bourgeois' in its nature. For the working class, the concept does not arise at all and is largely premature. Thus before any conversations could take place amongst the working class males about future trials, the first conversation that needs to take place must be about 'what options are there'. You cannot trial that which you do not know! The reason for 'what options are there' remains an elusive undertaking for working class youth goes to the very core of the notion of the capacity to aspire and the tools it requires. If you do not know 'what options are there' you cannot aim for them, you cannot wish for them, and most importantly, you cannot future trial for them. It is similarly the case for working class males with regards to the second element of the imposed form of space – time as space. What was common across the three working class male youth, was how stretched their time was. Time is not everything to them, but tends to be nothing to them. They were neither sure what they would do next in the following year, nor were they sure about their performance in the final exams. All they could tell me was that 'we will see'. They see their future as something distant, something they 'will see' hopefully, but not now. At the time, all they could see were parks, marijuana, beer, and girls. They lived in the moment and not towards the future. What they saw was what Appadurai calls 'immediate objects of aspiration', instead of seeing what feeds the 'meta-capacity'. For working class male youth, such time as space is loose.

The two elements of the intended form of space, hope and imagine, requires the ability to imagine, and see a future for yourself that does not yet exist in reality and at present. For some of the working class male youth to be able to imagine, they prefer 'to listen to music on my phone and be in my own space, there is too much out there that I have to block off'. Some instead have chosen to imagine the simple – being happy. Others imagine themselves in future 'as a philosopher, someone who gives people the advices of life. Like an adviser of how people should live, by doing good'. What was clear of the male working class youth was that their ability to imagine was either blocked off, simplified, or simply utopian. It is not the type of imagining that feeds the capacity to aspire. The overwhelming nature of their immediacy forced them to survive by blocking things out. Their attempts to imagine were so heavily shaped by their immediacy of unhappiness and the bad township life that they perceive themselves to have been exposed to in a manner that constraints them from seeing beyond. They believed that their space of poverty would not open any avenues of a future space of success. They believe that it is of no use for them to imagine a future of success when they do not have the privileges of middle class life like their counterparts in the suburbs.

Their hope was also burdened by hardship, which required of them to 'create a frequency. What you want in future you must pronounce yourself as having it now!' They also thought that 'positive thinking is half the work done', and that like 'the rose that grew from a concrete', they would persevere. This is not the 'hope to achieve' nor the 'politics of hope' or the 'ethics of possibility' that Appadurai (2013) spoke about. Neither is it the freedom that Sen (2001) refers to. It is what I refer to as the hope to survive, as opposed to Appadurai's (2013) notion of 'hope to achieve'. It is a negative, and not a positive hope. It is not the stuff the capacity to aspire is made of.

Cross Case of Youth Activities

There are 10 main youth activities that I have isolated for purposes of cross case analysis in this chapter. These include extramurals, role modelling, hobbies, peers, storytelling, prognostication, exposure, job shadowing, social media, and congregation. I deal with each of the 10 activities below applying the conceptual framework developed in the previous chapter.

The OATS of Extramurals

One of the key issues I explore is the extent to which teenagers understudy are engaged and/or involved in some kind of extramural activities within the school or outside school. The role and importance of extramural activities for these youths is looked at in the context of the central question of this research – 'what maps of the future do these youths have, and how their immediate environments in and out of school serve as instruments helping them interpret the maps'. It is an attempt to connect with Appadurai's positive quest to 'alter the terms of recognition' (2004), or conversely, Paul Willis, Barton, and Walker (1983) ethnographic account of how working class kids get working class jobs.

From the nine case studies, a pattern seemed to be emerging. It is clear that opportunities for exposure and participation in extramural activities are in abundance for middle class teenagers than they are for working class teenagers. This is to be expected and is a reality both in and out of school. Thus the options for middle class teenagers are many, whilst those for working class teenagers are extremely limited.

The richness of extramurals for middle class teenagers is deeper than that of working class teenagers – inclusive of facilities and organization. Thus the extent to which available extramural activities can feed the capacity to aspire for middle class youth is much more expansive than it is for working class youth. Whilst middle class female youth were actively involved in all kinds of extramural activities both in and outside school, the middle class males and working class youth tended to either not be involved at all or would be involved sporadically.

There are three middle class female youth sampled here – Karah, Wandi, and Naledi. What the case studies of these three middle class female teenagers show is both a great deal of commonality between them, as well as divergence among them. These youth were all involved in some or other form of extramural activity. Karah was consciously experimenting with leadership roles. Wandi on the other hand possessed a great deal of hope, which she had balanced with an assessment of realities and information about the consequences of hope itself. She had tempered hope with reality. Lastly, for Naledi, not everything was about the future – such as dancing which she does 'just to keep me fit'. However, she maintained her focus on the kinds of things she needed to do today to prepare for such a future, such as her participation in leadership committees of the school.

Karah played a lot of school sport such as tennis and netball at school and was also elected into the school leadership as the house captain for Fish Eagle house. She volunteered, and was subsequently elected into the leadership, so that she 'could stop complaining about what other people are doing wrong and start correcting the wrong things they were doing myself'. She also believed that participation in leadership spaces at school 'teaches you how to become a leader and makes you more informed on how to work with people'. So for Karah extramural activities are about three things – doing things yourself, becoming a leader, and working with people. These are generic skills that Karah is referring to, and are not available in a conventional school curriculum, but provide a unique set of qualities that she recognizes and aspires towards. These are the kinds of activities Appadurai refers to as 'altering the terms of recognition'. They create maps in that to do things you need to travel on some kind of journey of learning, to become a leader also requires some kind of journey of learning, and so is working with people. The traits and abilities that emerge from these three activities are central to a future leader who does things and can work with people in doing so – it is the cultural capital of being born middle class.

Just like Karah, Wandi had also been elected into the school leadership. But unlike Karah, Wandi's capacity to aspire and the role played by extramural activities in this regard is not through her school leadership participation, but rather her love of art.

> I can't make a career out of art, but I could but my parents will not support me just going straight off into art. I also feel that I can't live off art. Some artists can become really successful at first, but some people go through some rough times and live a terrible life and I don't want to go through that. I wanted to do what I love, but also find a practical way of doing it.

As a consequence, 'civil engineering will pay the bills, but art will make me happy'.

Wandi was very clear about her love and passion, which is art. At the same time, she was worried about how her passion could help alter her terms of recognition. This is where the concepts of hope and the ability to imagine become handy as part of the OATS theoretical construct. Where there is hope and an ability to imagine, we have grounds to see a future different from the current. Love and passion are emotions that are linked to both being able to imagine and having hope. As correctly observed by Aristotle, 'desire necessarily leads to action … the efficient cause of praxis (deliberate action) is prohaeresis (a certain kind of desire)' (Aristotle, 1959). Thus art serves as the 'cause of praxis' for Wandi to become a civil engineer. This is the 'practical way of doing' art for Wandi – becoming a civil engineer. Thus Wandi was using her extramurals in art to chart for herself a specific pathway – which illustrates her ability to imagine – into the future. Again, just like Karah – in taking advantage of her cultural capital of being born middle class – she was able to imagine a middle ground between her love for art and its risks for her into the future, as against the practicality of civil engineering and its possible advantages into the future. In a different manner from Karah however, Wandi was identifying a specific career pathway into her future which a typical school curriculum can assist her with, whilst Karah identified generic skills for her future that only extra-curricular activities could give her.

Just like Karah and Wandi, Naledi also benefited from the cultural capital of being middle class. She also served on one of the school leadership committees. Like Karah, she indicated that it 'assists me prepare for the future in terms of practicing my future's possibilities'. Thus for Naledi, participation in the school committee was about her future and exploring the possibilities it provides. Naledi was also very active in various extramural activities both at the school and outside school. She played netball at the school and did dancing outside school through a dancing academy in the city. However, this part of her life, according to her, had nothing to do with her future and was all about the present. 'Dancing for me is like a sport, something to keep me fit. It is not something I want to do like a profession'. Naledi was engaged in two kinds of extramural activities whose purpose she dissected – one for the future and the other for today. Her participation in the school leadership committees was mainly about preparing herself for the future, whilst her participation in dance was just for keeping fit. Even though

Naledi was herself not alive to the cross-fertilization abilities of the two extramural activities, their presence in her life nonetheless served to build a solid foundation for her future, which could alter her terms of recognition.

I would therefore argue that there is a lot of OATS built into the kinds of activities the black female middle class teenagers are engaged in above. Sport, particularly team sport such as netball, requires planning, discipline in execution, and ability to work with others in unison. These are the kinds of traits that are central to the OATS theoretical construct. For the netball team to be able to win games, it should be able to appreciate the relation between the wide range of ends and means – intermediate objects of aspiration – that would demand that the team must practise together, develop a winning strategy, and carry it out on the day of the game properly. It is an appreciation that winning is not a given and is not automatic, but requires hard work and practise over time to achieve the desired results. In the process, it is also about both the agentic transactions and capabilities. Playing in a team with other people, playing against other teams in various other areas – exposes these youth to a variety of agentic transactions that can shape their own outlook (capabilities) to their own future – an aspirational capacity. It also provides the tools for the future that these youth require, and not just the maps and navigational tools that Appadurai talks about, but also the windows that will expose the future to them.

Similarly, participation in extramurals for these youth creates the kinds of spaces that will stand them in good stead in building their own futures. It is a future trial of discipline, inter-personal relations, emotional intelligence (because you will loose and win some games both fairly and unfairly and how you carry yourself under all these trials builds you for a future that awaits), and dedication. It is about time as space, being able to manage when and how to peak at the right moment for the critical games that are a must win. It is also about hope and imagine, without these two there is no need for all the preparation for that most important game and anticipation to hopefully win the trophy. Thus the OATS theoretical construct cuts across all the key elements of participation in extramural activities for these youth, in a manner that allows them – as middle class youth – to maintain and possibly further upscale on their middle class life.

The opposite is true for working class female teenagers and middle class male teenagers. However, there are some important nuances that are worth highlighting.

For working class teenagers, two key elements arise. First, their reading of the context seemed to be different. Take the case of Mercury, he stopped participating in the extramural activity of playing in the brass band because he believed it was the cause of his poor performance at school. I argue that such a reading of the context could be wrong because such participation would have been an important map and navigational tool for him into the future both as a key skill (playing the instrument) and building his leadership abilities broadly. Their reading of the context could also be correct. Take the case of Thabang in this regard – for having stopped playing soccer so that he could improve his school performance. Thus depending on the kind of extramurals they were engaged in, these could be central to building their capacity to aspire or it could merely be a distraction.

I have earlier pointed to the impositions of working class life and its repro-ductive nature, a matter I shall not repeat here. I shall now turn to the implications this has on the role of extramurals for working class teenagers. This is a more nuanced aspect of working class life and is linked more directly to this quest – the perceived role of extramurals amongst the youth. Unlike middle class female teenagers, working class teenagers tend to perceive extramural activities as a distraction that is counter to growth and development. It is something that even if they were to be engaged in, it remains something they are prepared to stop doing as soon as it 'interferes' with their own development. Whilst both Nelo and Akhona simply did not participate in any extra murals, Thabang and Mercury used to be actively engaged in extramural activities until they consciously stopped so that they could focus on their studies. Thus they view extramural activities as an antibook to their development and better future, which is not necessarily the case in terms of the theoretical construct of OATS proposed here.

There are therefore some similarities and also differences between working class and middle class female teenagers and their relation to extramurals. What middle class female youth and their working class counterparts have in common is hope – with middle class females taking advantage of extramurals to further feed such hope. This is something missing from the middle class male youth as shown later. What however separates middle class female youth from their working class counterparts is their ability to imagine, as seen in how they relate to extramurals as an enabler for their future rather than the disabler that working class youth identify it with. Karah was able to imagine herself as a leader who will be doing things herself and working with people. Wandi was able to imagine herself as a Civil Engineer using her artistic abilities, love and passion. Naledi could also see herself as a possible leader having learnt the ropes from her participation in school leadership committees. These are all middle class females, they understand that they need other things in life towards building their intended future. The story for the working class is however different – they think the only way to the future is through school – with extramurals likely becoming a distraction. First, they can only imagine themselves in the narrow path of schooling and academics – nothing more, and everything else – such as extramurals – is a distraction from this narrow path. This narrow path is however not well defined and has no detail – no Civil Engineer, no Astronaut. In one of the long conversations I conducted with the working class teenagers we discussed the possibilities provided by the sky and the future it might hold for them – which none of them saw. The discussion was triggered by a conversation on the disadvantage of being working class, and these teenagers where impressing upon me how nothing around them gives them opportunities for the future. They pointed out the extramural resources middle class teenagers enjoy including swimming pools and the like. I then pointed out to them that the sky however remains the same for all of us and provides its own opportunities for the future, which they seemed to not be appreciating.

In my interview with Thabang, he indicated that 'since I am now in Grade Twelve, I just decided to stop playing soccer this year on my own so that I can focus on my studies'. Equally important, is the fact that Thabang participated in soccer as his extramural activity not to create a map and/or navigational tool, but was intended to solve a particular problem for him. Thabang told me that his participation

> ...in the soccer club was to avoid doing the wrong things. I have been playing soccer both to keep fit but more importantly to occupy my mind with something that will take me away from all the bad influences.

This is fundamental to Thabang's pathway of the straight and narrow. Thabang had however decided to stop playing soccer 'since I am now in Grade Twelve'. The literature on social and cultural capital helps us understand Thabang's sense of extramurals as a vehicle to 'avoid doing the wrong things' and as something to 'take me away from bad influences'. Whilst Naledi's, a middle class female youth, motivation for participating in sport and an extramural activity is simply to keep fit, Thabang on the other hand did so to avoid doing the wrong things.

Mercury used to belong to a brass band for many years. He informs me that

> I use my spare time over and above schooling, over weekends and holidays, to practice playing the trumpet with members of my brass band. Since I started Grade Eleven I stopped my participation in the band because my marks at school were dropping too fast, so I realised that I need to focus on my studies.

There is thus some form of hope embedded in Mercury's participation in the brass band. But unlike Wandi, who was able to build a bridge between her love of art and a future career as a civil engineer, Mercury had created a breakpoint between his love of brass band and his studies.

I would like to subject the OATS theoretical construct to this apparent contradiction between involvement in extramural activities and succeeding at school. Extramural activities are not just about the activity itself, whether it be soccer or the brass band as in the two cases above, they are more about OATS. The exposure they provide to youth, be it through internal disciplining or external influences, can be invaluable in feeding the capacity to aspire. These extramurals provide much easier access to the kinds of agentic transactions that can shape one's seeing of objects in a manner that opens up to intermediate objects of aspiration rather than immediate aspirational objects. They also tend to provide the tools, be it in maps and navigational tools as proposed by Appadurai or through the kinds of windows that I propose here, which are core to feeding the capacity to aspire. Such extramurals can also serve to alter the imposed spaces that working class youth are trapped in. There are many examples globally of youth whose paths changed for the better after participation in one or another local, national, and/or international competition – be it soccer or music. This logic is easily embraced and understood by middle class female youth, and not necessarily by the working class youth.

The logic of this analysis however gets even more complex when one expands it to look at middle class male youth – no hope and no ability to imagine. Take the case of Vuvu. Vuvu was neither in any leadership activities in the school, nor did he participate in any sporting activities. I was informed by the school that of the 60 pupils who applied to become the chosen leaders at the school for the following year, only one black boy applied. Vuvu was one of the boys who had been coaxed into participating in the study. None of the black boys attending this school had come forward with feedback on their participation in the study. Vuvu claimed to be 'lazy to run in athletics but I believe if I tried I would be good at it'. He was not interested in participating in any of the school's activities, be it sports – 'because I am lazy' or 'I am not fit', or school leadership activities – 'because I don't want to give up my lifestyle. I don't want to give up chilling with friends and something like that'.

The same is almost the case with Mzwandile. Mzwandile was not interested in participating in any sporting activities and/or school leadership responsibilities because

> I don't need it. Most people do those things because they think
> these things will help them with access to jobs and/or universities,
> but I don't need that in my life. To write and act and be a music
> icon I don't need school leadership or sports.

In analysing the difference between middle class female youth and their male counterparts, I first need to acknowledge the literature on adolescent behaviour and differences between adolescent males and females (Grotevant & Cooper, 1985).[1] An important developmental task of adolescence, in societies offering choices in these areas, is the formulation of a sense of identity, a cohesive set of personal values regarding career goals, relationships, political and religious beliefs (Erikson, 1950 in Grotevant & Cooper, 1985).

Here is the difference however between the logic proposed by middle class male youth and that proposed by working class youth. Whilst working class youth believe there is a contradiction between extramurals and success in school and later in life, middle class male youth do not believe that there is a contradiction. It is just that they believe they do not need extramurals for their future. Thus the agentic transactions and imposed space within which middle class male youth are located has resolved the myth of the extramurals' contradiction. It however cannot resolve the intended space and agentic capabilities that rely more on the middle class male youth themselves.

However, the story of extramurals is more complex. It is about hope and limitations. The hope talks to tomorrow, and envisioning a future different from the current – what Appadurai refers to as 'altering the terms of recognition'. It is

---

[1]See also Blakemore, Karah-Jayne, and Suparna Choudhury. Development of the adolescent brain: implications for executive function and social cognition. *Journal of Child Psychology and Psychiatry*, 47(3–4), 2006, pp. 296–312.

however also about the limitations of the current – what I refer to in my theoretical construct as the imposed space. This imposed space can be both tangible and intangible. Tangible as applicable to the working class, and their sheer lack of resources that would allow exposure to the kinds of extramurals that are building blocks to a better future. It can also be intangible, as in the sense of the middle class male teenagers who have all the resources and trappings of middle class life, but lack the guidance and its related agentic transactions from parents, and in particular their father-figure based agentic transactions.

The OATS of Role Modelling

Ramphele (2002) uses the term 'valuable regenerative resources' to define it. In a Netflix (2018) documentary on the renowned music producer and musician Quincy Jones, he explains that by the age of nine his dream and aspiration in life was to be a gangster leader. Probed further as to how he would aspire to such a bad thing in life his response was, 'You wanna be what you see' – referring to the dominance of gangsters in his life at the time. Being what you see – which Appadurai (2015) refers to simply as 'mediants', or valuable regenerative resources which Ramphele (2002) talks to, or simply role modelling as used in this study – all refer to the extent to which that which you are seeing shapes the future you espouse for yourself.

In a study on patterns of interactions in family relationships and the development of identity exploration in adolescence done by Grotevant and Cooper (1985), the authors' findings provide some insights into the essence of the OATS of role modelling. They found that for adolescent boys and their fathers, significant correlations suggested the potential role of reciprocated connectedness in identity exploration (permeability from adolescent to father and mutuality from father to adolescent) (Grotevant & Cooper, 1985). Grotevant and Cooper consequently conclude that, adolescents interactions with their fathers were associated with identity exploration, but in different ways for sons and daughters (1985). According to Grotevant and Cooper, these differences between girls and boys are attributable to the fact that 'sources of family influence on identity exploration may be more diverse for female adolescents than for males' (1985). Thus 'for girls, communication patterns in all four relationships were associated with identity exploration, whereas for boys, only father-son interaction patterns were related to exploration ratings' (Grotevant & Cooper, 1985). This finding helps us understand better the nuances between middle class females and their male counterparts with regards to the OATS of role-modelling as further elaborated below.

From the nine case studies, an interesting pattern emerged. The role models for the middle class females tend to be within the family. In the case of Naledi it is her mother. In the case of Karah it is her mother and sisters, and in the case of Wandi it is more interestingly herself. Wandi's case is more interesting in that her family has set her up to be her own role model. Thus what Ramphele refers to as valuable regenerative resources exist for middle class females within the immediate family, including self. For middle class male youth, and working class teenagers, there is a consistency in that where they have role models, these tend to be external to the family space – such as celebrities. It is thus not necessarily about the absence of Ramphele's valuable regenerative resources – as this would not be applicable to the middle class male youth – but more about Appadurai's mediants and the ability to see and not just look. Middle class male youth are looking at role models and the various valuable regenerative resources surrounding them, but they are not seeing them. However for the working class, it is more about the absence of these valuable regenerative resources that Ramphele talks about, thus they resort to celebrities as role models.

In the case of Naledi, she felt that her interest in neurology was influenced by her mother being a Microbiologist and her focus on business management stemmed from her father's influence as a businessman. Similarly with Karah, who had initially chosen Accounting as one of her school subjects because 'all members of my family have done Accounting and are good at it, and I was also good at it'. Thus the family influence from such a large family seems to have made a strong imprint on Karah, and most of her decision-making processes were linked to those of other members of the family. When it comes to role models, unsurprisingly, Karah's first role model is also her mother. The absence of her father in the list of role models she mentioned is however interesting, especially when assessed against her last statement, 'and have a good influence of me'. Karah's father's influence on her never gets mentioned, whether positive and/or negative. This is more interesting because her father in all likelihood fits the rest of the criteria of coming from a poor background, being hardworking, and overcoming adversity. In fact, other than being absent, he could be fitting the description of a role model more than her mother. Thus the issue, it would seem, relates more to 'influence on me'. Thus, to paraphrase Quincy Jones, you have to see it, for it to influence you. Therefore role modelling is not independent of the act of seeing, and to see you must not only be present, but do more than just looking – again using Appadurai's conception of mediants. This analysis is not only important in terms of understanding black middle class female youth such as Karah, but will become even more important when juxtaposing them against their middle class male counterparts. Vuvu and Mzwandile were surrounded by the same role models that surround Karah, Wandi, and Naledi, but they did not see them – with Vuvu resorting to a celebrity role model such as Gordon Ramsey. Just like Karah, who did not see her father as a role model but her mother, both Vuvu and Mzwandile did not see their fathers as role models – all of whom are in one way physically present but absent in all other ways. These other ways of absence of these fathers signal factors that shape the capacity to aspire, as conceptualized around the OATS theoretical framework proposed here. Equally important is the inverted role modelling outlook of Wandi. Unlike Karah who is focussing on others as her role models, Wandi is on the other hand focussing on herself as the role model. Wandi's parents want

> ...me to be the role model to my younger siblings and expect me to set the standard. It is also not that he doesn't trust me, it is more that he doesn't trust other people.

Thus there are two additional elements shaping Wandi's future – being a role model and setting the standard. Either way, as in Karah and Naledi's cases or the inverted role modelling of Wandi, there is an inherent OATS in role modelling.

For working class youth – both male and female – the OATS of role modelling is not as rich as it tends to be for middle class kids. For Thabang, Akhona and Mercury, role models are either simply absent or not ideal – such as in Thabang's case – whose role model is an ex-convict uncle who became a taxi driver. In the case of Nelo, her role model is a local celebrity – Bonang Matheba. This is because according to Nelo, Bonang Matheba 'is ambitious and independent and going places. She was doing a fashion show in New York recently and others'. Nelo herself seems to be drawn a lot into the beauty industry, with most of her posts on Facebook showing her in various poses and seemingly also joining one of the modelling agencies. Thus her identification with Bonang Matheba and issues of fashion and beauty do not come as a surprise. However, the OATS of this kind of role modelling can be very limited. Its path, what Appadurai calls maps and navigational tools, is at best grey – no clear educational requirements, no specific skill and/or ability, and more importantly, no duplicable or predictable trajectory. I am sure that even Bonang Matheba herself might be the first to admit that for her to have made so much success of herself has required multiple skills, paths, options and possibilities cutting across the modelling industry, the film industry, the radio industry, and various other sectors. It is a kind of role modelling that is filled with too many silences that preclude the OATS theoretical framework espoused hereon. The altering of the terms of recognition that Appadurai talks about as being central to the concept of the capacity to aspire is equally central to the OATS theoretical framework developed in this study. It is about the ability to differentiate and move from immediate objects of aspiration into intermediate objects aspiration. It is about future-building agentic capabilities and trans-actions. It is about tools that open new possibilities and provide the security to trial the future safely. It is also about spaces that project a future that is better than the current.

Middle class male youth again present a very complex picture with regards to the OATS of role modelling. This ranges from being indifferent to being focussed – both of which still result in a weak OATS. The case of Mzwandile is simply a case of indifference. Mzwandile is 'not sure' who his role model is as he

> ...would have to think about that. I don't know, maybe my cousin. He is somebody I grow around and he is the guy I try to watch closely and see how I can be able to do what he does. Now he is doing writing. He writes poetry and even performs it. He is always happy. I have never seen him unhappy or stressed and I want to also be like that, always happy and no stress and no debt.

What is interesting about Mzwandile's role model is that he does not seem to offer much in role modelling except happiness – an immediate object of aspiration. It also sounds like he is more of a carefree guy who does not seem to be bothered by whatever surrounds him, which is the map Mzwandile has in his head. This role model does not provide the requisite maps and navigational tools that feed the capacity to aspire and thus cannot alter the terms of recognition (Appadurai, 2004).

Vuvu's case is very interesting. His role model is Gordon Ramsey – the world renowned Chef. This is because, for Vuvu, Gordon Ramsey 'is just straight up. Says it like it is and tells it like it is and is the best Chef'. Gordon Ramsey is Vuvu's role model because Vuvu has the ambition of being a successful Chef one day. Vuvu indicates that, 'I did have an interest in being a Chef but culinary school is too expensive'. This is because 'my parents told me it is too expensive'. Vuvu's parents said what they want for him is to 'go to a normal university'. He had taken the time to check culinary schools out and 'there is one in Menlyn and I think it costs just over a hundred thousand'. This is a typical case for testing the OATS construct to its fullest. First, there is a clash between the agentic transactions that I talk about in my construct and the agentic capabilities. Vuvu is exercising the kind of agentic capabilities with regards to his aspirations of becoming a Chef that are core to the capacity to aspire. He has hope and imagine, and can locate himself in a future that is different from his current. Here is the twist however, the agentic transactions that Vuvu's parents are exposing him to are not in line with his agentic capabilities. Because they are middle class, Vuvu's parents can only identify with his agentic capabilities of wanting to become a Chef as regression, or a downgrade back into working class life. Unlike Wandi's parents who sought to inject some options and possibilities into her chosen path of drawing and shifting it into engineering, Vuvu's parents have chosen the path of blocking and dismissing his agentic capabilities. To achieve this, Vuvu's parents have ensured that no tools are available towards Vuvu's chosen path, and no spaces are created to enable the path Vuvu has chosen. In return, Vuvu is increasingly withdrawing his own agentic capabilities by being indifferent, trading online during class, not participating in any meaningful activities, and focussing on immediate objects of aspiration for instant self-gratification such as being 'a guys' guy'. It is these kinds of contradictions that make the OATS theoretical framework compelling as a construct that goes beyond the maps and navigational tools that Appadurai proposed.

Similarly, role modelling can take a totally different form in the absence of agentic transactions that feed the capacity to aspire. Both the working class youth and their middle class male counterparts seemed to identify with role models based on people who succeeded in ways that are not easy to duplicate. These role models tend to have succeeded mainly in the entertainment industry – those who succeeded through sheer hard work and luck and some who simply succeeded by chance. Hip-Hop artists such as Tupac and Nas as well as South African artists such as Black Coffee and Bonang Matheba dominated their outlook. However, when asked 'why do you regard Bonang Matheba as your role model and what are the things she has achieved and how did she achieve them in ways that could shape your own future trajectory?' – they drew blank. The best answer they could give is that 'you must socialise, but socialise and establish connections in a way that people follow you and you don't follow them such as DJs'. They believe that talent matters more than knowledge, 'so you follow your talent and passion. If you love something, you do it and follow it until you succeed'. Both middle and working class males did not seem to see any role for knowledge accumulation and its related advantages in building a future able to alter the terms of recognition. This kind of role modelling provides distorted agency and tools which does not feed the meta-capacity to aspire.

Role modelling relates to the OATS conceptual framework in various ways. The choice of role models and their availability relates in one way or another to the connection the youth under study have with either immediate or intermediate objects of aspiration. Nelo identifies with Bonang Matheba as her role model largely because of the immediate objects of aspiration that she presents to her with the celebrity lifestyle. It can be achievable now. The female middle class youth on the other hand relate and identify with role models, such as their mothers, who provide intermediate object of aspiration which are long term and provide a clear path towards a different future.

Role models also provide some form of agentic transaction that in one way or another feed agentic capabilities. The choices about the future that middle class female youth are making – which reflect their agentic capabilities – are shaped in some ways by the role models they have chosen. Wandi's love of Geography was shaped by the agentic transaction she received through her grandfather – who was a respected scholar and one of her role models. Similarly, when looking through Nelo's Facebook posts, you can trace the indirect influence of her role model in Bonang Matheba and her desire (agentic capability) to become a celebrity herself.

Role models also bring with them the tools such as windows and social safety nets. Because they have already travelled the path, role models are better placed to provide guidance and warning of pitfalls. Vuvu only had celebrity chef as his role model – which informed his agentic capability and hope to become a chef. However, in the absence of an agentic transaction that can open up his windows to see more of his path in a manner that Wandi's parents helped in managing her hobby in relation to her possible career, Vuvu remained with small windows and thus his capacity to aspire was stunted. Both Wandi and Vuvu, albeit with the same social safety nets, realized their capacities to aspire differently.

Lastly, role modelling is also about spaces – both as intended and imposed. The imposed space of role models for middle class youth was totally different from that of working class youth. In the absence of Ramphele's valuable regenerative resources in the townships, working class youth were only left with role models that are experienced through the media and far removed. This is the reality of the imposed space for working class youth with regard to role models. The reality for middle class youth is however different. Their imposed space of role models provides them with rich and valuable regenerative resources, to borrow Ramphele's phrase. All middle class youth have to do is to not only look – like the middle class male youth are doing, but to also see – as the middle class female youth are doing. By being able to see, only then can the ability to imagine and hope be realized – which is critical to the realization of the capacity to aspire. Equally important, in the presence of valuable regenerative resources, middle class youth are better placed to trial the future and experience tighter time as space, a luxury that is difficult to achieve for working class youth.

The OATS of Hobbies

Hobbies can take various forms or shapes, tapping on various activities across human life such as the arts, sports, entertainment, and the like. Thus what constitutes as a hobby to someone might otherwise constitute a career, a job, or a business for someone else. I relate to a hobby as different from an extramural activity to reflect the personal and agency basis of a hobby from a usually school based structured programme of extramural activities. Hobbies empower, give choice and agency.

The transition between a hobby as core to the OATS conceptual framework, and that which is noncore, can be both present and/or absent. A hobby can be good or bad in terms of feeding capacity to aspire – it all depends on the presence and/or absence of all the other elements of the OATS construct. Thus such activities, undertaken as hobbies, do tend to constitute an element of OATS in one way or another. Take the example of a sporting code such as golf. Most businessmen tend to play golf as a form of a hobby, to distress and unwind, in their adult life, in the heftiness of life. But what most of these businessmen will also tell you is the power of OATS that such a hobby brings with it in terms of facilitating business connections – what I call agentic transactions, opening avenues to new business ventures – what I call tools such as windows and Appadurai's maps and navigational tools, and opening new avenues – what I call intended spaces such as hope and imagine.

Similarly for youth, hobbies can form an important aspect of the OATS theoretical construct that informs their capacity to aspire. Whilst such hobbies can cut across the class divide, the extent to which they feed the capacity to aspire and thus benefit from OATS tends to be class based.

Take the cases of Karah and Wandi, who are middle class female youth. Karah likes to paint and considers herself an upcoming artist in that regard.

> I started drawing when I saw my sister doing it and I wanted to be
> like her. I started attending art classes and drawing and as I
> improved I loved it more and more.

Wandi also considers herself to be 'good at art' and wants to find the 'best way to do what I am good at'. Over and above studying, Wandi would like to pursue art and continue doing what she likes. More importantly however, which is where the OATS theoretical construct comes in, Wandi puts it that,

> I can't make a career out of art, but I could, but my parents will
> not support me just going straight off into art. I also feel that I

can't live off art. Some artists can become really successful at first, but some people go through some rough times and live a terrible life and I don't want to go through that. I wanted to do what I love, but also find a practical way of doing it.

As a consequence, 'civil engineering will pay the bills, but art will make me happy'. It has been a very difficult balancing act for Wandi though, between what she loves and what she has to do. Her parents have also been pushing her to focus on what will pay the bills without discarding what she loves. This is an important OATS theoretical construct at play here. It has enabled Wandi to enhance what is essentially her hobby into a related career option that alters her terms of recognition. Using her love of art as a hobby, Wandi is bridging this hobby into a career as a civil engineer – a career that will take advantage of the skills, abilities, and passion for her hobby in art. However, for this bridging to take place, it requires OATS. The kinds of agentic transactions that Wandi is exposed to through her parents have enabled her to exercise the agentic capabilities that have allowed her to differentiate between a hobby and a career and the related implications thereof. She has the tools to see beyond the hobby through the maps and navigational tools at her disposal, but equally important the windows in front of her that are wider and bigger. For her to know and recognize the civil engineering route as an option ahead required these tools. Both her imposed and intended spaces have been critical in creating this bridge that she is now utilizing in that she has hope and can imagine. Equally important are the future trials that she is exposed to that have opened up these possibilities and the tight time as space. This is why Wandi's objects of aspiration are more intermediate than immediate, as she tends to spend all her money feeding her hobby as it has now found space in her future. This is not the case with Karah (also middle class female), whose similar hobby in art has no space in her future.

The working class youth's story is however different in relation to its OATS location. As indicated earlier, hobbies know no class. Thus even working class youth have their own hobbies which at times are similar to those of middle class youth. Take the case of Akhona. Just like Karah and Wandi above, Akhona's hobby is in art and drawing. Like the middle class female youth above, Akhona loves drawing and art and spends a great deal of time nurturing and developing his hobby. Of course due to resource constraints, Akhona's drawings are not as colourful and expansive as he uses just ordinary note pad paper and an ordinary pen and pencil. The middle class female youth above spend thousands of Rands on equipment and resources to feed their hobbies. Despite the class divide, even though I am not an expert in this area, I would argue that Akhona's talent is more pronounced than that of the middle class female youth. Akhona spends 'a lot of my time in my room drawing because I enjoy and I feel I am good at, but it also helps me escape from my family space'. Here is the difference, whilst Wandi and Karah's love and ability in art is a means to the future, for Akhona, this same love and ability is key to escaping the current imposed space. Escape can only be about the current and has very little to do with the future. Escape is the antibook to the capacity to aspire, and evidence of the absence of OATS.

The same is closely the case for Mercury, also a working class youth. His hobby is not about escaping, but intended to create a path towards the future for him. However, this future is unrealistic as no real career of being a philosopher can be that easily pronounced, except perhaps as a motivational speaker. Mercury's main aim in life, as indicated earlier, is to become a philosopher, because 'I want to give people the ideas of life and the philosophy of how they can be'. He feels he can succeed as a philosopher 'because I like writing poems during my spare time, maybe before I sleep I write about two or three poems'. With solid agentic transactions, or some form of stepping stones, or even the opening of windows for him, Mercury – with his poetry writing and intention of being a motivational speaker – could see a path towards the future that could trigger his capacity to aspire and alter his terms of recognition. We have the makings of a hobby becoming central in shaping his capacity to aspire. However, as is the case with the working class, in the absence of OATS the translation of this hobby into something that can alter his terms of recognition becomes limited. The best that Mercury's mother could do, when she saw the possibility of this hobby shaping her son's capacity to aspire, was to encourage him to do more. The kinds of agentic transactions that Wandi's parents could facilitate for their daughter are not possible for Mercury's mother because these transactions tend to be class based. The kinds of tools that Mercury requires are not available, therefore as much as he has hope and imagine, the absence of windows and social safety nets constrain his ability to realize a positive future that feeds off his hobby as a poet. Mercury's spaces are also not conducive, with the lack of future trials and loose time as space. Thus the maps and navigational tools that he needs to navigate his way to the future are absent, and in their absence, Mercury thinks that to become a philosopher and poet is just something you decide upon and it happens. The routes and paths necessary to be travelled, similar to those travelled by his idol philosophers, are not known and remain a mystery.

For middle class male youth, unlike in all the other groups of youth studied here, what was striking was the general absence of hobbies. What Vuvu regards as his hobby is at best complex, in that he wants to

> ...use my hobbies to succeed like stocks, like investing in stocks. Not as a job, but like something on the side. This is something I can even do now and I am going to start during the coming holidays. I got money from my parents, like R4000, and I will just invest from there on an app. You just invest on the app.

'When the sun arises, I will just wake up and check on the app how it is going, I don't know, watch TV or something'. However, there was what I would regard as the silent hobby of Vuvu, which he does not recognize as such and thus was not verbalized. This is his interest, ambition, and more importantly, aspiration to become a Chef. This 'hobby' seemed to be so deep that it shaped a role model for him, and he spent a lot of time online watching videos about cooking. So Vuvu has a silent hobby of cooking, has the ambition to become a Chef, and his role model is a Chef. However, the OATS that surrounds Vuvu has sought to neutralize this outlook. The agentic transactions, the tools and the imposed spaces, are all in unison in negating what Vuvu is looking at, and consequently making it impossible for him to see. In the absence of his parents assistance to negotiate a path around his own vision (agentic transactions), non-exposure to the kinds of future trials he needs (imposed spaces), no windows and no social safety nets (tools) with the claim that chef school is expensive – Vuvu's capacity to aspire has become stunted. The same is similarly the case with Mzwandile, although with a slightly different nuance. Unlike in Vuvu's case, Mzwandile's parents are not necessarily opposed to his intended career, they are just silent about it. It is the case of the unguided hobby, again with no OATS. Mzwandile's aim when he finishes school was to become a writer or an actor. So far he had done a number of school shows in this regard. The absence of OATS in Mzwandile's hobby and its possible transition to shaping his future comes through when he says that he believes 'that you don't really need school to write'. Thus the kinds of agentic transactions that ultimately reshaped Wandi's love of art into engineering and further into institutions of further development, seems to be absent in the case of Mzwandile.

Hobbies relate to the OATS conceptual framework in various ways. As seen in the case of Wandi, her hobby has shaped how she relates to immediate objects of aspiration in in that it feeds into her intermediate objects of aspiration. The need to spend her money on drawing and art utensils in order to feed her hobby has overridden her desire to spend the money on shoes. With her hobby now increasingly linked to her future career, this investment in her hobby feeds her capacity to aspire and her focus on the intermediate rather than the immediate.

What is also clear in the case of Wandi and Karah who are middle class female youth, Vuvu as a middle class male, and that of Akhona as a working class youth, is the relation between hobbies and agency. Because of the kinds of agentic transactions both Karah and Wandi are exposed to, their hobbies seem to feed their capacities to aspire and strengthen their agentic capabilities. They are shaping their futures in dynamic ways such as Wandi's art hobby and its link to her engineering career. Vuvu's hobby of cooking is however not receiving the same agentic transactions that would enable his cooking to translate into career as a Chef, despite him being middle class as well. In Vuvu's case, the agentic transaction that he is receiving dissuades him from a path into the future simply because of the perception of class regression. Akhona's case, as a working class male, is different – the agentic transactions are simply absent and nearly impossible in his context.

Hobbies, more than any other activity, require tools. It takes big and wide windows to see the link between art and engineering as Wandi's parents have done. It also needs strong social safety nets to invest in art in ways that Wandi's parents have done as a path towards her 'chosen' career. Of course, Appadurai's maps and navigational tools are equally indispensable here, as the juxtaposition of Wandi against Vuvu in this case may show.

Hobbies are also about spaces – both as intended and imposed. The intended space of hobbies can be equally distributed amongst the working class and the middle class. Both Wandi – a middle class female, and Akhona – a working class male, share the same hobby in art. This inspires hope and the ability to imagine in two different ways. For Akhona, it is a way of escaping the hardship of the current – which, even if it were to succeed, does not open a path into the future. For Wandi, it is as way of enjoying her love for art and transferring it into her future as an aspect of her career. The imposed space of hobbies is however not equally distributed and tends to impact negatively on the working class. The greater part of Akhona's limitation to transfer his hobby into a clearer future is largely due to his imposed space of working class life. The opposite can also be true for Wandi as a middle class female. Wandi has opportunities to future trial her hobby, Akhona does not. Wandi's time as space is tighter, and that of Akhona is loose. These are all the elements that feed and/or limit youth capacity to aspire and the role of hobbies in this regard.

The OATS of Peers

Young people generally tend to value friends and friendships during their teen years. At the ages at which the youth study were identified, they were at the prime of their transition into adulthood. Thus friends and friendships played an important role in their lives.

These relationships are also critical in shaping young people's capacity to aspire and the possibilities that lie ahead for them. For middle class female youth, these friendships were not coincidental, but deliberate and seemed to be somewhat planned. They make conscious decisions (agentic capability), some with parental influence (agentic transactions), on who to befriend or not. Take the case of Karah as a starting point. Karah is very conscious of the fact that she associates herself with people who share her belief system and values which include being 'trustworthy, honest, and treating others as you would like them to treat you'. This is also the case with Wandi, who is close friends with Karah. Karah is close friends with Wandi and they tend to influence and shape each other's outlook on life because they 'became friends by association' – trustworthiness, honesty etc. Thus much as one sees a lot of agentic capability in the choice of friendships that both Karah and Wandi are exercising, it has also come with a lot of agentic transactions from their parents and families. Wandi's father's insistence on a set of rules at home and expectations of her becoming her own role model seemed to influence her choice of friends in the direction of somebody like Karah, whose strong sisterly and motherly guidance at home expected her to follow in everyone's footsteps. All four of Karah's sisters remained a strong influence on her in all aspects of her life and thus her choice of a friend in Wandi needed to enhance the kinds of values she is expected to carry by her family.

Middle class male youth on the other hand seemed to be operating from a blank slate. In the absence of any form of meaningful agentic transaction that they could absorb from their families, they exercised their own agentic capability as best as they know how. In the case of Vuvu, he decided to become 'a guys' guy'. What this meant was that Vuvu had to be popular with all his peers and derive his recognition from that. This approach seemed to have worked since boys such as Mzwandile held Vuvu in high regard and genuinely felt that he was a 'cool' guy.

But for Vuvu the costs of being regarded by his peers as cool were high – he had to stop paying attention in class and use that time to trade online during school hours under the guise of making money, he had to not participate in any of the school's extramurals at the cost of his own talent in athletics just to appear cool. Being a guys' guy is all about today, and has nothing to do with tomorrow – aspects of the capacity to aspire. Mzwandile, who is Vuvu's friend, held Vuvu in high regard as being the epitome of 'cool'. What was clear in both Vuvu and Mzwandile's decision-making process was peer influence, as shown in the following quote from Mzwandile regarding their participation in the study, 'one of my friends said that if three other friends of ours participate in the study then he will also join in'. Thus for them to agree to participate was more about their friends agreement influencing their own agreement and vice versa. The friends that Mzwandile was referring to are the same friends who formed a Hip-Hop group called *Usual Sxspects*, and belong to the WhatsApp group of about 10 boys who are members of this band. Mzwandile indicated that he and his friends at school

> ...only talk about the things we don't like, because it is natural. We talk bad about the school. Like my friends play hockey and they won the league but only received half colours from the school instead of them being given full colours. We also talk about life and our dreams and talk about girls and parties, and sometimes school.

There are a number of key differences between Karah and Wandi on the one hand, and Vuvu and Mzwandile on the other hand. Whilst all four youth are middle class and attend the same school, the first two are girls and the latter two are boys. First, the girls seemed to have a criteria that guides them on their choice of friends. The boys on the other hand had no criteria except popularity and acceptance in a group. The girls tended to consequently keep a few selected friends close, whilst the boys tended to belong to a bigger group with everyone being everyone's friend. The focus of friendship for the girls was likeness, shared values, shared outlook on the future, whilst boys on the other hand tended to focus on current events and activities such as parties and girls. The key difference between the girls and the boys that was most striking, and this is critical to our pursuit of the capacity to aspire, is the negativity surrounding the boys as against the positivity that was surrounding the girls. The very notion of aspire is by nature a positive outlook, hence the theoretical construct of hope and imagine. The friendship among middle class boys seemed to revolve around deeply negative constructs around their main life activity at their age – which is the school. As Mzwandile points out, we

> ...only talk about the things we don't like, because it is natural. We talk bad about the school. Like my friends play hockey and they

won the league but only received half colours from the school instead of them being given full colours.

So even a positive thing such as a major achievement of some of their friends who play hockey having won the league is clouded by the negativity of 'only receiving half colours'.

For working class youth, it is more about the imposed space of working class life rather than the intended space of a different tomorrow. The power and effect of the imposed space for them is too strong such that they have to either conform or spend most of their energies fighting back. For Akhona and Thabang the only solution for them was avoidance, which meant closing themselves out from the outside world. Due to their perception of being surrounded by negative influences, they chose not to have friendships and avoid their peers as much as they could. Even though Thabang played soccer, he still avoided establishing friendships with his playmates outside the soccer fields due to the fear of them being a bad influence on him. Whilst both Akhona and Thabang have made these choices and are sticking to them, Nelo on the other hand is dabbling in and out of friendships with her peers. She made the change in her life thus far – from keeping too many friendships to now having none – but remains at risk of falling back. 'It is not that I don't want to have boyfriends anymore, I just don't want a serious commitment for the sake of my future'. Nelo decided 'not to have any friends in the township, my only companions are my school mates'. She also decided to put aside 'all other negative spaces surrounding me as they tend to distract me from focussing on my future'. Nelo believes that she, and most of her friends, do not want to fall pregnant because 'we all worry about our parents and also because the boys deny it when they make the girls pregnant'. But the problem is that when 'girls get involved in a serious relationship with boys, even though we might use protection at the beginning, the boys end up demanding unprotected sex over time'. It is this power of the imposed space that is always present among working class youth that keeps them at risk of not altering their terms of recognition.

The OATS conceptual framework proposed here is a tool that is key in shaping the capacity to aspire. What was clear in all the cases studied was that the capacity to aspire does not happen on its own, it requires certain tools, in this case proposed as the OATS conceptual framework. Thus the framework equally applies to the choice of friends that youth make. Unguided by such a conceptual framework, such choices of friends are arbitrary and of no relation to the future. The future then happens on its own and by chance.

For middle class females, the choice of peers seems to be guided and somewhat controlled. The opposite seems the case for middle class males and working class youth. It therefore comes as no surprise that middle class female youth and their peers tend to possess intermediate objects of aspiration rather than their male counterparts, who seem convinced by immediate objects of aspiration. For the females, most of their objects of aspirations relate to tomorrow, whilst the males' objects of aspiration tend to relate to today, such as being 'a guys' guy'. Working class youth and their peers are also focussed on immediate objects of aspiration, and their imposed space almost makes it impossible for them to escape the imposition of the immediacy.

Thus largely due to the presence/absence and the type of agentic transactions, youth and their peers tend to exhibit related agentic capabilities. Middle class females, guided by the kinds of agentic transactions they receive, seem to exhibit clearer agentic capabilities about their future. The same is the case with the middle class youth and their peers, who have all joined a Hip-Hop group – *Usual Sxspects*. For the working class youth, the general absence of agentic transactions has placed more responsibility on them to exercise own agentic capabilities. The pressure they however constantly face is how to exercise such agentic capabilities in a manner that helps them escape peer pressure that leads to no future success. This is the challenge both Nelo and Thabang are constantly faced with.

The same is the case when focussing on tools. The windows of the middle class male youth are narrow, even though their social safety nets are strong. The narrowness of their windows impacts on them and their peers as their decision-making processes seem linked – such as whether to form and join the Hip-Hop group, and whether to participate as in this study. This limits their individual agentic capabilities. With wider windows and stronger social safety nets, middle class female youth are better able to exercise their agentic capabilities as they can see further and wider. For the working class youth and their peers, the class based nature of tools generally limits their ability to see further and explore more.

Overall, what is clear about the sampled youth and their peers is that both the intended and imposed spaces are shared amongst them. The imposed space of the working class youth tends to be the same, as is that of the middle class youth. The variations amongst the youth arise when one looks at their intended space. All middle class male youth were in a similar space of negativity with their peers. The opposite was the case with their female counterparts.

The OATS of Storytelling

Storytelling has historically been acknowledged in education as one of the key strategies to enhance learning. As Gramsci reminded us,

> The starting-point of critical elaboration is the consciousness of what one really is, and is 'knowing thyself' as a product of the historical process to date which has posited in you an infinity of traces, without leaving an inventory. The first thing to do is to make such an inventory.
>
> (Gramsci, 1973)

It is the making of such an inventory that triggers the need and importance of storytelling. Consequently, it is

> ...the characteristic features of storytelling – its *situatedness* and *specificity*, its *reflexivity* and *provisionality*, its focus on lived

experience – show that it is an indispensable means for remaining fully responsive to what is happening around us.

(Doecke, 2013, p. 11)

The situatedness, specificity, reflexivity, and provisionality of storytelling seems to not be lost among middle class female youth, and thus remains an indispensable means of remaining fully responsive to what is happening around them (Doecke, 2013, p. 11). Take the case of Karah. Karah's parents had a difficult life and upbringing back in the DRC, stories which they share frequently with her and her siblings. She indicated that her parents

> ...tell me stories like how they had to walk long distances to school and how they had to fetch water far away from their households at the river and walk like twelve kilometres for that. My mom had to also sell stuff in the streets so as to support her siblings and things like that.

For Karah, these are not just stories, but more importantly, they feed her desire to do better and alter her terms of recognition. As Doecke puts it, these stories are Karah's means for remaining fully responsive to what is happening around her (Doecke, 2013, p. 11). Similarly for Wandi, who indicated that for her these were not just stories, but further fed into the kinds of career choices she has been making for herself. Wandi indicated that she chose to study Geography amongst her subject choices because her 'grandfather was a Geography teacher in Nigeria'.

> Back then I didn't really know him (the grandfather) much, but people used to tell me he was a Geography teacher and I really didn't understand why he would choose Geography out of all these subjects. But then I thought let me take Geography and see. It however turns out that it is one of my most favourite subjects. It is not necessarily him who influenced me directly, I was just curious.

This is very important, Wandi never really met or knew her grandfather, she only knew about him through storytelling. It was this storytelling that made her 'curious' about this grandfather who was a Geography teacher that prompted her to explore taking Geography as a subject, which over time 'turns out that it is one of my most favourite subjects'. Just like in Karah's case, for Wandi

> ...back when they were younger in Nigeria and the country was experiencing a financial crisis it was hard for my parents and things were difficult for them. When he (father) moved here, he didn't have anything. He just scraped enough money for a plane ticket. And South Africa would not even let him practise medicine even with his qualifications. He had to get piece jobs in some shops to

survive. My dad has seen the rough side of life and doesn't want us to go through that.

All of this hardship of her father is not anything that Wandi herself experienced, but only knew about it through storytelling.

The case of Wandi and Karah could be easily dismissed as triggered by fresh memories of hardships and migration difficulties experienced by their parents. Such a narrative would however not be entirely misplaced, as the work of John Ogbu has shown in the context of migrant leaners in the United States. Ogbu's theory posits that 'differences in school performance between immigrant and non-immigrant minorities are partly due to differences in their community forces' (1990a). In Ogbu's minority typology, voluntary minorities, those who chose to immigrate to a host country, view the host societies' institutions, including schools, in terms of opportunity. They take an instrumental approach to schooling and view the schools in terms of what they can gain from them. They likewise view teachers as experts in specific areas and as the source of knowledge they need. Even if they face discrimination, they do not internalize the mistreatment, but rather remain focused on the opportunity to gain valuable knowledge and skills. They are also willing to learn, accept and adapt to the cultural norms of the majority group. They see no threat to their own sense of identity as a result of adopting new behaviours. In fact, they expect to learn new ways as necessary for their success in the host country. In Ogbu's conception, voluntary minorities are steady academic achievers (Ogbu, 1990b, p. 154).

But in South Africa, with the recent history of hardship under apartheid, one would assume that the same level of recent hardship memories among the parents of black South African youth would trigger similar story telling practices. But it would seem that for many South Africans, including many of the youth, the bitter past has had a profound negative psychological impact that manifests itself mainly through victimhood – as pointed out by Njabulo Ndebele (Ndebele, 2017). In the essay that attempts to find an explanation to the student protests of 2016, Ndebele argues that,

> ...a critical and sobering learning in state transformation since 1994 is how easily the visionary goals evolved over a century of struggle could be forgotten within a short space of time, and how the mechanisms of maintaining an oppressive society can be assimilated by those once oppressed, and reproduced as a feature of political and social behaviour such that their relative failure to create a new society according to the visionary specifications that have driven the struggle for that society for over a century is blamed on the racism of an ageing oppressor who is no longer in power. Visionary agency is given up precisely at that moment that it should be affirmed and intensified. Against this context 'black pain' in its current manifestations comes across to me more as an attribute of victimhood than of agency.
>
> (Ndebele, 2017)

This is more critical in that the history of apartheid South Africa and its recent transition to democracy is steeped in a lot of history and richness that one might easily assume lends itself to opportune moments for the kind of storytelling that would feed the capacity to aspire – what Ndebele simply refers to as 'visionary agency'. The case is however different for working class youth and middle class male youth.

Middle class male youth have a complete absence of the storytelling narratives I heard from their female counterparts. For middle class males, this absence seemed to create a complete ambivalence to their current state of privilege, let alone understanding it comparatively in the context of the country's recent transition from apartheid to democracy.

For the working class, their current state of poverty and hardship was also only understood in terms of the current with no link to the recent past. But more importantly, the kind of storytelling experienced by working class youth was different from the storytelling experienced by middle class female youth.

The OATS of storytelling varies in magnitude and depth. For storytelling to feed the capacity to aspire espoused by Appadurai and advocated in the OATS conceptual framework here, it needs to tick all the key boxes of the OATS conceptual framework – objects, agency, tools, and spaces. In the absence of the boxes being ticked, it remains limited, even though not useless. For Wandi, a middle class female youth, it allows for the kind of storytelling that provides characters like her Geography teacher grandfather who then shape her choice of Geography towards altering her terms of recognition. It is a higher order value proposition. For Thabang on the other hand, a working class boy, it is a different proposition all together, even though remaining valuable. Thabang's experience of storytelling came through mainly his uncle, who is an ex-convict. According to Thabang,

> ...my uncle tells me, 'don't be like me and end up stealing cars. You will be arrested and end up in jail like me. Look at me now I am driving taxis, you must be something better. Going to jail is not an easy thing and is not as romantic as some of the boys in the township make it out to be – it is tough and bad'.

Thus Thabang's entire framework on his life is avoidance and escapist. Therefore much as Thabang's storytelling experience through his ex-convict uncle does not provide him with the tools and spaces to achieve higher order aspirations similar to Wandi's, it nonetheless helps him to avoid the wrong things in life. It is limited, and does not necessarily alter his terms of recognition, but equally helps him avoid going deeper into the abyss of poverty and deprivation.

Through storytelling, Wandi's parents were able to plant certain likes and dislikes in her head. It was through storytelling that she discovered her grandfather's Geography specialization and developed a liking for the subject. Over time this story has connected with her art hobby and career in engineering. It is these steps, triggered by a single storytelling experience about her grandfather, which ultimately feed into her objects of aspiration being intermediate rather than immediate. Without the advantage of such storytelling experiences, both the middle class males and their working class counterparts find themselves stuck with immediate objects of aspiration, which are visible today and can be experienced immediately.

As shown in the case of Wandi above, and the same can be said with regards to Karah, storytelling is one of the key mechanisms of exercising agentic transactions, which ultimately feeds agentic capabilities. Agentic transactions do not happen by themselves, and they are not automatic. They have to be present in physical form (such as the presence of parents), and will have to be exercised (through deeds and words such as storytelling). Where both these elements are present, they are likely to impact on the capacity to aspire as envisaged by Appadurai. In cases where either one of these elements are absent – or aspects of them are absent – their probable impact on the capacity to aspire becomes limited. For middle class males, whilst one element of agentic transactions is present – that of physical presence, the other element of words is absent – blunting their capacity to aspire. For working class youth, both elements of agentic transactions tend to be absent in both physical presence, deed and words.

Whilst storytelling has less to do with social safety nets, it however has a lot to do with windows, maps and navigational tools. Windows, just like agentic transactions above, require both deeds and words. Youth can be shown the windows, or they can be told about them. Storytelling is central to telling youth about windows. By telling youth about the windows through storytelling, they are enabled to see further and wider. Their minds are opened to possibilities that the future holds, feeding them hope and allowing them to imagine. Evident in middle class female youth. The opposite is however true with regards to middle class male and working class youth.

Through storytelling, whilst it has limits in altering the imposed space, the intended space of youth can be influenced in ways that are central to their capacity to aspire. Where both Karah and Wandi see themselves in future, influenced by the stories their parents narrate to them, is totally different from where their parents come from. In Wandi's case, it has even shaped her desire to change the world and make it a better place which is more caring with less poverty and hardship. Thus her engineering career becomes just one step to a bigger future that she desires not only for herself but equally for the world.

The OATS of Prognostication

I am using the concept of prognostication to simply define in one word the kinds of conversations about the future that are necessary to one's realization of their capacity to aspire. This is different from the OATS of storytelling illustrated earlier, which tends to mainly be about the past and at best the present. Prognosticating is more about envisaging (and not prophesying), and thus in the context of the capacity to aspire, having the necessary conversations that envisage a future different from the past and current. It is equally at the core of

Appadurai's redefinition of culture as being less about the past and the present, but more about the future.

There are three key trends that have emerged from the nine case studies of the youth. The first is what I paraphrase as the 'higher order normative context' of the OATS of prognostication (Appadurai, 2013). It is linked to Appadurai's notion of intermediate objects of aspiration as 'a more complex experience of the relation between a wide range of ends and means'. This is evident in the parents of middle class female youth

> ...having a bigger stock of available experiences of the relationship between aspirations and outcomes, because they are in a better position to explore and harvest diverse experiences of exploration and trial, because of their many opportunities to link material goods and immediate opportunities to more general and generic possibilities and options.
>
> (Appadurai, 2013)

The second trend is the direct opposite of the first, which is a lower order normative context of the OATS of prognostication – affecting mainly working class youth. This lower order normative context of the OATS of prognostication is recognized for its existence and its equally important focus on the future – it however does not possess any maps or navigational tools that can alter the terms of recognition. For instance, Akhona's mother saying she will support art but not providing any real plan or vision. Its future orientation is thus based on risks and consequences rather than opportunities and options. The third and last trend is the sheer absence of the OATS of prognostication, which affects mainly middle class male youth and some of the working class youth – like Nelo's father not giving her anything to hold onto when she told him she wants to do nursing.

Middle class female youth are the main beneficiaries of the higher order normative context of the OATS of prognostication. These youth pronouncements about their futures tend to be prefaced with quotes such as 'my parents also', 'my dad says', 'my mom is', 'he (dad) tells me stories', 'see what he (dad) does', 'help him (dad) with stuff' and the like. These references all point to the provision of what Ball and Bok (Ball et al., 2002; Bok, 2010) refer to as family scripts and inheritance codes as inputs the families provide to these youth about their futures. Thus such prognostication allows for these middle class parents to exercise the kinds of agentic transactions that are key to building the capacity to aspire. Consequently, middle class female youth are conscious of and absorb these agentic transactions from parents, brothers and sisters, uncles and aunts who tend to be highly educated. These elders of the family also tend to be closely involved in their children's activities – 'she picks me up every day' and

> ...few weeks ago my dad asked me what I wanted to study one day. And my mom is also always asking me the same things. My parents are very supportive of my decisions.

It is what Lareau calls 'concerted cultivation'. Whilst the youth themselves might not be 'keen to talk to parents a lot about careers because it causes too much stress for me', these elders are nevertheless not relenting in engaging such youth about such matters – persistently and constantly rerouting and redirecting their agentic capabilities, opening windows and ensuring the presence of social safety nets. The influence and persistence of Wandi's parents in shaping her engineering career from just being about her art hobby is a case in point.

Take the case of Karah. Karah has had conversations with 'my mom' about her future and what she wanted to become. One of these conversations led to her mother arranging a visit to the BMW plant in Rosslyn because 'at the time I wanted to do mechanical engineering'. She was able to talk and work shadow an Industrial Engineer for the company. She finds such conversations extremely helpful; especially with her sister already practising in the field. Karah and Wandi, her friend, influence each other as friends and feed off each other's energies. They have serious conversations about their futures and options moving forward, as Wandi puts it, 'it always turns into a joke. We talk a lot about our aspirations but always turn them into jokes'. The same is the case with Naledi. She has conversations with her parents about her future and the options she is exploring,

> ...especially my mom because like she is into it. She calls us together to ask about what careers we want to follow because she wants to help us and stuff and she wants us to know now and be sure so that we can have time to ready ourselves. My mom also wants to expose us to the right people and find connections.

On the other hand Naledi's father

> ...is more like okay, whatever. If you change your mind today he just says okay, and if you change your mind tomorrow again he is like – okay. He won't like ask questions as to why you are changing your mind and are you sure.

The lower order normative context of the OATS of prognostication tends to affect more the working class youth rather than their middle class counterparts. In Thabang's case

> ...my uncles also guide me and teach me to do the right things. They are both supportive in their own way. They do talk to me about stuff and girls and how to avoid the wrong stuff. They also talk to me about education and encourage me to study hard and be myself and not be like him (the convicted uncle), and don't chase material things.

Thus the prognostication that takes place is more about what to avoid, the risks of not avoiding it, and the consequences of choosing the wrong path, as exemplified by the uncles themselves. To paraphrase Ball and Bok, it is about decoding the (un)inheritance codes. Whilst middle class parents are exemplary and keen to transfer the inheritance codes and family scripts, working class parents and/or guardians are not exemplary and thus use their inheritance codes and family scripts to, correctly, engender fear and avoidance into the youth.

Then there is the third trend of mere absence of the OATS of prognostication, which mainly affects middle class male youth and some of the working class youth. For the working class, the case of Nelo is relevant here. She has a father that she is aware of, who also stays elsewhere in the neighbourhood, but is not really involved in her life. Both her father and mother never really took an interest in her life and her future. She indicated that

> I don't know why, but my mother, even when she was alive, never really took any interest in what happens to me. I have relied on my aunt from even when I was young. My father supports me verbally and says I must go for it, but does nothing to help in a practical way. He always makes promises but never realises them.

The same narrative continues with middle class male youth. Vuvu reckons that

> I guess I sometimes have conversations with my dad, like once a month. It usually starts with my dad saying 'Vuvu you need to study and improve your future', something like that. But I don't enjoy such conversations with him because he says that so that he can start complaining about me and my marks. I think he assumes that I don't study simply because he does not see me study, but I do. But with my mom we don't usually talk about that.

Mzwandile, another middle class male youth, is not much different either because he too never had such a conversation with his father.

> Because I just tried it with my mom and it didn't work out. My dad also does not really like to talk about my future. My parents just want to make sure that my school is okay and that I will finish and like go to university. I only talk to my dad sometimes, like I don't really stay with him much, I am always in my bedroom and I spend more quality time with my mom and I speak more with her. I don't know, that is just how it is. She enjoys talking more.

Thus whilst Mzwandile's father is 'present' in the home, he is at the same time not really present, and Mzwandile made peace with that reality. A related online post from him also indicated that *'my parents when I was 8 "go to your room". My parents now "please come out of your room"'*. On two other occasions he posted: '*I fake sleep when my family members come in my room so they don't talk to me*' and '*my mom blames everything on my phone. "you failing?" cuz that phone*'.

There are various elements inherent in the OATS theoretical framework that arise with regards to the issue of prognostication as raised in this section.

Conversations about the future are key to differentiating immediate objects of aspiration from intermediate aspirational objects. It is when one is thinking ahead into the future and conversing about it that s/he gets to see the objects of the future, which from the current are intermediate. It helps one appreciate 'the relation between a wide range of ends and means' (Appadurai, 2013).

Prognostication is also about agency. It is a means by which agentic trans-actions can be exercised, feeding into the kinds of agentic capabilities that are key to one's realization of the capacity to aspire. As shown between the higher order normative contexts of such agentic transactions among the middle class as opposed to the lower order normative contexts of the working class, the exercise of this agency can either alter the terms of recognition or fail in this regard.

Prognostication is also as much about Appadurai's maps and navigational tools – what I simply refer to as tools – and the windows that I propose in my theoretical framework. It is during these conversations about the future that youth can be exposed to the opportunities that lie ahead – as in the case of middle class female youth, or the risks and pitfalls that await them – as in the case of working class youth. These are the windows that I propose as key to the third element of the OATS theoretical framework of tools.

Last and equally important, prognostication is also about both the intended and imposed spaces. In its core thrust, prognostication is about reflecting on the future – what I call the intended space. However, the realities of the imposed space tend to impact on the outlook of the intended space as part of the future reflection as shown in the differences between the middle class female youth and the working class. It is as much about hope and imagine as it allows for the middle class female youth as against working class youth.

The OATS of Exposure

I use the concept of exposure to broadly refer to the extent to which the youth are exposed to various other life experiences outside the classroom. In the literature such an analysis is periodically referred to as service learning. As argued, 'it is also common for educators, policymakers, and scholars to promote service learning as a means of fostering civic and political engagement' (Gibson & Levine, 2003). It is believed that this type of experience socializes young people to value and pursue civic activity and to develop social trust. Such activities are also thought to foster exposure to norms of behaviour and to develop skills that make engagement more likely (Youniss & Yates, 1997). In Paceman's classic formulation, 'the experience of participation in some way leaves the individual better psychologically equipped to undertake further participation' (p. 43). Finkel (1987), for example, found reciprocal effects between electoral and campaign participation and external political efficacy. Similarly, in their study of youth working in soup kitchens, Youniss and Yates (1997) showed how these experiences provided opportunities for agency (as students respond to social problems), social relatedness (as students join with others to respond to a societal need), and political-moral understanding (as students reflect on and discuss the societal issues with which they are engaged).

They argued that developing agency, social relatedness, and political moral understanding fosters the development of commitment to and capacity for civic and political engagement. While several quantitative studies have found strong relationships between service learning and civic outcomes (Hart, 2007; Kahne & Sporte, 2008; Metz & Youniss, 2005), not all studies of service learning have identified positive outcomes (Billig, Root, & Jesse, 2005; Melchior, 1998) (Kahne, David, & Nam-Jin, 2013).

Exposure also connects with Appadurai's notion of mediants, materiality, and normativity (2015). Exposure is essential for 'the eye (and its sensory-neural infrastructure)' to become 'the materiality through which seeing – as a practise of mediation – takes effect' (Appadurai, 2015). This happens in order to 'bring normativity back into the new materialisms', so that we can

> …recognise the dynamic materiality of mediants, seen as dividuals that interact to produce various materialities, ideas such as class, interest group, multitude, mass, and public will all need to be rethought.
>
> (Appadurai, 2015)

Both the notion of service learning that Kahne (2013) refers to, and that of mediants, materiality, and normativity that Appadurai (2015) raises are related and impact on the youth sampled in different ways.

First it is a class issue. Middle class youth have the advantage of more exposure with more depth – what Appadurai (2013) calls a 'higher order normative context' - than working class youth. Thus service learning derives a different meaning for the middle class to that of the working class,

> …because the better off, by definition, have a more complex experience of the relation between a wide range of ends and means, because they have a bigger stock of available experiences of the relationship of aspirations and outcomes, because they are in a better position to explore and harvest diverse experiences of exploration and trial, because of their many opportunities to link material goods and immediate opportunities to more general and generic possibilities and options.
>
> (Appadurai, 2013)

Secondly, exposure is also as much about mediants, materiality, and normativity as it is about service learning. For middle class male youth, their exposure seems different from that of their female counterparts, largely due to their inability to realize 'the materiality through which seeing – as a practise of mediation – takes effect' (Appadurai, 2015).

Karah, Wandi, and Naledi, as middle class female youth, have taken full advantage of the OATS of exposure due to its presence and their own 'practise of mediation' – what I refer to as agentic capability. Karah attended open days at various universities as per the school's guidance to learn more about her career of choice, which is industrial engineering. With her sister already practicing as an Industrial Engineer and Karah being keen to follow a similar career trajectory, she found a lot of inspiration from her sister. 'Even in the last open day at Tukkies, it is my sister who told me about it and that we should go and learn about our chosen career fields'. 'I have my sister, so if I ever need advice and knowledge she is there for me'. Karah also attended various sporting activities, meetings and other engagements both within South Africa and internationally – either as part of her family holiday travels, or as a school representative in the various leadership committees, or in the sporting codes that she participates in. The same is the case with Wandi, who hopes to go to a

> …University in America. It started with my dad wanting me to go. But now I feel like everyone stays here and if I also stay here and go to the same universities here with the same people I will not grow and meet new people and cultures. I also have family in Florida and I want to go and stay with them for a while and a lot of my dad's friends moved there. If I go and study in America, when I come back it is going to be much easier for me to get a job here. People will see that I have gone to a higher ranked university and made it there. Especially with the university I want to go to, which is the University of Florida. They have the best engineering faculty in the whole of Florida. So that is a good thing as I will have better facilities and better teachers.

The conversations with her parents and other members of her family do not seem to be in vain for Wandi because at her age she seemed to already have a personal sense of exposure to different people and cultures, she seemed to be alive to the unequal society we live in, she seemed to be alive to the rankings of universities and what it means for her, she seemed aware of her choices of universities and how best the faculty of her choice is. Naledi intends to study business management overseas because 'my parents also studied abroad. It will be a change of scenery, a new life style and different experience'.

Looking at the middle class female youth above as against their male counterparts, it shows a different picture. The exposure is the same but the OATS that is supposed to surround it is absent – thus the inability to see. Both Vuvu and Mzwandile have the same exposures as Karah, Wandi and Naledi, however they are not taking advantage of it to craft a different future for themselves. First with regards to their availability to exposure, they would rather opt out. None of them was involved in any of the school's sporting activities, and neither were they involved in any leadership committees of the school. Their only exposure was to themselves either alone or with each other. During school, their exposure was to each other through the Hip-Hop group *Usual Sxspects*. Their wish is for their parents 'to give us all the school fees money so that we can start our own Hip-Hop band with it'. After school, their only exposure was to themselves as individuals as Mzwandile put it, 'I fake sleep when my family members come in my room so they don't talk to me'.

For the working class, the first issue is that of exposure itself, which is very limited when compared to that of the middle class. Thabang is a case in point. He is

> …undecided as to where I am going in January but I have options of the things I can do. My options are around business. I could further study marketing and business management so that I can start my own business in future. I have applied to various institutions but all have told me that I do not qualify to study with them based on my subject choices and my performance at school.

Thabang however confessed that

> I do worry a lot about my future, seeing that I am about to finish school in two months. I mean it is my life on the line, I am depending on being given access to study at university, despite all my applications being rejected thus far. So it simply means if I don't succeed to study at university, then it means I must start looking for a job.

Thus the absence of exposure has meant a number of realities for Thabang. His choice of subjects are not aligned to his intended career choices. His performance at school has also not been up to the level warranting admission to his intended institution. As a result of all this, Thabang is 'undecided as to where I am going in January'. The same worries about the lack of exposure and its implications for the future affect Nelo. Nelo worries about the future every day.

> What if something goes wrong, I ask myself daily. I worry most about the financial issues and where my life is going. I am always thinking about the risks I must deal with every day, like what if I meet a guy who is going to spoil my future, before I know it I am pregnant and having children with no career and no money?

The fears that Thabang, Mercury and Nelo express are real. The exposure that working class youth tend to experience is that which easily serves as an antibook to the capacity to aspire. One of the early exposures in life for Nelo related to being sexually active at a young age of 14. Upon reflection of this kind of exposure, with hindsight at 17 years, Nelo believes it is a good thing for youth to be sexually involved from an early age 'because you learn a lot about yourself and others from an early age and you are able to manage relationships better when you are older'. She thus sees nothing wrong with her having been sexually active since she was 14 and also drinking alcohol at the time. This is all part, according to her, of gaining the necessary life experiences one might require later on in life.

Mercury in turn believes that part of the reason why most township youth and his friends misbehave is because of the exposure to, and influence of the local Hip-Hop industry. That is why

> ...because of these local musicians, they glamorise these bad behaviours since everybody is listening to music. They are destroying the community, to be honest. That is why youth these days always go to the parks and smoke marijuana and buy beers, busy with girls always. It is because of these musicians, they glamorise these things because there is no one who is not listening to music. Most youth are going to these parks drinking codeine and smoking, like 80%. This happens from an early age. It costs less than half of what nyaope (a drug) costs. A stash of nyaope costs R70 and you have to keep on buying more of it to remain high, which is why it makes people addicted to it and they start stealing from the community to feed their addiction.

The middle class female youth were decisive regarding their 'January' largely due to the OATS of exposure that advantages them. Middle class male youth on the other hand, as a result to their reluctance to take advantage of the exposure in front of them due to the absence of OATS, were undecided about their 'January'. Working class youth were all also undecided about their 'January', but mainly due to the utter lack of exposure that forms part of the disadvantage of working class life.

The OATS of Job Shadow

Job shadow forms

> ...part of career exploration in middle school or early high school years; students observe an employee at a workplace for a period of hours, a whole day, or in some cases, over several days, to learn about the business, industry or profession. Students do not perform productive work and are not paid for the experience.
> (Gray & Albrecht, 1999)

There is a lot of OATS embedded in the act of job shadowing itself, which is however class based. Much as schools as institutions of learning can embrace and encourage the job shadowing, its realization however relies significantly on families as separate institutions to the school. It is usually the family, or more specifically the parents, that facilitate the act of job shadow for school going youth. As a consequence, children of working class parents, who in the context of South Africa might themselves not be employed, tend to automatically be at a disadvantage compared to their middle class counterparts – whose parents are likely to either be employed or are employers themselves.

In both Karah and Wandi's cases, who are middle class female youth, their parents are not only employed but are employers themselves. Karah did job shadowing every year since Grade Nine as part of the school programme.

> Once I went with Wandi to see a Medical Doctor in Grade Nine.
> This year we had to go for two days, I went to see a Neurologist
> and I went to see my uncle who is a Mechanical Engineer in
> aeronautics.

Thus Karah and Wandi do job shadow in other fields not necessarily related to their intended fields of study. In Karah's specific case, she never felt the need to specifically job shadow her sister who works in her intended field of study. Naledi, also a middle class female, 'work shadowed in neurology at Steve Biko Hospital and I actually fainted during the work shadow process. Then I realised that neurology is not for me'. She is now aspiring to do business management. From these middle class female youth there are a number of key elements that emerge in their specific cases. Firstly is the broad range of job shadow experiences that they go through over multiple years of their high school life. What this broad range does is expand their horizons about what is out there and what is possible, I refer to this element of the OATS theoretical construct as a tool, and more specifically the notion of windows that I propose. It is about building windows around these youth that enable them to see further and wider. This broad range of options also transfers agentic transactions which in turn inform rich agentic capabilities. Thus Naledi's notion of 'then I realised that neurology is not for me', is a rich agentic capability that she is exercising ahead of making choices about her future. It thus prompts a different intended space for her – capacity to aspire – in a different field of business management.

Contrast the three middle class female youth with their male counterparts – then you have a case of job shadow gone wrong in Vuvu's case. Whilst the agentic transactions of job shadow are important and necessary, they must however not be to the detriment of agentic capabilities that would still need to be realized on their own. Naledi's agentic capability, which triggered a different intended space, can only be realized and experienced by her, but not imposed through an intransigent agentic transaction – as is the case with Vuvu. Vuvu, despite his middle class life, does not 'want to work in an office, I'd rather just do that (online trading) than work in an office'. But the job shadow opportunities that Vuvu was exposed to were all office based work opportunities – which is something he did not like. Vuvu's ambition and purpose, of being a Chef, is a path that does not mirror that of his parents. As a consequence, Vuvu does not feel he gets opportunities to practise his future because the things he wants to do in future are not the things his parents and the school are teaching and preparing him for. So he seems to have consciously decided to switch off because his main interest is to become a Chef – he 'does not want academics'.

For the working class, job shadow opportunities are largely limited. None of the youth have had any job shadow opportunities either through school or their respective families. Thus for Thabang, the implications of this absence has been that even in his own choice of human resource management – which he upfront points out 'is not a scarce skill area', he faces the same risks of not being able to alter his terms of recognition. Thus Thabang's career choice is not based, as is the case with middle class female youth – on a broad range of options or what is for them or not – but 'because it is easy'. This in Thabang's view is also caused by the

> ...career limiting choices we are given by the school. During career guidance, we are shown very few career options that we can follow, so we do not know what is out there. They never come to our school and show us options we have never heard about, it is always the same old things that everybody has done. Even the teachers do not seem to know more than us, as long as you can get a job; that is all everyone is worried about. Even our elders themselves; they are struggling and have no idea what options are there.

Thus the entire OATS theoretical construct and its realization through job shadowing is absent for working class youth.

The OATS of Social Media

Subrahmanyam and Greenfield (2008) remind us that,

> ...for today's youth, media technologies are an important social variable and...physical and virtual worlds are psychologically connected; consequently, the virtual world serves as a playing ground for developmental issues from the physical world.
> (Subrahmanyam & Greenfield, 2008)

Ahn (2011) further points out, referencing Ito et al. (2009) and Jenkins (2006), that 'many scholars suggest that students learn in new ways using social media and that educators should embrace these new platforms'. Ahn further suggests that, SNS (Social Network Site) use is related to self-esteem and psychological well-being. Adolescents who frequently use an SNS have more friends on the site and also more reactions on their profile (i.e. friends posted more comments and wall posts). In addition, researchers report that having more positive reactions on one's SNS profile is correlated with higher self-esteem, and higher self-esteem is significantly correlated with satisfaction with life. The results highlight the emerging sense that the use of SNS itself does not cause feelings of well-being. Rather, the positive or negative reactions that youth experience within the site are a key mechanism for their social development (Ahn, 2011). Thus social media, associated with the 'reactions that youth experience' (Ahn, 2011), can be a key lever towards one's realization of the capacity to aspire. The OATS of social media can thus serve as a platform for resistance and/or confirmation.

Among the middle class female youth Karah, unlike Wandi, was allowed to have a cellphone since she was 12. She has Instagram and WhatsApp accounts. She uses Instagram 'just to look at peoples photos and get ideas on what to paint' in terms of her art projects. She shares her drawings online to elicit the kinds of 'reactions that youth experience'. Wandi on the other hand mainly uses Facebook to post pictures of herself and various pictures of the art she draws to elicit the same reactions.

Middle class male youth are also active on social media, but in slightly different ways. Vuvu uses social media to stream and watch various content that is posted online. He 'prefers streaming rather than TV'. The main channel that he tends to stream is '*buzzfeed*'. This is the site Vuvu indicated he uses to 'watch videos about food and how it is cooked'. From another different website I came across Vuvu's drive to make money beyond the binary options and the school fundraisers – the www.olx.co.za website. Vuvu has an open account on olx.co.za which he uses to sell some of his used PlayStation games. Mzwandile also prefers to stream videos on the internet through YouTube and *Buzzfeed*.

> The channels I tend to watch on *Buzzfeed* are those that do various kinds of experiments. For example you can go to a person and recite lyrics and see if they can recognise them.

There is thus a more utilitarian aspect to middle class male youth's use of social media which is different from the female middle class' use which is reaction dependent. Both these uses are however key to feeding the capacity to aspire.

For middle class female youth, the reactions that they experience with regards to the art they post seems to provide them with a sense of confirmation that feeds their capacity to aspire. More directly so for Wandi than Karah. Wandi's ultimate choice of career – civil engineering – is closely tied to her artistic abilities, whose social media confirmations can only serve to enhance and solidify. For Vuvu – a middle class male youth – he is attempting to ensure that 'the virtual world serves as a playing ground for developmental issues from the physical world' (Subrahmanyam & Greenfield, 2008). His aspiration to become a Chef and businessman, outside the office, can only be experienced in the virtual world since the physical world seems to be blocking him. Thus *Buzzfeed* serves as Vuvu's intended space whilst his imposed space is different. For Mzwandile it is the exposure to experimentation that attracts him the most to *Buzzfeed*. Thus notions of agency, tools, and spaces that are inherent in my enhanced theoretical construct feature meaningfully in the OATS of social media espoused in this section.

For the working class however, social media provides a different platform. It seems to mainly feature as a platform to look for motivation, and/or inspiration and/or guidance. This search at times take a social tone, at other times a political tone. The main players providing such inspiration and/or guidance tend to be artists – mainly musicians – but also include authors and scholars and/or motivational speakers. Even though this search does not seem to provide the kind of meta-capacity that Appadurai talks about, it nonetheless provides some level of looking towards a future that is different from the current. For Thabang, according to his Facebook posts, '*positive thinking is half the work done*', or posts of Tupac Shakur and Nas' music. He seemed to be looking for some guidance towards calmness from his favourite artists. One of his posts referred to, '*Paranoid Stoners -_- Just be calm and ride along*'. Thus music for Thabang, which he accesses through social media, must do more than just provide sound – it is more importantly about the message. What I found telling was his attraction to Nas' music 'telling us to keep calm when we see white kids having plenty of stuff but you can't get them'. It is about deprivation and inequality, but keeping calm about it. This calmness permeates all of Thabang's life and informs his acceptance of many aspects of his life. These aspects include the family, the school, the government and society at large. Bragging by South African artists about money and girls did not get to him maybe because it might have enraged him when he needed to keep calm. What is very interesting about Nas music is that it is very sparse on instruments. What drives most of his music are the lyrics, which of course all of Rap music is based on, but his are deeper and more importantly, somehow uninterrupted. Nas is also a much older Rap artist and like Tupac, I would not have expected a 19-year old youth to listen to and enjoy.

Similarly for Thabang, he posted a lot of status updates linked to where he was and what he was doing, and commented on various other societal developments such as new song releases by his favourite Rap artists and soccer related developments. He also used the space to share his views on the political issues in the country and his views on them, such as commenting on the State of the Nation Address, '*Zupta must Fall!!! Zuma and Guptas!!! 2016 STATE OF THE NATIONA ADDRESS!!'* Akhona on the other hand used social media to look for guidance from various authors and motivational books. He told me that he

> ...bumped into this book when I was surfing the internet and bumped into some quotes by Michael Beckwith, who is a philosopher and I liked his quotes, which were so inspirational. So I discovered that he has a book and I downloaded it and saved it as a PDF file. I was shocked to discover the things he has written about.

All of Akhona's lessons and attitude were triggered by an ordinary surfing of the internet, bumping into a few inspirational quotes online, discovering books by specific inspirational authors, and reading them. He indicated that

> ...this is what this book has taught me. We all have choice, everyone has a choice, you just have to make your own choice and follow it. Everybody must read this book, it changed my life. Everything is a choice in life. The thoughts people have now are just under one thing and they don't realise who they are and their capabilities, which are endless and limitless.

Mercury, just like Thabang, is looking towards his favourite Hip-Hop artists for guidance. Also a fan of Tupac, Mercury posted the following lyrics of Tupac Shakur on his timeline

> I see no changes / wake up in the morning and I ask myself / Is life worth living? / Should I blast myself? / I'm tired of bein poor and even worse I'm black / My stomach hurts so I'm looking for a purse to snatch / Cops give a damn about a negro? / Pull the trigger.

For Mercury, the reason he is such a big fan of Tupac Shakur, an American Hip-Hop artist is because

> I think my life of being a philosopher is related to his. Tupac believed in fighting for the States and what he does not like about how they treated people. He was always thinking about the community and the people.

Thus in his endeavour to become a philosopher, there seems to be a strong philanthropist element permeating through Mercury's wishes. His goal is closely linked to a notion of society, a feeling of doing good, and a drive to fight for the downtrodden and marginalized. Mercury felt that

> South African Rap artists are not inspiring. They are always rapping about girls and money. I like people who give advice to the community, not people who destroy. I don't like their lyrics. Like Casper Nyovest, he only sings about money and girls.

Mercury believes that 'music is not just music. Music means a lot, to be honest. I don't feel comfortable supporting local music when I don't get what I am expecting'.

In some way it would seem that the guidance working class youth were looking for online was linked to the realities of their working class lives. They were aware and conscious of their circumstances and the need for something to change either through 'positive thinking' (Thabang), making 'your own choice' (Akhona), or even pulling 'the trigger' (Mercury). It is this kind of consciousness that is supposed to feed the capacity to aspire. However, without the necessary OATS that injects it with agentic transactions, with the absence of tools, and limiting imposed spaces, it is unlikely to result in the kind of meta-capacity as espoused by Appadurai.

Social media impacts on both youth objects of aspiration, be they immediate or intermediate, in a number of ways. For Nelo, Thabang and Mercury – all working class youth – social media seemed to be playing an important part in shaping their objects of aspiration. Thabang saw all these objects of aspiration as being immediate, and sought to extract himself from them without much success. Mercury used such immediate objects of aspiration to attempt a connection with more intermediate objects of aspiration through becoming a philosopher and a poet – similar to the poets he saw online – also without much success. Nelo on the other hand seemed to embrace the immediate objects of aspiration that social media provides through her role model identification with celebrities such as Bonang Matheba. For Vuvu on the other hand, through online trading, he could see the immediacy of immediate objects of aspiration.

Social media also brings with it the power of agentic transactions. In the absence of valuable regenerative resources in the townships, working class youth increasingly used social media to access the kinds of agentic transactions that they would not have ordinarily had access to. Nelo's access to a celebrity such as Bonang Matheba is a case in point. Through this celebrity, there seemed to be a transfer of agentic transactions which shaped Nelo's agentic capabilities, and thus her prospects for the future and what she herself posts online. Her own beauty and how she presents it online with the hope to realize similar dreams to those of Bonang emerged. Thabang, Mercury and Akhona used social media to access agentic transactions from celebrities such as Tupac Shakur, who 'tells us to be calm'. They own these lyrics and post them as reflecting their intended spaces, which I return to later below.

Social media can also serve as a window into the future. The kinds of books that Akhona started reading, which he indicated as key to changing his life, form part of the exposure social media presents. To use Appadurai's metaphor, social media can present a map of the future, even though it is unlikely to provide the required navigational tools.

Social media is also more about the intended space rather than the imposed space. Social media only features as an imposed space in terms of the kinds of resources it requires – mobile instrument and data. These requirements bring with them the kind of class divide that benefits the middle class and disadvantages the working class. Limited as the access for the working class might be due to the resource constraints, social media however remains an important feature for the working class in South Africa, thus access remains present. It therefore seems to shape the intended space of both working and middle class youth – feeding hope and their ability to imagine.

The OATS of Congregation

I am using the concept of congregation here in an attempt to capture an assembled group, which is usually a community of some form or another – usually religious. The youth under study belong to various forms of congregations which serve, or are intended to serve, different purposes.

In the case of middle class female youth such as Wandi, she and her family belong to a church and prayer group, whose members are very close to each other. Some of these families have become Godparents to Wandi and her siblings. Wandi indicated that she derived most of her values and beliefs from church because 'we are actually very big on church' at home. Much as Wandi believes in the church and attends all activities associated with the church, she however does not agree with everything that the church preaches and what her parents say to her.

> ...For instance, they don't believe in transgender people and that they are born like that. They believe that it is just an excuse. They just have an old fashioned way of thinking and haven't really adapted to the new world we leave in.

Wandi believes that transgender people are born like that and that it is not just an excuse but who they are and must be accepted as such. 'It is not our place to judge, like in the bible it says God will judge them, not us. We shouldn't treat them any differently'. For Naledi, she and her family also attend church services every Sunday and are part of the broader church community. Her grandfather is also a preacher, which has significantly influenced the family. As part of the church, they do a lot of outreach programmes and visit various communities to support and reach out. Naledi values 'honesty, prayer, and respect for everybody, and not to look down on people and speak up for yourself because life is short; and be loving and caring'. Thus for both Wandi and Naledi, being part of and participating in their respective congregations seemed to have triggered both agentic transactions and agentic capabilities – not always in sync but at times in conflict. Wandi seemed to have exercised her agentic capabilities by choosing which aspects of the agentic transactions she was receiving from her congregation to accept, and which ones to reject. Thus, much as she accepted most of the values and beliefs that were transacted, she however rejected those transactions that she regarded as 'old fashioned'. These agentic transactions of the congregation that both Naledi and Wandi experience also impact in various ways on their choice of objects – which tend to be intermediate, and provide tools and put them in spaces that feed the capacity to aspire. Not judging and being caring, as both Wandi and Naledi put it respectively, is as much about hope as it is about an intended space.

The same is however not the case for middle class male youth. Much as both Vuvu and Mzwandile also form part of a congregation, their extraction of the OATS theoretical construct from it in a manner that feeds their capacities to aspire is largely absent. Vuvu attends church every Sunday with his parents, though there is

> ...nothing I am getting from the church. I only attend church because my parents say we must go. I would have only preferred for my parents to force me to attend only school and not church on top of that.

Even though Vuvu would indicated his preference for school rather than church, his apathy towards school on the other hand nullified his contrasting of school with church. In Mzwandile's case, he attends church every Sunday with his parents in the same area. He further reckoned that church

> …helps me define my relationships with others and how to respect
> and nurture them; also with my family. These are the kinds of
> teachings I take with me from attending church.

Unlike Vuvu, who seemed to gain nothing from the congregation he belongs
to, Mzwandile seemed to be taking something out, albeit not translating as much
into his everyday life.

The practise of belonging to a congregation could also be found among
working class youth. Nelo attends church frequently, as do most members of her
family. She goes to church most Sundays. She however did not regard herself as

> …necessary religious. It is just that that is how I have been brought
> up. Everybody goes to church at home on Sundays. Church also
> teaches you certain things that you cannot find elsewhere. So it is
> not necessary useless.

Nonetheless, she felt parents tend to overplay the role of the church and the
difference it makes in one's life. This is because 'parents however do not understand us, they call us the *X generation*. They expect us to do things the way they
did them, and we are different'. For Thabang, his biggest apprehension was more
with the broader community within which he was located than the church itself.
Thabang felt that the broader community's role is negative on his life. 'The
community is just waiting for you to fail, *ke yona nthwe ba e shebileng fela* (that is
all they are looking for)'. He attributed this to the prevalence of failure in the
township. 'Because everybody else fails in the location, they also want you to fail'.
As a result,

> I was raised to be stereotyped and focus on one thing all the time –
> like church. When I was brought up I was told that church is the
> only way to be on the right path, which is not true and I don't want
> my children to be stereotyped like that. There are many people
> who do not go to church but who are on the right path, and many
> others who go to church but are on the wrong path.

This branching out seems to have informed the choices Thabang has made on
his own about his future path and how to traverse it. On the other hand, as a
regular church goer, there are things that Thabang felt he learnt from church
which have helped shape his outlook on his future in a positive way. He felt what
he learnt from church includes 'faith and trust and how to share with others'.
These are aspects of his church life that he continues to embrace. For Mercury, it
is the abundance of failure in the township that every other member of the
community

> …wants everybody else to fail because they themselves have failed.
> Because their children are failures, they also want and wish that I
> should fail just like their children. If you are doing a good thing,

they will still just have something negative to say about you just to bring you down.

Thus among the working class youth there is a deeper questioning of the role of the congregation, both church and community, of which they are members. This seems to be limiting the kinds of agentic transactions that could materialize, the tools that could be provided, and the intended spaces that could be created.

Congregation can be both imposed and intended space. For most youth, it is imposed on them without much choice – they have to attend church as instructed by their parents. It is also an intended space in many respects as it attempts to feed hope through preaching. This seems to affect both working and middle class youth equally.

Congregation is also about agency. It is one way in which – through both deeds and words – agentic transactions can take place. These agentic trans-actions are equally an attempt to shape agentic capabilities in specific ways, which are not always realized as intended. Many of the youth seem to exercise their own agentic capabilities which are not always in line with the agentic transactions provided.

Conclusion

It is generally accepted that 'working class schools in the black African townships are likely to persist in reproducing working class school leavers, with a few exceptional cases of upward social mobility' (Robins & Fleisch, 2014). Bowles and Gintis also make a powerful case along these lines (Bowles & Gintis, 2002). The absence of opportunities and resources to engage in extramural activities for the working class is well documented. The literature on social capital and cultural capital has over time helped us understand better the disadvantages inequality and poverty imposes on the working class. As pointed out by Bourdieu, social capital is 'the aggregate of the actual or potential resources which are linked to possession of a durable network of more or less institutionalised relationships of mutual acquaintance or recognition' (Bourdieu, 1985, p. 248). According to Bourdieu, these relationships and networks, which allow individuals to 'claim access to resources possessed by their associates', are minimal or simply absent for the working class both in terms of amount and quality (Schuller, 2000, pp. 1–39). The same can be said about cultural capital, as shown by Lareau in her study on social class differences in family-school relationships and the importance of cul-tural capital (Lareau, 1987, pp. 73–85).

The case studies of working class youth are not much different in this regard. The converse is also assumed to be correct, that as a consequence, middle class schools persist in reproducing middle class school leavers, with a few exceptional cases of downward social mobility. This is the argument that is equally central to Arjun Appadurai's conceptualization of the capacity to aspire – which is mainly about the working class and how to trigger their upward mobility through them changing 'their terms of recognition' (Appadurai, 2014).

This study is informed by nine case studies of black South African youth, four of whom are working class and the other five being middle class. Based on these nine cases, I can therefore not claim generality. I however, offer new knowledge in a number of instances. First, what it shows is that whilst it largely confirms what the literature says about the reproduction of working class school leavers, the cases of all middle class male youth seem to challenge mainstream literature when it comes to the reproduction of middle class school leavers. The reproduction of black middle class male school leavers seems to not be as given as the reproduction of middle class female school leavers and that of the working class youth.

However, I pursued an important nuance, which is not necessarily about class reproduction itself. This nuance is about the 'kinds of things' that feed and/or can break class reproduction itself – upwardly for the working class, and downward for the middle class. These kinds of things that feed the capacity to aspire are inherent in the OATS theoretical framework proposed. Whilst I do not provide evidence in any form regarding the future outcome of the youth under study, I nonetheless point to the centrality of the capacity to aspire, as further enhanced, as key to defining a different future. The notion of the capacity to aspire used thus goes beyond the conceptualization originally proposed by Appadurai. Appadurai had used poverty stricken communities in Mumbai, India to explore how, by providing such communities with the necessary maps and navigational tools, they could alter their conditions of poverty. I take this theoretical construct further by suggesting that what the capacity to aspire requires is more than just maps and navigational tools. Using both middle class and working class school going youth in South Africa, I propose the theoretical construct of OATS. In this construct, I suggest that we need to equally focus on *objects*, and *agency*, as much as we agree with Appadurai on the *tools* that he proposes, and further suggest that we appreciate the *spaces* that equally inform the capacity to aspire. I illustrate the applicability of this theoretical construct based on the youth studied in the nine case studies. Let me first expand a bit on the applicability of the OATS theoretical construct.

Just like the capacity to aspire, I am proposing OATS as a tool that could be used to realize such capacity, but more importantly, as a tool that is critical to altering the terms of recognition. Appadurai introduced the concept of the capacity to aspire as a way of understanding culture differently, as not only being about the present and the past, but more importantly about the future. This study has embraced this analysis and provides no further insight in that regard. Appadurai went further and introduced two concepts that he regards as the necessary tools to realize such capacity – maps and navigational tools. Whilst I accept these two tools proposed by Appadurai, I however argue that we need more than just the two tools. It is in this context that I propose the OATS conceptual framework. In my OATS conceptual framework I subsume Appadurai's maps and navigational tools into the third aspect of the theoretical construct, which is titled tools, and further suggest two additional tools that we need to realize the capacity to aspire. These are *windows* – which enable us to see further and wider into the future, and *social safety nets* – which allow us to make the necessary jumps assured of a safe fall should we miss our landing. In the first aspect of the OATS conceptual framework is objects, in which I differentiate between two kinds of objects, *immediate objects of aspiration–* which refers to short term wants which tend to take the form of material goods, and *intermediate objects of aspiration–* which are medium to long term and tend to show an appreciation of the relation between a wide range of ends and means. The second aspect of the OATS conceptual framework talks about agency, here I also propose two types of agency which include *agentic capabilities –* which focus on one's internal agency and the decisions and indecisions one is capable of making on their own, and *agentic transactions –* which focusses on the kinds of external transactions (interactions) one needs in order to make the decisions they are required to make. The last aspect of the OATS conceptual framework is spaces, again proposing two forms of spaces which are *imposed spaces –* which are about the current and the possibilities it provides of trialling the future and managing time as space, and *intended spaces –* which are about the future and how it is shaped through hope and imagination.

In this section, I used the OATS conceptual framework to delve deeper into the nine case studies. The aim was to understand and explain these case studies in relation to the value and applicability of the theoretical construct, and the extent to which both the cases and the construct can enhance the notion of the capacity to aspire.

Of the nine case studies, five of the teenagers' stories were very telling. A lot emerged from the comparison of the teenagers studied on the notion of the capacity to aspire – three of the middle class female teenagers, and the other two who are working class males. What was common among all these five teenagers was a strong presence of hope and their ability to imagine – the key precursors to aspirational capacity.

Hope is as futuristic a concept as Appadurai's conceptualization of culture as futuristic is. Intangible as it is, it is the only thing or feeling human beings can possess today, about tomorrow. With hope, human beings are able to locate themselves in a future they want to see and aspire towards. It is rarely concrete and does not provide any specific outlook, except a feeling. The ability to imagine however goes beyond hope. The ability to imagine is the process of putting the building blocks of the future today. It provides a specific outlook and gives shape to the future one aspires towards. In more specific terms, whilst one might simply hope for a bright and productive future, on the other hand one might also imagine him/herself as an astronaut or successful businessman/woman in the future. Hope and the ability to imagine are theoretical constructs highlighted as key to one's realization of the capacity to aspire. These constructs borrow heavily from Appadurai's conceptualization of 'the politics of hope'.

Both working class teenagers and the middle class girls were quiet hopeful about their own future and were able to imagine themselves in that future in one way or another. For the middle class girls, this hope and ability to imagine would be about maintaining middle class life. For working class teenagers, it was about escaping working class life and altering their terms of recognition. Secondly, all these youth have their own presence into the future in common, even though they see the future with different eyes. Middle class female youth see the future and the possibilities it holds for them, whilst working class youth see the future and the obstacles that lie ahead.

There was quiet a differences between the three middle class female youth and two working class teenagers under study. Whilst middle class female youth tend to understand that their future requires a combination of various skills and abilities over and above those offered in the traditional school and academic environment, working class teenagers on the other hand tend to have a self-defined, very narrow path that limits them to only school and academics. Secondly, middle class female youth could see their pathways in more specific career terms, with the richness of possibilities, options, expectations, requirements, and implications. Working class teenagers on the other hand tended to lack the necessary career details.

What can we learn from the five teenagers about the capacity to aspire? And what implications do these cases carry for the OATS conceptual framework?

Three categories of the case studies undertaken in this project serve to confirm the abovementioned conceptual framework. In three of the four groups studied, it would seem true and applicable, except in the case of the middle class male youth. The reproduction of family scripts and inheritance codes, which fall under what I call agentic transactions, is clearly visible when looking at black middle class female youth. These youth's choices of the future and its possibilities is shaped by those before them who are located within the family structure.

Parents generally seem to have a major influence on these middle class female youth's capacities to aspire. They constantly indicate how their parents influenced them. As Naledi indicated with regards to her inheritance codes, her 'mom influences me a lot cause she is a Scientist – a Microbiologist'. On the other hand Naledi's father provides her with the family scripts in that,

> ...my dad owns his own small micro lending business. Hopefully I will run my own business one day, but my dad says 'it is tough to start your own business. But when running your own business things will go wrong and you must take risks and invest. But if you are sure then go for it'. His friend owns Roman Pizza and he tells me stories about how he managed. He takes me to his work sometimes, now and then; just to see what he does because that is hopefully something I want to do and to see how it is done. I help him with stuff and he says I will be a great assistant.

Evident in their choice of subjects from Grade 10 onwards, there seemed to be a strong family influence. Some of the middle class female youth's choices of subjects were influenced by their 'grandfather who was a Geography teacher himself', 'sister who also majored in Accounting', and other related members of the extended family. When probed further as to what about the fact that her grandfather was a Geography teacher and would have pulled her into choosing the same subject, the reasoning from Wandi's inheritance code was not much deeper than 'I was just curious as to why my grandfather became a geographer'.

In most of these youth pronouncements about their futures, they constantly talked about 'my parents also', 'my dad says', 'my mom is', 'he (dad) tells me stories', 'see what he (dad) does', 'help him (dad) with stuff' and the like. These references all point to the provision of family scripts and inheritance codes as inputs the families provide to these youth.

As a consequence, reconnecting with Ball's notion of family scripts and inheritance codes, it would seem that middle class female youth are conscious of and absorb these agentic transactions from parents, brothers and sisters, uncles and aunts who tend to be fairly educated. These elders of the family also tend to be closely involved in their children's activities – 'she picks me up every day' and 'few weeks ago my dad asked me what I wanted to study one day. And my mom is also always asking me the same things. My parents are very supportive of my decisions', which provides for what I would call map and navigational tool provision opportunities and spaces; and what Lareau calls 'concerted cultivation'. Whilst the youth themselves might not be 'keen to talk to parents about careers because it causes too much stress for me', these elders are nevertheless not relenting in engaging such youth about such matters – persistently and constantly rerouting and redirecting their agency and tools.

Chapter 5

Conclusion

Introduction

This research was informed by case study methodology. There are nine case studies informing it, comprising black urban young men and women at the crossroads of their lives. The black youth that were chosen were between the ages of 16 and 18 years, and were in their last two years of schooling – Grades 11 and 12.

What these youth had in common was age, race, and an urban South African setting. They however had other traits not in common. The first being gender – four of them girls and five others boys. The second being class – five of them middle class youth, and the other four working class youth. Their urban setting also varied due to their class status.

The four working class youth were from Phiri Township in Soweto (South of Johannesburg). This is the area where I was not only born and grew up in, and thus a community which I am familiar with, but it is an area where I have also done detailed ethnographic work looking at the culture of learning. Thus through my networks in the community and knowledge of the area, I was able to secure random access to the youth that form part of the case studies covering working class youth.

The five middle class youth on the other hand were selected from Pretoria East, a wealthy suburb east of the capital city of South Africa, populated by top government officials, politicians, businessmen and diplomats. This area has been part of my adult life over the last 20 years of my working life as an aspirant middle class black South African. The youth randomly chosen in this setting attended the same school as my son, and live in the same area under generally similar settings.

The conceptualization of the notion of the capacity to aspire is grounded in the life of the working class. Amartya Sen – on capability, and Arjun Appadurai – on capacity – both grounded their work in the working class communities in India. Appadurai used this conceptualization to study slum communities in India (Mumbai) and how, by enabling their capacities to aspire through providing them with maps and rich navigational tools, they could reclaim their citizenship and extricate themselves from poverty and deprivation (Appadurai, 2004).

Thus over time, scholars have naturally tended to concentrate mainly on the working class in their further development of the concept, though increasingly

Black Youth Aspirations, 171–187
Copyright © 2022 Botshabelo Maja
Published under exclusive licence by Emerald Publishing Limited
doi:10.1108/978-1-80262-025-220211005

applying the work among working class late adolescents, and young adults. These include work undertaken by Aslaam Fataar in South Africa on a young Fuzile Ali and how religion helped him negotiate his own transitions in the city. Fataar's work was an attempt to open a window onto the lives of young persons' educational navigations in a democratic South Africa (Fataar, 2010). His analysis of a young boy's encounter with his schooling across the rural and urban land-scape, relates that his life circumstances were incommensurate with his desire to become educated. In Australia this conceptualization is being used to study learners from low socio-economic status with the aim of enriching their aspira-tional maps to participate and succeed in higher education. Some of the work done in this area in Australia has since been adopted into government policy (Bok, 2010; Commonwealth of Australia, 2009; Prodonovich et al., 2014). Thus most scholarly work on the capacity to aspire has similarly been about the absences of resources that would restrict people's acquisition of skills, knowledge and values that would translate into a unique capacity – the capacity to project oneself into a productive future.

As a consequence, the working class bias of most of the work on the notion of the capacity to aspire has meant that little comparative work has been done on class broadly, and gender in particular. It is this broad focus on class, and equally the specific focus on gender, that gives us new insights into what the capacity to aspire is about – and how it can be realized. Based on the work done by Appadurai, we had come to appreciate the importance of maps and navigational tools in shaping one's capacity to aspire, as per the navigational metaphor he utilized. Fataar also helped us understand how these maps and navigational tools could be imposed in describing how Fuzile Ali had to overcome difficult material cir-cumstances and forced mobility to realize his capacity to aspire for better edu-cation. With the broader class lens and gender focus of this research, we have been able to develop new insights into the notion of the capacity to aspire, but also new tools key to its realization.

There are three key new insights that I provide on the capacity to aspire, which I shall describe broadly first and later provide their related evidence.

- The first insight is about class. Contrary to mainstream analyses on the capacity to aspire thus far, the challenge of realizing aspirational capacity does not only affect the working class, it is a phenomenon that can also be a challenge for the middle class.
- Secondly, for young people such as those studied here, gender seems to play a key determinant in shaping one's capacity to aspire.
- Thirdly, for black urban South African middle class boys, there seems to be an additional element of alienation that has engulfed their lives, blunting their capacity to aspire.

Let me reconnect with the evidence to support these three observations arising out of my research. I shall begin with the issue of class. I shall first confirm the argument presented by Appadurai, Sen, and Fataar. The inability to see a different future and alter the terms of recognition through the realization of one's capacity to aspire seems to affect the working class the most. Of all the working class young men and women covered, none were able to see a different future. This despite them looking and having the desire to escape their current realities of poverty and hopelessness. Similarly, middle class female youth confirm Appadurai, Sen, and Fataar's contention that the middle class, due largely to their position of privilege, tend to possess the necessary capacity to aspire and realize a different future. I shall return to these two observations about the working class youth and middle class girls in more detail later.

The new insight which I want to focus on is about middle class young men. Despite their position of privilege and advantage, middle class boys did not possess much capacity to aspire. Not only were these young men unable to see anything, they were evidently not looking. The juxtaposition of looking and seeing is borrowed from Appadurai. Appadurai recently conceptualized what he terms mediants, materiality, and normativity. He argues that you can look, but not see. You can hear, but not listen. He posits that the eye (and its sensory-neural infrastructure) is the materiality through which seeing – as a practice of mediation – takes effect (Appadurai, 2015). To be able to imagine a future different from your current setting, in a manner that enables you to alter the terms of recognition, requires you to not only look, but to have the ability to see the future 'as a practice of mediation' taking effect. Middle class boys attended one of the most exclusive and most expensive private schools in South Africa, but they hated their presence there. Their wish was for their parents to give them the school fees so that they could start their own Hip-Hop band with it. They had already formed this Hip-Hop group and named it *Usual Sxspects*. One of them, Vuvu, saw a future for himself involving online trading – where all he would be required to do would be to trade online in binary options. As a result, they had already opened accounts to trade in binary options and used their time in class to practice and perfect their intended future careers. These actions do not alter the terms of recognition for a better future. Binary options are simply a gambling hobby that anyone can practice, it does not feed the capacity to aspire to bigger goals in life – what I call intermediate objects of aspiration. Hip-Hop and the celebrity life it provides does not necessarily alter the terms of recognition, the best that it provides is access to immediate objects of aspiration– bling, nice cars, nice clothes, alcohol and other material things – what Appadurai refers to as 'wants rather than needs'. The most immediate and visible inventory of wants which often led students of consumption and of poverty to lose sight of the intermediate and higher-order normative contexts within which these wants are gestated and brought into view (Appadurai, 2013).

The role of gender in shaping one's capacity to aspire is the second new insight that this research provides, as evidenced among the middle class young men and women. This insight would not have been possible had one only used working class case studies. This is because for the working class, some of these nuances are easily lost in the bigger picture of the challenges confronted by working class youth of poverty – inclusive of mere absence of parents (see for example the report

State of South Africa's Fathers by the Human Sciences Research Council and Sonke Gender Justice, 2018), and lack of a roof over one's head amongst others. It also became evident that Appadurai's argument of the need to provide maps and navigational tools has a gender bias for black middle class youth. Middle class girls seemed more receptive to maps and navigational tools provided by their mothers, whilst middle class boys seemed more receptive to maps and navigational tools provided by their fathers. When mothers are providing these maps and navigational tools, and fathers are not doing the same – then you have the disjuncture evidenced between middle class girls realizing their capacities to aspire and middle class boys not realizing theirs. The presence of middle class mothers in feeding the young girls capacities to aspire is evident in what these girls said both online and during the interviews conducted, as was similarly the case with the middle class young boys' absence of similar provision from their fathers. Whilst this absence could be explained, such as most fathers being the main sources of income for their homes and the mothers being stay-at-home-moms, the impact it appeared to be having among middle class boys in blunting their capacity to aspire was clearly evident as proven earlier. This leads me to my third observation.

The third new insight provided is the apparent alienation of middle class boys. Middle class boys are not only lacking in looking and seeing, they also seemed to feel alienated. This alienation proved to have invoked an element of anger and disconnection from the real world. Much as the same alienation and anger was picked up among working class boys, for working class boys it only confirmed what the literature has already been telling us, whereas it was new and unexpected amongst middle class boys. These middle class boys seemed to view their condition as that of disadvantage and no belonging. They felt that they did not belong to the school, they felt that they did not belong to their home, and felt that no one cared about them or understood them. At school, they were more comfortable to gather together after school at the students Wendy house under the tree and chit chat about their Hip-Hop group and how to get it going. Their school performance was poor and they did not want to participate in any of the school's extramural activities – unless forced to. At home they would rather lock themselves in their rooms and pretend not to see or hear anyone around their home. They only did and participated in things they were forced to participate in such as going to church. No one seemed to be communicating or connecting with them, especially not their fathers.

The case studies of young people, black young men and women from different positions within the class system, shows the extent of very differential access to the resources and opportunities that impact the capacity to aspire. The cases provide a compelling picture of how structural circumstances can expand, make no difference, but also limit young people's capacity to aspire. Confirmation of existing research was found in the way in which the case studies proved how middle class girls acquired and came to possessing the well-developed capacities to aspire. In contrast, despite many of the same advantages and resources, middle class boys displayed a different pattern. There was a marked contrast in how they used the same resources to aspire differently from their female counterparts. This is a particularly important finding as much of the existing research had assumed that class and race rather than gender would be decisive in the acquisition of the capacity to aspire.

In order to understand all of these new insights and nuances, I have built on the work of Appadurai and Fataar to create new tools that are key to shaping the capacity to aspire. These tools are in the form of a newly developed theoretical construct of *objects*, *agency*, *tools* and *spaces* – abbreviated as OATS. I am hopeful that these new tools have not only provided a deeper theoretical construct on the notion of the capacity to aspire, but that they will also help explain how structural circumstances relate to dreams that define a different future. Middle class males had the resources that come with middle class advantage, but lacked the dreams that could help enhance their own future differently. Working class youth on the other hand lacked the resources, but had the dreams and aspirations for a better life. Without the OATS however, both these groups of youth are doomed to a future of failure.

There are four key elements to the OATS theoretical construct.

The first is about aspirational Objects. I identify two kinds of objects of aspiration – *immediate objects* of aspiration and *intermediate objects* of aspiration. Immediate objects of aspiration do not feed the capacity to aspire, whilst intermediate objects of aspiration tend to feed the capacity to aspire. Examples of immediate objects of aspiration include material things such as expensive cars, clothes, alcohol – which according to Appadurai, often lead students of consumption and of poverty to lose sight of the intermediate and higher-order normative contexts within which these wants are gestated and brought into view (2013).

Intermediate objects of aspiration on the other hand may include a career, a profession, an expert, or some form of philanthropy. They are about higher-order normative contexts within which these wants are gestated and brought to view (Appadurai, 2013). There is a difference between wanting to buy the most expensive Nike shoe (immediate aspirational object) and wanting to develop the most expensive Nike shoe (intermediate aspirational object).

The second aspect of the theoretical construct is about Agency. I propose two kinds of agency. The first is what I call agentic capabilities, and the second I refer to as agentic transactions. The key difference between these concepts is that which talks to capabilities versus transactions. The concept of agency itself is well established in the literature (Marx, Weber, Bourdieu, Bandura, and lately Sen and Appadurai). Capabilities as a form of agency is mainly about the actor, or in this case, the aspirant – the black urban youth. It focusses on the kinds of agentic capabilities that they are able to exercise in the choices they make and routes they take towards their desired future. These choices were expressed both through the interview processes and online activity observed as part of the data collection process.

Transactions on the other hand are experienced from the outside, and are more about the spaces around the aspirant – what Appadurai refers to as the thickness of social life (2004). Ball and later Bok use the notion of transgenerational family scripts or inheritance codes to define how parents' own life journeys tend to inform and shape the paths their children ultimately follow (Ball et al., 2002; Bok, 2010).

The third aspect of the theoretical framework is about Tools. This concept seeks to expand on Appadurai's navigational metaphor of maps and navigational tools. I am proposing two additional tools over and above Appadurai's navigational tools, these are windows and social safety nets. I suggest that we need these additional tools for the following reasons: To be able to aspire you need to know what is out there. For you to know what is out there necessitates that you be surrounded by windows as enablers, rather than walls. The working class tend to be surrounded by walls unlike the middle class who tend to be surrounded by windows. However, as already shown through the middle class boys, the presence of windows does not in itself and on its own guarantee a capacity to aspire, one still needs to look through the windows and see what is out there.

Social safety nets on the other hand relate to one's ability to trial the future. Trialing involves risk taking, and no risks shall be taken without the comfort of available social safety nets. This too was a differentiator between the working class and the middle class. The middle class had available to them social safety nets that encouraged risk taking and trialing of the future as opposed to the working class, whose lack of social safety nets could mean disaster should their attempt to trial a different future fail.

The last aspect of the theoretical framework is about Spaces. Here again I identify two types of spaces – one imposed and the other intended. At the heart of the youth's imposed space is the concept of future trials. Future trials are mainly about the opportunities one gets, and the options one has, to test the future in the immediate. Future trials are imposed in the sense that they are they can be readily available to middle class kids rather than working class kids. They come in various forms such as job/work shadow and taking girl/boy children to work. They are an important element in shaping the capacity to aspire by not only showing what is possible in the future, but also doing it in advance of the future itself. Secondly, again as an imposed space, is the notion of time as space. I propose time as space as an imposed space in that it tends to be bound by the middle class/working class dichotomy, thus more prevalent among the working class. However, middle class boys also struggled with the notion of time as space. Time as space is elongated for some, and short for others. Those with a meta-capacity to aspire have so much to do in a day and so little time, whilst it is the opposite for those without any aspirational capacity.

Secondly in the aspect of intended space. There are two elements to intended spaces, one which I simply refer to as imagine, and the other which I refer to as hope. The capacity to aspire requires the ability to imagine, and see a future for yourself that does not yet exist in reality and at present. Thus Appadurai's conceptualization of the notion of mediants, materiality, and normativity comes to the fore here, which somehow connects with Einstein's theory of relativity. One can look, but not see. You can listen, but not hear. Derived from Appadurai's position that 'the eye (and its sensory-neural infrastructure) is the materiality through which seeing – as a practice of mediation – takes effect' (Appadurai, 2015); to be able to imagine a future different from your current, in a manner that enables you to alter the terms of recognition, requires of you to not only look, but to have the ability to see the future 'as a practice of mediation' taking effect. Looking alone does not allow for this practice of mediation to take effect, and thus stunts one's ability to imagine differently, and thus aspire differently. As a consequence, I suggest that the future is not as much of a 'loose leash' as one would assume, especially for the working class. One needs to have 'things' present in the visual space that feed the capacity to aspire. One must also be able to see these 'things', rather than just look at them, in order to imagine. The pressures and pain of the present do not seem to allow sufficient room or the luxury to imagine a future of a different kind.

The concept of hope borrows heavily from Appadurai's notion of 'hope to achieve' (2015), which is also about the 'politics of hope' (Appadurai, 2013). The concept of hope is also intrinsically linked to Amartya Sen's notion of freedom. It is thus not equally distributed, even though not an imposed but intended space. It is not determined, but influenced. Similarly, to hope without aspiring is the same as having a plan that you don't execute. Aspiration takes us closer to Nussbaum's concern with 'the exercise of function' (1997) or Appadurai's notion of 'materiality'. Similar to the 'meta-capacity' that Appadurai refers to (2013), the hope that I refer to here is also some sort of meta-hope. It is the hope which, as an intended space, allows one to 'reach valuable states of being' (Sen, 1993).

As a consequence, it would seem that middle class youth life does not guarantee a middle class future in the absence of OATS. Although, working class life proved to constitute a trap into future working class life. The key differentiator in this regard proved not to be class or race - but OATS. It is beyond the scope of this research to indicate why this is the case. Based on the case studies however, the presence and/or absence of OATS seemed to be gender based. With regards to boys, it appeared to have to do with their relationship with fathers, which is plausible, but remains at the level of hypobook.

Contribution to the Field

This research hopes to contribute to the field in three ways. First by confirming key aspects of Appadurai's notion of capacity to aspire and how it relates to the poor and their in/ability to 'alter their terms of recognition' (Appadurai, 2013). Secondly, it will seek to extend Appadurai's theoretical construct on the capacity to aspire by doing two things;

- It introduces a systematic conceptual framework to the concept of the capacity to aspire. Key elements of the systematic schema being introduced to the concept of the capacity to aspire are objects, agency, tools, and spaces – OATS.
- It presents the gender based bias of the concept of the capacity to aspire. It would seem that the feeding of aspirations for the youth is gender based.

Thirdly, this research challenges Appadurai's class-based analysis of the capacity to aspire – that of it being the preserve of only the middle class. Middle class male youth under study serve as a case in point in refuting such a class based analysis.

Confirm

In his attempt to explain how a capacity to aspire gets cultivated, Appadurai points out that, '...to aspire, like any complex cultural capacity, thrives and survives on practice, repetition, exploration ...the opportunities for such conjecture and refutation with regard to the future are limited' for the poor (Appadurai, 2013). Thus the rich tend to have ample opportunities to practice, repeat, and most importantly, explore the future they hope and envisage for themselves even before they reach it. These trials of the future consequently enrich the maps and navigational tools of the middle class than they would for the working class.

Aspiration is about desire, hope, longing, yearning and wishing – all of which are future oriented verbs. Thus the capacity to aspire as elucidated by Appadurai is futures based.

> It is in culture that ideas of the future, as much as of those about the past, are embedded and nurtured. Thus, in strengthening the capacity to aspire, conceived as a cultural capacity, especially among the poor, the future-oriented logic of development could find a natural ally, and the poor could find the resources required to contest and alter the conditions of their own poverty.
>
> (Appadurai, 2004)

Thus opportunities to practice, repeat, and explore – in the context of an attempt to illustrate the notion of the capacity to aspire – are all future oriented. As a consequence, the role and importance of trialling the future in shaping the capacity to aspire becomes critical.

Thus in confirming Appadurai's theoretical construct as indicated here, all middle class female youths had sufficient opportunities to trial the future, as against the working class youth who did not. Black female youths from the middle class institutionalized trialling of the future both within and outside the school. Their time as space as a consequence was also tight – the future for them was immediate. They did things immediately, including trials of their future, which would shape and impact on their future ahead.

The opposite is true for working class youth. They could not trial their future and could only live for the day. As a consequence, working class youth's time as space tended to be stretched, whilst that of middle class youth tended to be tight. For working class youth, tomorrow seemed like never. As Karah pointed out, we

> ...do work shadowing every time. The school also expects us to start work shadowing from grade nine. Choices of work shadow

vary from year to year and not always related to area of interest or future trajectory – it is nice to know and learn about other professions.

Parents played a role with regards to futures trials, as shown in Karah's case,

...sometimes I ask my mom to take me to places for work shadow and tour; and once I asked her to take me to the BMW factory because there was a time I wanted to do mechanical engineering.

Thus beyond the institutionalized school work shadow programme, the family based trialling of the future provides ample opportunities for practicing the future and its options. Thus all the middle class female youth interviewed had multiple opportunities to practice the future, even though they were not always aware that such spaces were in themselves opportunities to practice the future.

The opposite is however true for the working class. All of these youth have never seen and or met anyone already working in their intended fields of study. In the case of Thabang, in the absence of job shadowing arrangements both at school and home, he never had an opportunity to practise his intended field of study, 'except from soapies on TV'. Thus Thabang's view of his future – and the related 'practice', 'repetition', and 'exploration' – is all informed and based on what he saw on TV. Thus Appadurai's class based theoretical construct of the poor having less opportunities to practice, repeat and explore their futures as opposed to the rich holds for black working class youths whilst the opposite holds for the black middle class female youth. The class based theoretical construct however does not help us explain the patterns for black middle class male youth.

Appadurai's class based construct equally holds with regards to the presence of stepping stones and custodianship. All middle class youth had sufficient stepping stones and enjoyed the presence of custodianship – albeit more from mothers than fathers, whilst all working class youth had none. Working class youth also had no windows to enable them to see far and beyond, neither did they have any social safety nets to secure them when taking risks by venturing out. Working class youth also tended to focus on what Appadurai refers to as 'immediate objects of aspiration', whilst middle class youth – especially female middle class youth, tended to focus on what I refer to as intermediate objects of aspiration. Lastly, both what I refer to as agentic capabilities and agentic transactions also tended to be class based. Appadurai talks to this when he refers to Albert Hirschman's notions of 'loyalty', 'exit', and 'voice' (Appadurai, 2013; Hirschman, 1970). The aspect of voice is more prudent, especially in relation to what it represents in shaping the capacity to aspire. As pointed out by Appadurai, 'the faculty of "voice" in Hirschman's terms, and what I am calling the capacity to aspire, a cultural capacity, are reciprocally linked' (Appadurai, 2013). Appadurai further points out that

Voice is a critical matter for my purposes since it engages the question of dissensus... voice is vital to any engagement with the

poor (in this case youth), since one of their gravest lacks is the lack
of resources with which to give 'voice', that is, to express their
views and get results directed at their own welfare.

(Appadurai, 2013)

Thus the 'sort of meta-capacity' (Appadurai, 2013) that Appadurai talks to
when referring to the capacity to aspire, is in essence, a class based concept –

...because the better off, by definition, have a more complex
experience of the relation between a wide range of ends and
means, because they have a bigger stock of available experiences
of the relationship of aspirations and outcomes, because they are
in a better position to explore and harvest diverse experiences of
exploration and trial, because of their many opportunities to link
material goods and immediate opportunities to more general and
generic possibilities and options.

(Appadurai, 2013)

Middle class female youth, through their various opportunities to future trial –
work shadow – 'are in a better position to explore and harvest diverse experiences
of exploration and trial'. As a consequence, they have 'a bigger stock of available
experiences'. They have a 'complex experience of the relation between a wide
range of ends and means', and have 'opportunities to more general and generic
possibilities and options', through their demonstrated understanding in quotes
such as this, 'Sometimes I ask my mom to take me to places for work shadow and
tour and once I asked her to take me to the BMW factory because there was a
time I wanted to do mechanical engineering' Appadurai's quest to provide for
'real progress on the relationship between culture, poverty, and development'
remains as much a quest for this study as it was for him (Appadurai, 2004).

Extend

Appadurai proposed the notion of the capacity to aspire in the context of the
work he was doing focusing on slum dwellers in Mumbai, India. In proposing the
concept, he sought to provide some broad definitions of the capacity to aspire. He
defined it first as a cultural capacity – culture again understood here differently
from its everyday meaning. The capacity to aspire is a 'cultural capacity' and not
an 'individual motivational trait', and it is consequently shaped by knowledge and
experience (Appadurai, 2004). It is about changing 'the terms of recognition' for
the poor and marginalized groups of our society 'within which they are generally
trapped, terms which severely limit their capacity to exercise voice and to debate
the economic conditions in which they are confined' (Appadurai, 2015). It is
about 'how human beings engage their own futures' (Appadurai, 2004), and is an
attempt to extend Amartya Sen's (1980) notion of capability as 'a strong feature

of cultural capacity, as a step in creating a more robust dialogue between "capacity" and "capability"' (Appadurai, 2004).

Inherent in Appadurai's conceptualization of the capacity to aspire are two key concepts – capacity and aspire. In further elaborating on this conceptualization, Appadurai gives provides some deeper analysis of one concept and very little on the other. The concept that Appadurai defines a bit further is that of aspire. Appadurai uses what he refers to as a 'navigational metaphor' to elucidate further the concept of aspire. He sees the concept of aspire as requiring what he calls maps and navigational tools. According to Appadurai, the presence of maps and navigational tools – which are not equally distributed – is a form of capacity that is central to shaping aspirations. Appadurai's navigational metaphor helps us deal with the notion of aspiration at its basic level. It allows us to know where to go and how to get there. The youth sampled here should know what subjects to choose, for what career options, and what pass and entrance requirements are linked to their future trajectory. Maps and navigational tools however don't help us with complexity and detail, such as why we need the careers we have chosen (why we must go there) and what likely impact they will have on our lives and those of others (the consequences of us getting there or not getting there). To further enrich Appadurai's conceptualization, I propose that we need more than just the navigational metaphor of maps and navigational tools used thus far.

This research is in congruence with the broad definitions of the capacity to aspire as espoused by Appadurai. What Appadurai has however not done is to define in more detail what I refer to as a systematic conceptual framework of the capacity to aspire. Appadurai tells us that the capacity to aspire is a 'cultural capacity' (culture here understood as futuristic), and that it is shaped by 'knowledge' and 'experience' (Appadurai, 2004). To help us understand this conceptualization of the capacity to aspire better, Appadurai utilizes what he refers to as a 'navigational metaphor' (2013) of maps and navigational tools as key to shaping the knowledge and experience that is key to the realization of the capacity to aspire. This work extends Appadurai's theoretical construct by providing a systematic conceptual framework that shapes the 'knowledge' and 'experience' Appadurai refers to as critical to shaping the capacity to aspire. It further extends, through the systematic conceptual framework of the capacity to aspire as proposed, Appadurai's navigational metaphor of maps and navigational tools.

I have proposed that we define in more detail, the key elements of capacity, as against the key elements of aspiration, both of which are central to 'altering the terms of recognition' (Appadurai, 2013).

I presented these elements, both of capacity and those of aspiration, diagrammatically – with all four categories of youth studied plotted as per the analysis provided, informed by the case study findings (MCG = Middle Class Girls; MCB = Middle Class Boys; WCG = Working Class Girls; WCB = Working Class Boys) (Figs. 5.1 and 5.2).

I proposed to extend Appadurai's theoretical construct by proposing a systematic conceptual framework referred to as OATS, comprising of objects, agency, tools, and spaces.

Fig. 5.1.   Capacity/Tools and Aspiration/Objects Axis.

The first element of aspiration has to do with what I referred to as objects. I extended Appadurai's theoretical construct by more systematically differentiating between two types of objects – immediate objects of aspiration and intermediate objects of aspiration– by providing additional features of the construct. Immediate objects of aspiration are the kind that

> …emerge only as specific wants and choices: for this piece of land or that, for that marriage connection or another one, for this job in the bureaucracy as opposed to that job overseas, for this pair of shoes over that pair of trousers.
>
> (Appadurai, 2013)

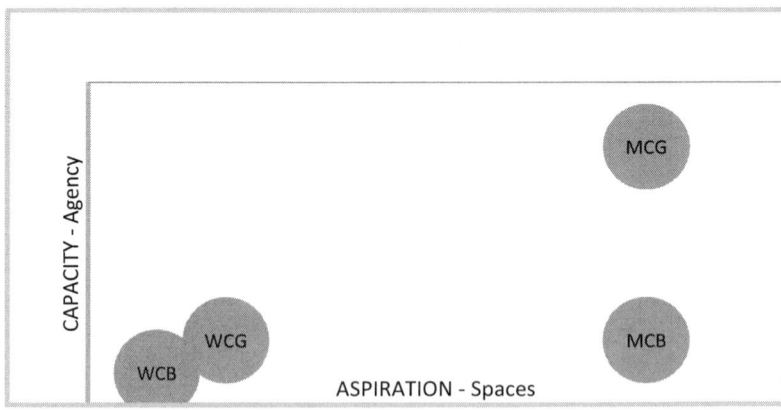

Fig. 5.2.   Capacity/Agency and Aspiration/Spaces Axis.

As Appadurai has correctly pointed out,

> This last, most immediate and visible inventory of wants has often led students of consumption and of poverty to lose sight of the intermediate and higher-order normative contexts within which these wants are gestated and brought into view.
>
> (Appadurai, 2013)

Intermediate objects of aspiration on the other hand focus on what Appadurai refers to as 'higher order normative context' (Appadurai, 2013). Put differently, intermediate objects of aspiration are about

> ...a more complex experience of the relation between a wide range of ends and means, because they have a bigger stock of available experiences of the relationship between aspirations and outcomes, because they are in a better position to explore and harvest diverse experiences of exploration and trial, because of their many opportunities to link material goods and immediate opportunities to more general and generic possibilities and options.
>
> (Appadurai, 2013)

Secondly, I proposed that capacity to aspire must also deal with another element, that of agency. Agency as a form of capacity must in essence deal with two key aspects. The first is the aspect of what I call agentic capability – which is more inward looking, and the second focusing more on what I refer to as agentic transactions – which is more outward looking.

Thirdly, I proposed that capacity must also deal with the concept of tools. Appadurai only deals with tools as part of what he calls a navigational metaphor – maps and navigational tools. I suggested that we need more tools than only those navigational to better feed the capacity to aspire. I have proposed two additional tools which are, windows and social safety nets.

The fourth and last key element of aspiration has to do with what I referred to as spaces. These are both what I refer to as imposed spaces and intended spaces. Imposed spaces are the inheritances of today and the realities they present to us either as enablers of future trials and time as space, but also the efficiencies that they either create or block in this regard. Intended spaces on the other hand look to the future in a manner that opens and/or closes our eyes to hope and imagine. Thus spaces form one element of aspiration.

I refer to this systematic conceptual framework of the capacity to aspire as the OATS conceptual framework of the capacity to aspire. The OATS conceptual framework, which I believe provides us with a systematic conceptual framework that feeds the capacity to aspire, is essentially about objects, agency, tools and spaces. These are shown in Fig. 5.3.

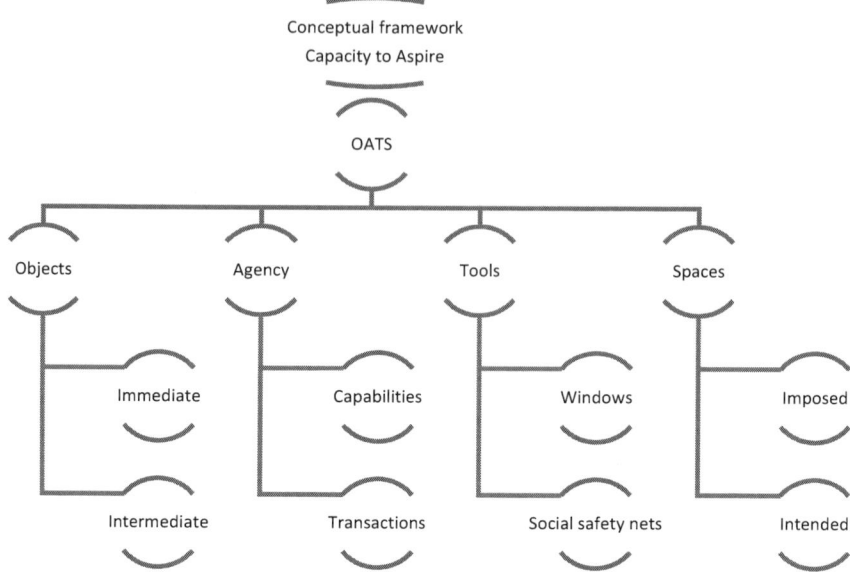

Fig. 5.3.   Conceptual Framework: Capacity to Aspire.

Challenge

There are three additional elements to the capacity to aspire, which go beyond just the class analysis Appadurai provides us with.

First is the issue of gender which seems to cut across class. From the case studies, it would seem that gender can be more important than class in defining one's capacity to aspire, especially for the middle class. Female middle class youth have role models whom they were able to hold onto for guidance – OATS. Male middle class youth seemed not to have role models that they could hold onto for guidance – OATS. The mothers were present for the middle class female youth and the fathers were absent for the middle class male youth. But unlike in the case of working class youth – where fathers were literally absent, for middle class youth these fathers were literally present, yet absent. Most studies on the capacity to aspire, including Appadurai's data, missed this element of gender because the construct has thus far only been used to understand the working class better, with no comparative analysis focussing also on the middle class. Thus the main challenge to Appadurai's construct is that, race, class, and most importantly gender seem to be key differentiators in feeding the capacity to aspire – and not just race and class as posited thus far.

The middle class at times also had no agency – what I call agentic capability, and also no 'voice' – using Appadurai's take on Hirschman's concept. Being middle class comes with certain expectations and pre-determined paths such as top private schools, top universities and top blue collar jobs. Middle class male youth seemed not to fit into any of these expectations and rituals, yet they had no voice, no agentic capability to choose their own paths. Even the middle class female youth had very limited voice and agentic capability in exploring their own paths. Thus the only exercise of voice for the middle class youth was through social media, where a great deal of their agentic capabilities and voice was coming through. Thus the assumption that middle class, based only on their class status, have agentic capabilities and voice can be challenged.

In terms of the choices they made, middle class female youth chose a conformist approach to charting their paths whilst middle class male youth chose a rebellious approach to charting their own paths. The class based argument of Appadurai has further been enhanced by literature (Ball et al., 2002; Bok, 2010) which has argued that youth who are born and grow up in families that have achieved the highest levels of education, economic and social status, are more likely to also achieve levels commensurate with their family standing. Pattillo has however, countered this argument with her theoretical construct of 'downward mobility' (Pattillo, 2013). The inverse is thus equally true for both middle and working class youth – displacing the class notion professed by Appadurai, Ball and Bok. Thus middle class male youth, a gap in the literature thus far, buck the 'inheritance codes' trend. What this shows is that what Ball describes as 'trans-generational family scripts' can also become what I refer to as transgendered family gaps created by the absence of OATS. Middle class male youth also experienced what I would call a future trials mismatch – which challenges Appadurai's class based argument. Their future trials did not seem to match their hopes and wishes, and no attempt to bridge this gap seemed to be in place. Working class youth on the other hand experienced a future trials gap. They simply did not get any form of opportunities to trial the future – no work shadowing, no role models and no proper career guidance. Thus their only opportunities to trial the future, as in the case of Thabang, was through television.

The second issue relates to Appadurai's construct with regards to provision versus extraction of what he calls maps and navigational tools. Two factors seemed to shape this phenomenon for middle class black male youth. First is their reluctance to extract, to use Appadurai's navigational metaphor, maps and navigational tools for own use. Thus again, unlike in Appadurai's argument, the responsibility to extract available maps and navigational tools remains the responsibility of the aspirator. But this still does not explain why middle class female youth were keen to extract available navigational tools and maps whilst their male counterparts were reluctant to extract the same maps and navigational tools for themselves – which I earlier argued is gender based. This talks to the second factor for middle class male youth – what Ramphele refers to as 'the absence of valuable regenerative resources', I refer to this simply as custodianship. It would also seem that the capacity to aspire, and the existence of maps and navigational tools, does not equate to their automatic utilization. It is key not only to study the existence/absence of maps and navigational tools, but also their utilization and/or lack thereof. Appadurai seems not to nuance the utilization aspect of maps and navigations tools sufficiently, especially in a context of young people of the age studied in this project. The middle class female youth studied have rich aspirations and have and are utilizing their rich maps and navigational tools. Informed by the narratives of their parents, the utilization of such maps and navigational tools seems to be partly shaped by acceptance and fear of poverty and suffering that they have never experienced themselves but only heard through storytelling. They attend the richest school, live in the richest estate, and yet they have as close a psychological affinity to poverty and deprivation which has only been narrated to them by their parents. On the other hand their male counterparts, who are equally middle class, again seemingly in the absence of fatherly engagement and lack of role modelling, chose not to utilize the maps and navigational tools availed in their space. What this shows is that the extraction of maps and navigational tools is not automatic and requires its own theorization in this regard, which I argue, has a strong gender influence.

The last issue with regards to Appadurai's construct is about pathways. Appadurai argues that the working class have 'rigid, less supple, and not strategically valuable' pathways. Equally, middle class black youth can also have as much 'rigid, less supple, and not strategically valuable' pathways as is the case with working class black youth. Middle class male youth seemed to emerge from families that did not provide pathways to them that were more strategically valuable, yet they were equally rigid and less supple. Take the case of Vuvu, who indicated that his main interest was to become a Chef – as he 'does not want academics'. He had raised this matter previously with his parents and asked that they remove him from an academic school and send him to a chef school.

This case in point has various dimensions. The intension of this middle class male youth to become a Chef is clear, and the determination is strong. However, it is also a reality, which could be informing his parents' rigidity and less suppleness in opening pathways, that there is very little space for celebrity Chefs to succeed. However, even if this were the circumstances informing the parents' rigidity in this regard, in this case, these parents – similar to working class youth and the poor – are equally providing pathways that are 'rigid, less supple, and less strategically valuable' (Appadurai, 2013). These parents, if Appadurai's theoretical constructs was holding for the middle class, could be exploring other 'chef' pathways for this middle class male youth. These could include business studies (leading to running own restaurant), they could include media studies (leading to conceptualizing own media programme) linked to being a Chef, and various other pathways which Appadurai would describe as flexible, more supple, and most importantly, more strategically valuable.

Future Research/Implications

This work has brought about multiple future research implications that are briefly indicated here. Firstly, the very conceptualization of the capacity to aspire, as originally espoused by Appadurai, opens up a great deal of scope in our attempts to not only understand poverty and underdevelopment, but more importantly on how we could turn it around for a better future. In the South African context burdened by decades-old oppression of the black population – whose legacy remains stubborn after 24 years of our democratic dispensation – realizing our black youth's the capacity to aspire can go a long way in 'altering the terms of recognition' (Appadurai, 2013). More work however remains to be done:

- The research is informed by case studies of nine black youth in an urban setting of both middle class life and working class realities. A spread of case studies and some additional triangulation with more survey based data that could cover more representative samples of black youth could go a long way in deepening our understanding in this regard. Rural youth could also present different dynamics from urban youth, which remain unstudied.
- The emergent black middle class in South Africa since 1994 needs more research beyond the economics of this group. Much as a lot is known about this group economically, very little is known about this group culturally – utilizing Appadurai's notion of culture as being about the future and not the past.
- With the youth forming the majority of the population in South Africa and globally, it is about time more and more research is dedicated to studying youth dynamics and their future prospects.

Bibliography

Ahn, J. (2011). The effect of social network sites on adolescents' social and academic development: Current theories and controversies. *Journal of the American Society for Information Science and Technology*, *62*(8), 1435–1445.

Anthony, G. (1984). *The constitution of society: Outline of the theory of structuration*. Berkeley, CA: University of California Press.

Appadurai, A. (Ed.). (1988). *The social life of things: Commodities in cultural perspective*. Cambridge; New York, NY: Cambridge University Press.

Appadurai, A. (1990). Disjuncture and difference in the global cultural economy. *Theory, Culture & Society*, *7*(2), 295–310.

Appadurai, A. (1996a). *Global ethnoscapes: Notes and queries for a transnational anthropology*. (pp. 48–65). Minneapolis, MN: University of Minnesota Press.

Appadurai, A. (1996b). *Modernity al large: Cultural dimensions of globalization* (Vol. 1). Minneapolis, MN: University of Minnesota Press.

Appadurai, A. (2004). The capacity to aspire: Culture and the terms of recognition. In V. Rao & M. Walton (Eds.), *Culture and public action* (pp. 59–84). Palo Alto, CA: Stanford University Press.

Appadurai, A. (2006). *Fear of small numbers: An essay on the geography of anger*. Durham, NC: Duke University Press.

Appadurai, A. (2013). *The future as cultural fact. Essays on the global condition*. London and New York: Verso.

Appadurai, A. (2014). Thinking beyond trajectorism. In M. Heinlein (Ed.), *Futures of modernity: Challenges for cosmopolitical thought and practice* (pp. 25−32). Bielefeld: Transcript-Verlag.

Appadurai, A. (2015). Mediants, materiality, normativity. *Public Culture*, *27*(276), 221–237.

Archer, M. S., & Archer, M. S. (1996). *Culture and agency: The place of culture in social theory*. Cambridge: Cambridge University Press.

Archer, M. S., & Archer, M. S. (2000). *Being human: The problem of agency*. Cambridge; New York, NY: Cambridge University Press.

Archer, M. S., & Archer, M. S. (2003). *Structure, agency and the internal conversation*. Cambridge: Cambridge University Press.

Aristotle, & Webster, E. W. (1923). *The works of Aristotle*. Oxford: Clarendon.

Aristotle, J. (1959). *Éthique à Nicomaque*. Paris: Vrin.

Aristotle, W. D. (1949). *Aristotelous Analytika=Aristotle's prior and posterior analytics*. Oxford: Clarendon Press.

Aristoteles, et al. (1959). *The works of Aristotle*. Oxford: Clarendon.

Atkinson, P. (1988). Ethnomethodology: A critical review. *Annual Review of Sociology*, *14*(1), 441–465.

Auerbach, C. F., & Silverstein, L. B. (2003). *Qualitative data: An introduction to coding and analysis*. New York, NY: NYU press.

Baillergeau, E., & Duyvendak, J. W. (2016). Social inequality and young people in Europe: Their capacity to aspire. In *World social science report*. ISSC and UNESCO, Paris, France.

Ball, S. J., Davies, J., David, M., & Reay, D. (2002). Classification and judgement: Social class and the cognitive structures of choice of Higher Education. *British Journal of Sociology of Education, 23*(1), 51–72.

Bamberg, M. (2011). Who am I? Narration and its contribution to self and identity. *Theory & Psychology, 21*(1), 3–24.

Bandura, A. (2001). Social cognitive theory: An agentic perspective. *Annual Review of Psychology, 52*(1), 1–26.

Bandura, A., & Walters, R. H. (1977). *Social learning theory* (Vol. 1). Englewood cliffs: Prentice Hall.

Barbarin, O. A., & Richter, L. (2013). *Mandela's children: Growing up in post-apartheid South Africa*. Oxfordshire: Routledge.

Barnett, C. (2004). Yizo Yizo: Citizenship, commodification and popular culture in South Africa. *Media, Culture & Society, 26*(2), 251–271.

Biko, S. (1973). Black Consciousness and the quest for true humanity, pp. 87–98.

Black, I. (2006). The presentation of interpretivist research. *Qualitative Market Research: An International Journal, 9*(4), 319–324.

Blumenfeld-Jones, D. (1995). Fidelity as a criterion for practicing and evaluating narrative inquiry. *International Journal of Qualitative Studies in Education, 8*(1), 25–35.

Bogatsu, M. (2002). Loxion Kulcha: Fashioning black youth culture in post-apartheid South Africa. *English Studies in Africa, 45*(2), 1–11.

Bok, J. (2010). The capacity to aspire to higher education: "It's like making them do a play without a script". *Critical Studies in Education, 51*(2), 163–178.

Bourdieu, P. (1973). *Cultural reproduction and social reproduction* (pp. 178). London: Tavistock.

Bourdieu, P. (1984). *A social critique of the judgement of taste (Traducido del francés por R. Nice)*. Londres: Routledge.

Bourdieu, P. (1986). The forms of capital. In I. Szeman & T. Kaposy (Eds.), *Cultural theory: An anthology 2011* (Vol. 1, pp. 81–93). Malden, MA: Wiley-Blackwell.

Bourdieu, P., & Passeron, J. (1990). *Reproduction in education, society and culture*. California: Sage.

Bowles, S., & Gintis, H. (2002). Schooling in capitalist America revisited. *Sociology of Education, 75*(1), 1–18.

Brewer, J. (2000). *Ethnography*. New York, NY: McGraw-Hill International.

Bruner, J. (1991). The narrative construction of reality. *Critical Inquiry*, 1–21.

Buckingham, D., & Willett, R. (Eds.). (2013). *Digital generations: Children, young people, and the new media*. Oxfordshire: Routledge.

Carrim, N. (1999). School effectiveness in South Africa. *International Journal of Qualitative Studies in Education, 12*(1), 59–83.

Carrim, N., & Shalem, Y. (1999). School effectiveness in South Africa. *International Journal of Qualitative Studies in Education, 12*(1), 59–83.

Carter, P. L. (2003). "Black" cultural capital, status positioning, and schooling conflicts for low-income African American youth. *Social Problems, 50*(1), 136–155.

Castells, M. (2011). The rise of the network society: The information age: Economy, society, and culture.

Chabedi, M. (2005). Governing the ungovernable: Policing, vigilante justice, crime and everyday life in a post-apartheid city (Soweto). In IFRA conference, Nairobi.

Chatterjee, P. (2004). *The politics of the governed: Reflections on popular politics in most of the world.* New York, NY: Columbia University Press.

Christie, P. (1998). Schools as (Dis) Organisations: The 'breakdown of the culture of learning and teaching in South African schools. *Cambridge Journal of Education, 28*(3), 283–300.

Clifford, G. (1973). *The interpretation of cultures* (pp. 412–453). New York, NY: Basic.

Cohen, L., Manion, L., & Morrison, K. (2011). *Research methods in education.* Milton Park; Abingdon: Routledge.

Collins, P. H. (2006). *From Black power to hip hop: Racism, nationalism, and feminism.* Philadelphia, PA: Temple University Press.

Commonwealth of Australia. (2009). *Transforming Australia's higher education system.* Barton: Australian Government.

Corbett, M. (2016). Rural futures: Development, aspirations, mobilities, place, and education. *Peabody Journal of Education, 91*(2), 270–282.

Côté, J. (2014). *Youth studies: Fundamental issues and debates.* East Sussex: Macmillan International Higher Education.

Cross, M. (1991). Youth culture and resistance in South African education: A theoretical review. *Perspectives in Education, 12*(2), 33–48.

Cross, M. (1993). Youth, culture, and politics in South African Education: The past, present, and future. *Youth & Society, 24*(4), 377–398.

Cupchik, G. (2001). Constructivist realism: An ontology that encompasses positivist and constructivist approaches to the social sciences. *Forum Qualitative Sozialforschung/ Forum: Qualitative Social Research, 2*(1).

Dalton, P. S., Ghosal, S., & Mani, A. (2016). Poverty and aspirations failure. *The Economic Journal, 126*(590), 165–188.

Dass-Brailsford, P. (2005). Exploring resiliency: Academic achievement among disadvantaged black youth in South Africa: "general" section. *South African Journal of Psychology, 35*(3), 574.

De Certeau, M., & Randall, S. (1984). Walking in the city. In R. A. Guins & O. Z. Cruz (Eds.), *Popular culture: A reader* (pp. 449–461). London; Thousand Oaks, CA: SAGE Publications.

Deleuze, G., & Guattari, F. (1987). *A thousand plateaus B. Massumi (Trans.).* Minneapolis, MN: University of Minnesota Press.

Deleuze, G., & Parnet, C. (1987). *Dialogues.* London: Athlone Press.

De Munck, V. C., & Sobo, E. J. (Eds.). (1998). *Using methods in the field: A practical introduction and casebook.* Lanham, MD: Rowman Altamira.

DeJaeghere, J. (2018). Girls' educational aspirations and agency: Imagining alternative futures through schooling in a low-resourced Tanzanian community. *Critical Studies in Education, 59*(2), 237–255.

Delius, P., & Glaser, C. (2002). Sexual socialisation in South Africa: A historical perspective. *African Studies, 61*(1), 27–54.

Denscombe, M. (2008). Communities of practice a research paradigm for the mixed methods approach. *Journal of Mixed Methods Research, 2*(3), 270–283.

Denzin, N. K. (1970). *The research act in sociology.* London: Butterworths.

Denzin, N. K. (2008). The new paradigm dialogs and qualitative inquiry. *International Journal of Qualitative Studies in Education, 21*(4), 315–325.

Department of Education, Republic of South Africa. (1994). Draft white paper on education and training. *Government Gazette, 351*(15974).

Department of Higher Education and Training, Republic of South Africa. (2014). Fact Sheet on NEETs: Analysis of the 2011 South Africa census.

Dlamini, S. N. (2006). Youth and identity politics in South Africa, 1990–94. *Canadian Journal of Sociology*.

Dlamini, J. (2009). *Native nostalgia*. Johannesburg: Jacana Media.

Doecke, B. (2013). Storytelling and professional learning. *English in Australia, 48*(2), 11.

Dolby, N. (1999). Youth and the global popular: The politics and practices of race in South Africa. *European Journal of Cultural Studies, 2*(3), 291–309.

Dolby, N. (2001a). White fright: The politics of white youth identity in South Africa. *British Journal of Sociology of Education, 22*(1), 5–17.

Dolby, N. (2001b). *Constructing race: Youth, identity, and popular culture in South Africa*. New York, NY: SUNY Press.

Dreze, J., Sen, A., & Hussain, A. (1995). *The political economy of hunger: Selected essays*. Oxford: Oxford University Press.

Eddington, A. S. (1921). *Espace, temps et gravitation*. Paris: Hermann.

Elmore, T. (2010). *Generation iY: Our last chance to save their future*. Norcross, GA: Poet Gardener Publishing.

Emirbayer, M., & Mische, A. (1998). What is agency? *American Journal of Sociology, 103*(4), 962–1023.

Erikson, E. H. (1950). *Growth and crises of the healthy personality*. New York, NY: W.W. Norton and Company.

Escobar, A. (1992). Culture, practice and politics. *Critique of Anthropology, 12*(4), 395–432.

Everatt, D., & Jennings, R. (Eds.). (1996). *Developing a policy framework for out-of-school youth in South Africa*. Johannesburg: CASE.

Everatt, D., & Sisulu, E. (1992). *Black youth in crisis: Facing the future*. Johannesburg: Ravan Press of South Africa.

Fataar, A. (2006). Policy networks in recalibrated political terrain: The case of school curriculum policy and politics in South Africa. *Journal of Education Policy, 21*(6), 641–659.

Fataar, A. (2007a). Educational renovation in a South African "township on the move": A social–spatial analysis. *International Journal of Educational Development, 27*(6), 599–612.

Fataar, A. (2007b). Schooling, youth adaptation and translocal citizenship across the post-apartheid city. *Journal of Education, 2*(4), 17–32.

Fataar, A. (2009). Schooling subjectivities across the post-apartheid city. *Africa Education Review, 6*(1), 1–18.

Fataar, A. (2010). Youth self-formation and the 'capacity to aspire': The itinerant 'schooled' career of Fuzile Ali across post-apartheid space. *Perspectives in Education, 28*(3), 34–45.

Fine, M., & Ruglis, J. (2009). Circuits and consequences of dispossession: The racialized realignment of the public sphere for US youth. *Transforming Anthropology, 17*(1), 20–33.

Fine, M., & Sirin, S. R. (2007). Theorizing hyphenated selves: Researching youth development in and across contentious political contexts. *Social and Personality Psychology Compass, 1*(1), 16–38.

Finkel, S. E. (1987). The effects of participation on political efficacy and political support: Evidence from a West German panel. *The Journal of Politics, 49*(2), 441–464.

Flechtner, S. (2014). Aspiration traps: When poverty stifles hope. *World Bank Inequality in Focus, 3*(1), 1–4.

Fornäs, J. (2017). *Defending culture: Conceptual foundations and contemporary debate.* New York, NY: Palgrave Macmillan.

Foster Michael, K. (2004). Coming to terms: A discussion of John Ogbu's cultural-ecological theory of minority academic achievement. *Intercultural Education, 15*(4), 369–384.

Fraser, N., & Honneth, A. (2003). *Redistribution or recognition?: A political-philosophical exchange.* New York, NY: Verso.

Furlong, A. (Ed.). (2009). *Handbook of youth and young adulthood: New perspectives and agendas.* Oxfordshire: Routledge.

Furlong, A. (2012). *Youth studies: An introduction.* Oxfordshire: Routledge.

Gage, N. L. (1989). The paradigm wars and their aftermath a "historical" sketch of research on teaching since 1989. *Educational Researcher, 18*(7), 4–10.

Gale, T., & Parker, S. (2015). To aspire: A systematic reflection on understanding aspirations in higher education. *Australian Educational Researcher, 42*(2), 139–153.

Gans, H. J. (1968). The participant observer as a human being: Observations on the personal aspects of fieldwork. In *Institutions and the person* (pp. 300–317). Oxfordshire: Routledge.

Garfinkel, H. (1967). *Studies in ethnomethodology.* Englewood Cliffs, NJ: Prentice Hall.

Gibson, C., & Levine, P. (2003). *The civic mission of schools.* New York and Washington, DC: The Carnegie Corporation of New York and the Center for Information and Research on Civic Learning.

Giddens, A. (1984). *The constitution of society: Outline of the theory of structuration.* Berkeley and Los Angeles, CA: University of California Press.

Gill, J., & Zipin, L. (2017). *Identity, neoliberalism and aspiration: Educating white working-class boys* (pp. 619–625). Oxfordshire: Routledge.

Glaser, D. J. (2009). Teenage dropouts and drug use: Does the specification of peer group structure matter? *Economics of Education Review, 28*(4), 497–504.

Glaser, D. (2011). The new black/African racial nationalism in SA: Towards a liberal-egalitarian critique. *Transformation: Critical Perspectives on Southern Africa, 76*(1), 67–94.

Gold, R. L. (1958, December). Roles in sociological field observations. *American Sociological Review, 23*(6), 652–660.

Gorard, S., & Smith, E. (2006). Combining numbers with narratives. *Evaluation & Research in Education, 19*(2), 59–62.

Gorard, S., & Taylor, C. (2004). *Combining methods in educational and social research.* New York, NY: McGraw-Hill International.

Gould, S. J. (1987). *Time's arrow, time's cycle: Myth and metaphor in the discovery of geological time* (Vol. 2). Cambridge, MA: Harvard University Press.

Gray, W. W., & Albrecht, B. (1999). *Mentoring youth for success.* Publication Sales, Wisconsin Department of Public Instruction.

Gramsci, A. (1973). *Letters from prison: Selected, transl. from the Italian, and Introduced by Lynne Lawner.* London: Harper & Row.

Grotevant, H. D., & Cooper, C. R. (1985). Patterns of interaction in family relationships and the development of identity exploration in adolescence. *Child Development, 56*(2), 415–428.

Harber, C. (2001). Schooling and violence in South Africa: Creating a safer school. *Intercultural Education, 12*(3), 261–271.

Harrison, A., Xaba, N., & Kunene, P. (2001). Understanding safe sex: Gender narratives of HIV and pregnancy prevention by rural South African school-going youth. *Reproductive Health Matters, 9*(17), 63–71.

Hart, G. (2007). Changing concepts of articulation: Political stakes in South Africa today. *Review of African Political Economy, 34*(111), 85–101.

Hebdige, D. (1995). Subculture: The meaning of style. *Critical Quarterly, 37*(2), 120–124.

Hebdige, D. (1999). The Function of subculture. *The cultural studies reader, 2,* 441–450.

Hirschman, A. O. (1978). Exit, voice, and the state. *World Politics, 31*(1), 90–107.

Holston, J. (2009). Dangerous spaces of citizenship: Gang talk, rights talk and rule of law in Brazil. *Planning Theory, 8*(1), 12–31.

Howell, S., & Louise, V. (2014). Licking the snake – The i'khothane and contemporary township youth identities in South Africa. *South African Review of Sociology, 45*(2), 60–77.

Ito, M., Horst, H. A., Bittanti, M., boyd, d., Herr Stephenson, B., Lange, P. G., … Robinson, L. (2009). *Living and learning with new media: Summary of findings from the digital youth project.* Cambridge, MA: The MIT Press.

Jansen, J. D. (2009). *Knowledge in the blood: Confronting race and the apartheid past.* Stanford, CA: Stanford University Press.

Jenkins, H. (2006). *Fans, bloggers, and gamers: Exploring participatory culture.* New York, NY: NYU Press.

Josselson, R. (2006). Narrative research and the challenge of accumulating knowledge. *Narrative Inquiry, 16*(1), 3–10.

Kahne, J., David, C., & Nam-Jin, L. (2013). Different pedagogy, different politics: High school learning opportunities and youth political engagement. *Political Psychology, 34*(3), 419–441.

Kahne, J. E., & Sporte, S. E. (2008). American educational research. *American Educational Research Journal, 45*(3), 738–766.

Kao, G., & Tienda, M. (1998). Educational aspirations of minority youth. *American Journal of Education, 106*(3), 349–384.

Kennelly, J., & Dillabough, J.-A. (2008). Young people mobilizing the language of citizenship: Struggles for classification and new meaning in an uncertain world. *British Journal of Sociology of Education, 29*(5), 493–508.

Kreutzer, T. (2009). Generation mobile: Online and digital media usage on mobile phones among low-income urban youth in South Africa. University of Cape Town.

Lam, D., & Seekings, J. (2005). Transitions to adulthood in urban South Africa: Evidence from a panel survey. In IUSSP General Conference.

Lareau, A. (1987). Social class differences in family-school relationships: The importance of cultural capital. *Sociology of Education, 60*(2), 73–85.

Lareau, A. (2011). *Unequal childhoods: Class, race, and family life.* Berkeley, CA: University of California Press.

Latour, B. (1996). On actor-network theory: A few clarifications. *Soziale Welt, 47*(4), 369–381.

Latour, B. (2012). *We have never been modern.* Cambridge, MA: Harvard University Press.

Le Compte, M. D., & Preissle, J. (1993). *Educational ethnography and qualitative design research.* Cambridge, MA: Academic Press.

Lebra, T. S. (1992). Self in Japanese culture. In *Japanese sense of self* (pp. 105–120). Cambridge: Cambridge University Press.

LeCompte, M. D., Preissle, J., & Renata, T. (1993). *Ethnography and qualitative design in educational research.* Cambridge, MA: Academic Press.

Lewis, P. R. (1966). A 'city' within a city – The creation of Soweto. *South African Geographical Journal, 48*(1), 45–85.

Lincoln, Y. S., & Guba, E. G. (2001/1985). *Naturalistic inquiry.* VALLES, M. Técnicas. London: Vallentine Mitchell.

Lyotard, J.-F. (1984). *The postmodern condition: A report on knowledge* (Vol. 10). Minneapolis, MN: University of Minnesota Press.

Maggs-Rapport, F. (2000). Combining methodological approaches in research: Ethnography and interpretive phenomenology. *Journal of Advanced Nursing, 31*(1), 219–225.

Maja, B. I. (1994). *The breakdown in the culture of learning: A case book.* Johannesburg: Urban Foundation.

Maja, B. I. (1995). *The future trapped in the past: A case study of a Soweto secondary school.* Johannesburg: National Business Initiative.

Marks, M. (2001). *Young warriors: Youth politics, identity and violence in South Africa.* Johannesburg: Wits University Press.

Maxwell, J. A. (1992). Understanding and validity in qualitative research. *Harvard Educational Review, 62*(3), 279–301.

McAdams, D. P. (1993). *The stories we live by: Personal myths and the making of the self.* New York, NY: Guilford Press.

McMillan, H., & Schumacher, J. (2006). *Research in education evidence-based inquiry.* Oxford: Pergamous Press.

Metz, E. C., & Youniss, J. (2005). Longitudinal gains in civic development through school-based required service. *Political Psychology, 26*(3), 413–437.

Miles, M. B., & Huberman, M. A. (1984). *Qualitative data analysis.* Beverly Hills, CA: Sage.

Mokwena, S. (1992). Living on the wrong side of the law: Marginalisation, youth and violence. In D. Everatt & E. Sisulu (Eds.), *Black youth in crisis. Facing the future* (pp. 30–51). Johannesburg: Ravan Press.

Moloi, K. C. (2005). *The school as a learning organisation: Reconceptualising school practices in South Africa.* Pretoria: Van Schaik.

Morrow, W. (1988). Democratic schooling and the continental nuisance. *South African Journal of Education, 8*(3).

Morrow, W. (1989). *Chains of thought.* Johannesburg: Southern Book Publishers.

Morrow, W. (1992). Educational authority and community in a transforming society. Paper presented at the 3rd conference of the International Network of Philosophers of Education, Bulgaria.

Morrow, W. (1994). Restoring the culture of teaching. *Die Suid Afrikaan in Depth*, SAIDE, OER Courseware, Reading 6.

Motala, S. (1993). *Towards transitional governance: Policy and conflict in South African education and training*. Johannesburg: University of the Witwatersrand. Education Policy Unit.

Motala, S. (1995). Surviving the System-a critical appraisal of some conventional wisdoms in primary education in South Africa. *Comparative Education, 31*(2), 161–180.

Mundell, P. H. (1992). *Secondary schools in Soweto: A strategic appraisal*. Pretoria: University of South Africa.

Narsing, Y. (1989). *Learning in Limbo: Experiences of Schooling in Soweto, January–June, 1989*. Johannesburg: Education Policy Unit, University of the Witwatersrand.

National Treasury. (2011). Confronting Youth unemployment: Policy options for South Africa. Discussion paper.

Ndebele, N. S. (2017). They are burning memory. *Critical Arts, 31*(1), 102–109.

Nkomo, M. O. (1984). *Student culture and activism in black South African universities: The roots of resistance*. Westport, CT: Praeger.

Nkomo, M., & Vadeyar, S. (2009). *Thinking diversity, building cohesion: A transnational dialogue on education*. Pretoria: UNISA Press.

Ntshingila-Khosa, R. (1994). Teaching in South Africa: Observed pedagogical practices and teacher's own meanings. In Proceedings of a Seminar on Effective Schools, Effective Classrooms. Improving Education Quality Project, Cape Town.

Nussbaum, M. C. (1997). Capabilities and human rights. *Fordham L. Rev, 66*, 273.

Nussbaum, M. C., & Sen, A. (Eds.). (1993). *The quality of life*. Oxford: Oxford University Press.

Ogbu, J. U. (1990a). Minority education in comparative perspective. *The Journal of Negro Education, 59*(1), 45−57.

Ogbu, J. U. (1990b). Minority status and literacy in comparative perspective. *Dædalus*, 141–168.

Ogbu, J. U. (2003). *Black American students in an affluent suburb: A book of academic disengagement*. Oxfordshire: Routledge.

Ogbu, J. U. (2008). *Minority status, oppositional culture, & schooling*. Oxfordshire: Routledge.

Ogbu, J. U. (2013). Cultural boundaries and minority youth orientation toward work preparation. In *Adolescence and work* (pp. 107–146). Oxfordshire: Routledge.

Parlett, M., & Hamilton, D. (1976). Evaluations as illumination: A new approach to the book of innovatory programs. In Glass, G. (red.), *Evaluation studies review annual* (Vol. 1).

Pattillo, M. (2013). *Black picket fences: Privilege and peril among the Black middle class*. Chicago, IL; London: University of Chicago Press.

Patton, M. Q. (1990). *Qualitative evaluation and research methods*. Newbury Park, CA: SAGE Publications.

Pelser, E. (2008). Learning to be lost: Youth crime in South Africa. In *Discussion papers for the Human Sciences Research Council (HSRC) youth policy initiative* (pp. 1–14). Pretoria: HSRC Publisher.

Pinnegar, S., & Daynes, G. J. (2007). Locating narrative inquiry historically. In *Handbook of narrative inquiry: Mapping a methodology* (pp. 3–34). Thousand Oaks, CA: Sage Publishing

Polkinghorne, D. E. (1988). *Narrative knowing and the human sciences.* New York, NY: SUNY Press.

Powell, L. (2012). Reimagining the purpose of VET–Expanding the capability to aspire in South African further education and training students. *International Journal of Educational Development, 32*(5), 643–653.

Prodonovich, S., Perry, L. B., & Taggart, A. (2014). Developing conceptual understandings of the capacity to aspire for higher education. *Issues in Educational Research, 24*(2), 174–189.

Putnam, R. (2001). Social capital: Measurement and consequences. *Canadian Journal of Policy Research, 2*(1), 41–51.

Ramphele, M. (2002). *Steering by the stars: Being young in South Africa.* Cape Town: Tafelberg.

Randall, W. L. (2014). *The stories we are: An essay on self-creation.* Toronto: University of Toronto Press.

Ray, D. (2006). Aspirations, poverty, and economic change. In *Understanding poverty* (pp. 409–421). Oxford: Oxford University Press.

Reay, D., & Ball, S. J. (1997). Spoilt for choice: The working classes and educational markets. *Oxford Review of Education, 23*(1), 89–101.

Reynolds, P. (1995). Youth and the politics of culture in South Africa. In *Children and the politics of culture* (pp. 218–240). Princeton, NJ: Princeton University Press.

Rheingold, A. A., Smith, D. W., Ruggiero, K. J., Saunders, B. E., Kilpatrick, D. G., & Resnick, H. S. (2004). Loss, trauma exposure, and mental health in a representative sample of 12-17-year-old youth: Data from the national survey of adolescents. *Journal of Loss and Trauma, 9*(1), 1–19.

Richman, A. (2007). The outsider lurking online: Adults researching youth cyber cultures. In *Representing youth: Methodological issues in critical youth studies* (pp. 182–202). New York, NY: New York University Press.

Ritchken, E. (1990). *Learning in Limbo: Experiences of secondary schooling in Mapulaneng District, Lebowa, 1989. No. 4.* Education Policy Unit, University of the Witwatersrand.

Robins, S., & Fleisch, B. (2014). Mediating active citizenship and social mobility in working-class schools: The case of equal education in Khayelitsha, Cape Town. In B. Von Lieres & L. Piper (Eds.), *Mediated citizenship* (pp. 128–145). London: Palgrave Macmillan.

Rule, P. (1990). *Learning in Limbo: Student perspectives.* Johannesburg: Education Policy Unit, University of the Witwatersrand.

Runciman, C. F. (2012). *Mobilisation and insurgent citizenship of the Anti-Privatisation Forum, South Africa: An ethnographic book.* Diss. Glasgow: University of Glasgow.

Schenk, J., & Seekings, J. (2010). *Locating generation X: Taste and identity in transitional South Africa.* Cape Town: Centre for Social Science Research.

Schenk, J., & Seekings, J. (2012). Locating generation X. In *Generation X goes global: Mapping a youth culture in motion*. Oxfordshire: Routledge.

Schuller, T. (2000). *Thinking about social capital. Global Colloquium of Lifelong Learning*. Milton Keynes: Open University.

Seekings, J. (1995). Media representations of Youth and the South African transition, 1989-1994. *South African Sociological Review, 7*(2), 25–42.

Seekings, J. (1996). The lost generation: South Africa's youth problem in the early 1990s. *Transformation, 29,* 103–125.

Seekings, J. (2003). *Do South Africa's unemployed constitute an underclass?* Cape Town: Centre for Social Science Research, University of Cape Town.

Seekings, J. (2006). Beyond heroes and villains: The rediscovery of the ordinary in the book of childhood and adolescence in South Africa. *Social Dynamics, 32*(1), 1–20.

Seekings, J. (2014). The social and political implications of demographic change in post-apartheid South Africa. *The ANNALS of the American Academy of Political and Social Science, 652*(1), 70–86.

Seekings, J., & Everatt, D. (1993). *Heroes or villains?: Youth politics in the 1980s.* Johannesburg: Ravan Press.

Seekings, J., & Thaler, K. (2010). *Socio-economic conditions, young men and violence in Cape Town.* Cape Town: Centre for Social Science Research.

Selikow, T.-A. (2004). We have our own special language. Language, sexuality and HIV/AIDS: A case study of youth in an urban township in South Africa. *African Health Sciences, 4*(2), 102–108.

Selikow, T.-A., Bheki, Z., & Cedra, E. (2002). The ingagara, the regte and the cherry: HIV/AIDS and youth culture in contemporary urban townships. *Agenda, 17*(53), 22–32.

Sen, A. (1980). Description as choice. *Oxford Economic Papers, 32*(3), 353–369.

Sen, A. (1985). Well-being, agency and freedom: The Dewey lectures 1984. *The journal of philosophy, 82*(4), 169–221.

Sen, A. (1992). *Inequality re-examined.* Oxford: Clarendon Press.

Sen, A. (1993). Capability and well-being. In *The quality of life*. Beverly Hills, CA: Sage Publications.

Sen, A. (1999). *Commodities and capabilities.* Oxford: OUP Catalogue.

Sen, A. (2001). *Development as freedom.* Oxford: Oxford Paperbacks.

Sen, A. (2005). Human rights and capabilities. *Journal of Human Development, 6*(2), 151–166.

Solomons, I., & Aslam, F. (2011). A conceptual exploration of values education in the context of schooling in South Africa. *South African Journal of Education, 31*(2), 224–232.

Sorabji, R. (1974). Body and soul in Aristotle. *Philosophy, 49*(187), 63–89.

Soudien, C. (2007). *Youth identity in contemporary South Africa: Race, culture and schooling.* Pretoria: New Africa Books.

Spindler, G., & Spindler, L. (1992). Cultural process and ethnography: An anthropological perspective. In *The handbook of qualitative research in education* (pp. 53–92). Cambridge, MA: Academic Press.

Spohrer, K. (2016). Negotiating and contesting 'success': Discourses of aspiration in a UK secondary school. *Discourse: Studies in the Cultural Politics of Education, 37*(3), 411–425.

Stahl, G. (2015). *Identity, neoliberalism and aspiration: Educating white working-class boys.* Oxfordshire: Routledge.

Standing, G. (2011). *The precariat: The new dangerous class.* London: Bloomsbury Academic.

Standing, G. (2014a). Why the precariat is not a bogus concept. *Open Democracy.*

Standing, G. (2014b). *A precariat charter: From denizens to citizens.* A&C Black.

Stats, S. A. (2011). *Statistics South Africa. Formal census.* Pretoria: Statistics South Africa.

Stats, S. A. (2012). Census 2011. In STATSSA (Ed.), *Statistical release* (pp. 301).

Stats, S. A. (2018). *Quaterly labour force report.* Pretoria: Statistics South Africa.

Stephens, S. (Ed.). (1995). *Children and the politics of culture.* Princeton, NJ: Princeton University Press.

Strelitz, L. (2004). Against cultural essentialism: Media reception among South African youth. *Media, Culture & Society, 26*(5), 625–641.

Strelitz, L. (2005). *Mixed reception: South African youth and their experience of global media.* Pretoria: UNISA Press.

Subrahmanyam, K., & Greenfield, P. (2008). Online communication and adolescent relationships. *The Future of Children, 119*–146.

Swartz, D. (1997). *Culture and power: The sociology of Pierre Bourdieu.* Chicago, IL: University of Chicago Press.

Taylor, C. S., & Taylor, V. (2004). Hip-hop and youth culture: Contemplations of an emerging cultural phenomenon. *Reclaiming Children and Youth, 12*(4), 251.

Teddlie, C., & Abbas, T. (Eds.). (2009). *Foundations of mixed methods research: Integrating quantitative and qualitative approaches in the social and behavioural sciences.* Thousand Oaks, CA: Sage Publications Inc.

Trahar, S. (2009). Beyond the story itself: Narrative inquiry and auto ethnography in intercultural research in higher education. *Forum Qualitative Sozialforschung/ Forum: Qualitative Social Research, 10*(1).

UNICEF. (2014). *Generation 2030 Africa: Child demographics in Africa.* New York, NY: UNICEF.

Van Manen, M. (1990). *Researching lived experience: Human science for an action sensitive pedagogy.* New York, NY: SUNY Press.

Van Zyl Slabbert, F., Malan, C., Marais, H., Olivier, J., & Riordan, R. (1994). *Youth in the new South Africa.* Pretoria: HSRC Publishers.

Walker, J. C. (2007). Learning (not) to labour?: *Youth transitions from vocational education in post-Soviet Russia.* Dissertation, University of Birmingham.

Ward, C. L., et al. (2012). Violence, violence prevention, and safety: A research agenda for South Africa. *South African Medical Journal, 102*(4), 215–218.

Weber, M. (1978). *Economy and society: An outline of interpretive sociology* (Vol. 1). Berkeley, CA: University of California Press.

Willis, P. (1977). *Learning to labor: How working class kids get working class jobs.* New York, NY: Columbia University Press.

Willis, P., Barton, L., & Walker, S. (1983). Cultural production and theories of reproduction. In L. Barton & S. Walker (Eds.), *Race, class and education* (pp. 107–137). London: Routledge.

Willis, P. E. (1981). *Learning to labor: How working class kids get working class jobs.* New York, NY: Columbia University Press.

Youniss, J., & Yates, M. (1997). *Community service and social responsibility in youth.* Chicago, IL: University of Chicago Press.

Zipin, L., Sellar, S., Brennan, M., & Gale, T. (2015). Educating for futures in marginalized regions: A sociological framework for rethinking and researching aspirations. *Educational Philosophy and Theory, 47*(3), 227–246.

Index